Once I Was A Teenager

Jonquil Graham

2013
© Jonquil Graham
Edited by Susan Tarr
Cover design and layout by Richelle Allely, Printing.com

ISBN 978-0-9941022-0-1   Paperback
ISBN 978-0-9941022-1-8   ePub
ISBN 978-0-9941022-2-5   Mobi

The Little Red Hen
Community Press
PO Box 13-533
Tauranga Central 3141
New Zealand—Aotearoa

Contents

Author's Note

The best gift I ever received was a diary from my dad when I was nine years old. Every birthday he gave me another until I grew up and bought my own. They recorded childish events in pencil and ballpoint before the writing became smaller and sometimes in shorthand, in case Mum read my teenage yearnings.

Mum was a Kiwi and Dad was a Pom who worked in Sydney. We had frequent sea voyages to England and several trips to New Zealand.

I now live in New Zealand, but enjoy catching up with friends and family in Australia and reminiscing about the crazy things we got up to in the 1960s.

I would like to thank some special people who helped with the book.

Pidge, (Christine James), my SCEGGS Redlands classmate, for her encouragement.

Dr. Vic Eastman for computer help.

Jenny Argante of Argante Literary Services for her cheerful expertise.

Little Pattie, the Aussie singing legend - and still performing today - for her contribution.

And my husband Bryan for his ongoing support.

Foreword by Little Pattie

It's often said that if you remember the Sixties, you weren't really there!

However, much has been written about those wonderful times and Jonquil's writing reminds me so beautifully of my own upbringing. Her light-hearted and warm memoir of life in the Fifties and Sixties will resonate with other readers, too.

I remember those years with great affection. Even during the conservative Fifties life for me was all about primary school, which I loved, lots of friends and carefree weekends.

There wasn't much money around but my brother and his mates managed to build 'the best billy carts in the world.' They were perfectly balanced for us lightweight little sisters to ride down the steep hill where we lived. We even had our brothers strategically placed at the end of our block to stop the traffic so we could have our billy cart races uninterrupted.

Try doing that today!

Along came the Sixties, and, as Bob Dylan so famously wrote, 'the times, they are a-changing.' I loved being able to question my parents' beliefs and values. We were watching world events on television and we wanted to know more.

We even had opinions!

By 1963 I was a 14 year old professional performer. I didn't plan this at all. My ambition was to be a doctor, but after winning a talent quest one afternoon at the local surf club, a scout from EMI Records convinced my parents to allow me to make a record. It was entitled 'He's my Blonde Headed Stompie Wompie Real Gone Surfer Boy' and we were all surprised when it went to the top of the charts.

My life changed forever.

There were to be no more carefree days at the beach with my girlfriends. I truly missed the sea water, the smell of the coconut oil, the hot chips and Coca Cola for lunch and, most all, I missed the giggling.

Thankfully, Jonquil has taken me back there and I know you will all love this book as much as I do.

Pattie Amphlett

Once I Was A Teenager

Prologue

Pittwater Road in Sydney stretches 30 kilometres from North Manly, snaking through the suburbs of Brookvale, Dee Why, Collaroy, Narrabeen, Warriewood, Bayview and Church Point. Collaroy, halfway between these beach suburbs, is where my family lived during the 50s and 60s.

We lived at 1046 Pittwater Road, which was opposite the Salvation Army's Darby and Joan Home. Ours was nestled between other houses on the proverbial quarter-acre section with its expansive weeping willow, a mulberry tree and outside dunny tucked behind the garage next to the chook yard. The suburbs along Pittwater Road had a tropical feel with their Norfolk Pines, grassy verges called nature strips, the continuous rolling surf crashing onto coarse golden sands, and small shops tucked side by side.

There were no supermarkets or shopping malls at Collaroy, just the beach. The surf club, golf course, milk bar and cinema provided ample entertainment. It was an era where neighbours chatted and freckle-nosed children roamed freely. Traffic was much lighter then and even little Donny from next door crossed the road at a young age, reciting, "Look to the *white* (sic), look to the left, and you never get *wunned* (sic) over."

The new technology was Dictaphone machines, electric typewriters, transistors, televisions, and cars with fins and boots large enough to hold a crate of beer. There were no cell phones, home computers, unemployed youth, racial gang violence, terrorist threats and kids with ADD. Mothers were lionesses, priding themselves on cooking, washing, cleaning and chiding offspring. Fathers were the indisputable head of the household and women ran themselves ragged to keep their family intact and happy.

Living in that era seems like a long sleepy dream that today's travellers can still find if they are prepared to leave modern technology behind.

Chapter 1
The Back Verandah

One late sizzling Australian afternoon I came home to a shocking sight.

Mother was prostrate on the sofa on the back verandah, tangled up in the laundry. I could tell she was alive because the newly-laundered sheets, Wild Flowers of Scotland tea towel and my sister's pyjamas with their frolicking pinto-pony pattern were rhythmically rising in shallow bursts. A strangulated sobbing sound emanated from the confused mound.

"Mum!" I cried. "What's the matter? Why are you nose down in the washing? You'll suffocate."

I'd never seen a hidden mother before. At sunset she was normally in the kitchenette ladling lard into a fry-pan, swatting blowflies and sipping a sherry to the strings of Mantovani or My Fair Lady on the radiogram in the adjoining dining room. The dining room housed a table, chairs for five, a Kelvinator refrigerator and an upright piano.

Silence. Then a muffled moan.

"What are you doing home?"

"I'm home, Ma, because I live here. How long have you been lying like this?"

I shook the warm bulge and the garments tumbled revealing Dad's Y-fronts, his white office shirts and a couple of Mum's nylon bras—or umbrassas, a moniker used since I was a tot and couldn't pronounce the strange garments hanging from the washing line.

"What happened? Are you ill? Did Daddy drop dead at the office? Did he get run over by a bus?"

"No. No," she sniffed, still entombed. "Much worse than that."

What could be worse than losing the breadwinner of the family, even if he had bad-tempered spasms reminding his family we were ungrateful wretches and the world would be a better place if more people spoke the Queen's English and played cricket.

I patted the lump. Then a relief of realisation swept over me.

"Oh, I know why you're crying. You're going to have a baby. Don't worry. I'll help you look after it."

Mother shot bolt upright.

"God, no," she barked. "What a ghastly thought. I'd cut my throat if that happened. You know your father and I can't stand children."

She looked like a startled bird of paradise bedecked in undies and sun drenched towels.

"What then, Ma? Don't keep me in suspenders—I mean suspense."

Our family liked fooling around with words; we played Scrabble. Mother might say she was *diluted* about something instead of delighted and if she was in a playful mood said *pissabolity* for possibility. My sister giggled at scatological quips and my brother enjoyed suspect word conversion—bosomberries for boysenberries, Vegemite became vagina-mite and penis-butter for peanut butter, then saying, "Oops! Sorry, must have slipped out," and cock a leg and say "Oops!" again.

And Mum would sigh, "Did your father spend a fortune on your education so you could bring our family down to the lowest common denominator?"

Then she'd smile indulgently; Jasper was the only son.

I couldn't imagine what ghastly words might creep from Mum's mouth. For a moment my world stopped despite the incessant sound of croaking cicadas outside the fly-screened windows, the odd cackle of a kookaburra perched in the mulberry tree and the next door neighbour shouting in the heat to her little boy, "Donneeee! Teatime, lovey. Quick sticks."

Traffic rattled outside our beach villa on Pittwater Road like continuous snoring, comforting yet detached. But Mother was clearly perturbed, possibly disturbed. I didn't know how to mother Mother. It was odd seeing her so vulnerable.

She made me feel afraid. In all my teenage years I'd never seen her weep, even when she reclined on another back verandah at our previous house at North Curl Curl and nodded off reading to the three of us when we were babies. When she awoke from her nap and found a large knitting needle embedded in her thigh, she calmly soothed us amid gushing blood and told my father to deal to his hysteria while

4

she dealt with her leg. No doctor was called. Dad thought Mother was brave and unflappable and pretty good for a little farming woman from the back-blocks of that land across the ditch renowned for earthquakes and geysers.

Mum rolled her cornflour blue eyes at his teasing. She was born into a well-regarded and established family from Nelson, New Zealand. He knew perfectly well he'd married a prize.

"Your mother comes from good stock," he'd remind us, and give her a squelchy kiss on the side of her face.

"Stop it, Fairley," she'd giggle. "The children are looking."

Good breeding or not, she was Mum, he was Dad, and it was their job to love and feed the three of us kids and be happy with each other and life. But now she was behaving strangely.

"Tell me why you're sad. Did I do something?"

Mum's tanned arm dug through the Rinso-scented sheets.

"Read this."

She delved into the deep pocket of her flowery apron then wiped her nose on a Made in Ireland lace hankie.

I took the creased envelope.

"What does insubordinate mean, Mum?" I asked, scanning the official letter.

"It means your brother has been booted out of the navy. He won't apply himself and the silly fool has given up a glorious naval career."

It didn't seem like the end of the world to me.

"Your father and I tried our best to get him into the navy. And what happens? He's blown his chances. He's a disappointment. We'll never get over this. Your father's right. He's a beach bum. We should never have moved to Collaroy. God, I hate this country."

Although I empathised with Mum, I was reluctant to embrace her hurt and my brother's lamentable behaviour. My brand new boyfriend with Beatle haircut and flirtatious brown eyes encircled with long eyelashes was causing my own teenage palpitations. Mothers were supposed to be rock solid, not have problems and not do strange things like sobbing into the washing.

Mum had two brothers in the Navy, one a Commander and the other a Rear Admiral. They had pulled strings to get my brother, Jasper, into the naval college at Jervis Bay. And she longed to see her blonde, blue-eyed charismatic sixteen-year old son in uniform, even if it was with the Australian Navy.

Jasper would be launched and her job as a mother practically done. He'd greet us wearing black epaulettes and a perky peaked hat with badges; face bronzed and dimpled as he flashed a wide smile against a flotilla of warships. Jasper's mere presence would exude success. He'd introduce cadets who pronounced their vowels nicely and came from 'good homes.' We'd be invited to cocktail parties and marry delicious naval men—not trades' people like pastry cooks, assistant plumbers and grocery store-hands. Our family status would be elevated despite living opposite the Salvation Army at Collaroy, where some neighbours waddled up the road with their hair in curlers to the corner shop and said haitch for H. The only son would carry on a naval tradition and make the whole family proud.

"He couldn't even last out the year," she moaned. "His school won't take him back. He's a juvenile delinquent."

"Oh, Mum," I implored. "Try to be happy. You've got me. I'll do the dishes tonight."

"I'm going to talk to your father when he comes home from the office. I'm sick of this country. I want to go back to New Zealand or England to decent people. Just get away from it all."

"But what about me, Mum? What about the kids?"

"We'll all go. Maybe we can get your brother into a naval college in England."

"But, Mum, I quite like Australia."

"You'll like England better. You'll meet a nice Englishman and have trips to the Continent. I'll help you."

"But what's wrong with Australian men?"

"They're a bit *too* Australian," she sighed. She arose from the faded sofa, smoothed her coarse brown hair and began folding the washing.

"I'll do the folding, Mum. I'll do anything you ask me."

I couldn't bear to see my normally cheerful mother behave abnormally. Would Dad ship Mother off to a funny farm? I'd heard it was a place for people who cried a lot and had brain disorders. In extreme cases they were given electric shock treatment.

How awful, I fantasised, for poor Mummy to be rigged up to a machine. Her crying out, "I'm feeling better now," before starting to apply her lipstick. I imagined she'd become a strapped-down shuddering doll, her eyes bulging with fright.

But now she was one disappointed weeping wreck. These days you'd call it Menopausal Mums but the term wasn't invented then.

"Just peel the spuds and do the beans," she said. "There's something I must do."

The verandah door wobbled on its hinges as she disappeared into the garden.

What was she up to? What was on her mind?

While chopping up the coarse beans, I glimpsed unusual activity through the Venetian blinds. Mother was wielding an axe.

"Mummy," I screamed like an infant. "Don't do anything silly. Are you killing yourself?"

"Better than that, darling," she shouted back in the growing darkness. I heard a sudden thwack intermingled with excited muffled gasps and heavy breathing bordering on exhilaration.

Young Donny from next door must have succumbed to his mother's call for his tucker and not abseiled up the voluptuous choko vine that spread its tentacles over the tall fence. He was becoming a good little climber and often gazed longingly at the noisy activities in our backyard, chucking the odd choko over the fence, just like his mother.

"We don't like them. You can have them," he'd squeal in delight.

Chokos—those innocuous green marrows, slightly prickly—made good target practice. As far as Australian kids were concerned, they should have been eradicated like polio and scarlet fever since they caused infantile panic all over God's Country, ruining many a Sunday roast. Mum tried to disguise the slimy vegetable on our plates by splattering gravy made from flour and vegetable water all over it. Her veiled warning, "Think of the starving millions. You're lucky there's food on the table. Eat up if you want pudding."

The African kids with their soulful eyes and protruding bellies became a fleeting image as we three children grabbed glasses of water, pinched our noses and bravely ingested it. But

I was old enough to be annoyed by Donny's mother throwing the execrable vegetable over the fence, calling out, "Can't stand the bloody things. George won't eat them. Pity to see them go to waste."

But if George, her ample-bellied, crimson-faced husband who sported a wiry grey moustache and slicked back hair couldn't stomach them wasn't it cruel to inflict them on the defenceless kids next door?

In revolt we formed the Choko Gang. Whenever Donny's mum chucked some chokos our way, our visiting scabby-kneed friends hurled them right back. It caused a bit of tension until Mum, disliking unresolved tension, found an excuse to hail her over the fence. Or Donny's mother tottered over to borrow a cup of sugar. Then they'd be nattering over cups of tea like conjoined twins.

"Are you all right, Mum?" I called when Mother clambered up the back concrete steps with a lop-sided satisfied grin. She looked more composed and less demented.

"Something I should have done a long time ago," she said. "That deserves a drink. God, look at the time! Your father will be home soon and we'll be in hot H20 if his dinner's not on the table in time."

I liked the way Mum included me. *She* was the mad crying vixen. I didn't even know how to cook.

"I hope you didn't chop up the cat or do anything silly out there."

Mother said, "Do you think I'm mad?"

I said, "Hmm." I didn't know what else to say.

I always wondered what might happen when Dad walked in the door. He was a creature of habit and anything that negatively changed his routine gave him an apoplectic fit. Catching the Sydney to Palm Beach express bus later than most office workers meant he didn't need to gallantly offer his seat to a woman, and he could do the cryptic crossword in the evening paper. Then he could face a household with a wife who hatched new plans daily, three hormonal teenagers, and a panting German Shepherd wearing underpants if she was on heat.

Initially we gave Dad a wide berth, unsure of his mood. After an hour long bus ride, he looked forward to a tasty meal and a devoted wife who'd showered, changed into a floral frock and slapped on vermilion lipstick. She'd be sympathetic and soothe bruised feelings, despite looking vacant about the intricacies of his accounting job at The Firm where he slaved for the family.

Mum wasn't a doormat though.

She was intuitive and knew it was easier to agree than rattle a hungry man. His change-into clothes would be neatly folded on the bed, his pipe and tobacco on the bedside table and a slug of alcohol newly poured. This tacitly said, 'Welcome home, my worthy husband. You are appreciated.' Possibly more than he felt at the office. There he spent half his life poring over figures in a box room, dictating letters to a buxom spinster wearing a twin-set, an amethyst brooch and a strand of Australian harvested pearls.

After Dad hung up his felt hat, changed out of his three-piece suit, and said, "Christ, I've had a helluva day," Mum said, "I think you should tell The Firm you want to go back to England."

"Why?" he asked, confused.

When Mum thrust the official letter at Dad, he acted like a thoughtful accountant. He sat in his chair in the lounge and polished his spectacles. Then he tapped his pipe on the small silver ashtray, peered inside it at the clogged debris before poking at it with a pipe cleaner. Striking a match, he inhaled deeply, until small rings of circular grey puffs appeared.

"What do you expect, Dot?" he said, after reading the letter. "I've told you before. Your son is a beach lout. Can't take discipline. Dislikes authority."

"He's your son, too. Where did we go wrong? Why has he blown his chances? He's taken after your side of the family."

A parental discussion ensued on the genetics of our family, until I hissed, "Mum, the spuds are burning and have you told Dad what you've done?"

"Sssh," she said. "I might have been a bit hasty."

Hasty? She'd done something mad, quite out of character. I was curious to see what mischief she'd got up to.

After dinner my work-weary dad, and my disappointed mother clutching a torch, shone a weak beam onto our backyard. At first it was unclear what all the colourful bits were.

"What did you do, Ma? What's the mess? Animal, vegetable or mineral?"

Another game our family played.

We all stared speechless in the dark. She had done something no other mother dared do in Collaroy. It was an act every 60s surfing youngster dreaded. She'd taken an axe to my brother's surfboard and chopped it to smithereens.

Chapter 2
A Kiwi Bride

The 60s hit my parents like a sledgehammer. Three teenagers immersed in the exhilarating surfing and music culture overran their home, once a domain of domestic bliss. For a decade they remained puzzled, confused and grumpy.

"There's no worse pain than having children," Mum said on several occasions. "And I don't mean the actual part of having them, it's what happens after."

"Why did you bother begatting us?" I'd snarl.

"Didn't know you'd all turn out so ghastly, darling," she'd reply.

Whenever our back verandah was invaded by Jasper's surfing mates, twelve foot surfboards, old cars jamming the driveway and cigarette butts stuck in the dregs of coffee cups, she'd sigh.

"Marry if you must, but for God's sake don't have children. They'll ruin your life."

Her veiled warnings were dished out with loving concern.

"And try not to marry a short man. They become pompous bullies and use their voice to make up for it."

We'd glance through the hatch separating the dining room from the lounge. After Dad's 'blow-up' he'd calmly smoke a pipe, check out the latest cricket score and playfully bellow out for a nice cuppa.

"Let's keep the old boy happy," she'd say. "Anything for a bit of peace and quiet."

"Why'd you marry him?" I'd ask after one such blow-up.

Mother looked thoughtful.

"I was fond of him. It was wartime. War makes people do mad things. And he made me laugh."

"Are you laughing now, Ma?"

Mum would change the subject or say they never argued before having children.

My parents, who met on a ship during World War 2, were born on opposite sides of the world—she from New Zealand and he from England—and both from very different backgrounds.

Mother was from Nelson. She was sandwiched amongst six children. Her father was Dr Washbourn, and her mother had been a nurse. It was a carefree happy household with the surgery attached to an imposing two-storey house. There was a maid and home help, and holidays with a bachelor uncle by the sea where the kids fished and swam, and ate around a campfire.

Grandma loved babies and peered into every pram to inspect the infant who'd most likely been delivered by her husband. What embarrassed her children most were her wrinkly brown stockings, which drooped around her ankles as she poked her nose into the pram. I liked the sound of Grandma but she died before I was born. Mum said she was gentle, kind and rarely scolded them.

"She'd laugh if we were naughty. She thought we were funny."

As a tot, the youngest daughter, Sydney, nibbled on raw liver. It was so revolting she became a vegetarian for the rest of her life and no one made a fuss about it. John, the baby of the family, was a quiet mischievous little imp. As soon as he realised one of his sisters was whispering down the phone to a beau, he played the popular song *Love in Bloom* loudly on the record player he wound by hand.

The family lived next door to the Masonic Temple where men arrived furtively at night, gave funny handshakes and drank lots of whisky.

"We heard them being sick in the flowerbeds," recalled Mum, "but, oh, the food they had. Wonderful parties. You should have seen all the leftover cakes in the bins the next day."

The Washbourn children attended Nelson College. Mum barely missed being hit by a bust of Julius Caesar during the 1929 Murchison earthquake when it toppled from a classroom shelf.

In those days women didn't need to pursue a career. It was expected they'd marry early to a man of promise, who'd provide financially in return for a devoted wife who cooked, cleaned, bore children and was not stingy on conjugal rights.

To fill in time, Mum attended art school, dabbled in photography and spurned adoring suitors. When war broke out she was engaged to a naval officer and drove army trucks. She had an impulsive restless streak and yearned for adventures. As a schoolgirl she was asked what she wanted to be when she grew up. A tourist, was her emphatic reply.

Dad was born in Colchester, Essex, in 1909, and was raised by older sisters. His father died when he was a baby and his mother spent her days confined to bed in delicate health. Aged three, he remembered the massive headlines in newspapers and endless speculation on the sinking of the Titanic, but little about World War 1. His sisters said he had beautiful golden curls and wore a black velvet frock at that age.

As an ex-soldier of the Royal Scottish Fusiliers sporting thin strands of black hair, it was hard to imagine him as a cherubic toddler.

Dad was employed by Lord Vestey's firm, which had shipping and meat works around the world. He was sent to Argentina as a young man where he learnt to speak and swear in Spanish, and ride large yellow horses. Perhaps they were a different colour; the miniature sepia photos have faded over the years. He was shortish, bespectacled, prematurely balding, and resembled a pleasant-looking Tibetan monk.

We pored over encyclopaedias. And we wondered if Daddy was a throwback to some funny foreign country; his face was as familiar as the black and white pictorial photos with unpronounceable names. His head was moon-shaped. He never had a moustache that captured beer froth from the tops of schooners and middies. Daddy had a long space between his nostrils and lips.

Mother said those were unattractive features. The best-looking people had curved, upturned noses with a *short* space between nostrils and lips, she said, which sent me scuttling to the oval mirror in my attic bedroom to examine my genetic imperfections. I tried wooden pegs clipped together but it gave me a rash and a bout of teenage gloom.

Mum said at least I'd inherited her blonde hair although, at that stage, she'd gone bottle-brunette and was battling dandruff.

The way my parents met is cinematic nostalgia viewed at the beginning or closing of old romantic movies. She could have been Grace Kelly, with her haughty nose, and he a hybrid of Mickey Rooney and Andrew Lloyd-Webber, but taller and better looking.

On that fateful England-bound voyage Mum was fed up with being pursued by the captain and randy officers, for she was beautiful and desirable on that woman-drought ship.

A solitary man in thoughtful repose was leaning over the railings gazing at the expanse of grey choppy seas. She tapped him gently on the shoulder, saying, "Excuse me. Do you mind if I stand next to you for a while?"

Dad recollected how his eyes bulged out like organ stops at the vision of such loveliness.

"No, madam, I'd be delighted."

And so he became her protector for the remainder of the trip, and beyond.

While the bombing raid continued in London, my parents married at a stone registry office. Mum wore a smart suit nipped in at the waist, with a feather attached to a jaunty hat. Dad wore a kilt and a triumphant smile.

They didn't have time for a honeymoon for Dad's division ordered him to fight *the enemy* on Italian soil and Mum answered an advertisement for the dream job; a wealthy elderly Jewish socialite sought a companion with typing skills. Since Mum looked classy and efficient she was hired and the two women swanned off to America and the West Indies.

I don't think Mum did much except photograph horses with long ears poking through straw bonnets in Bermuda, or languish on foreign beaches, a lifetime away from the war and the troublesome kids she would later produce. The old lady had connections to the rich and famous and introduced Mother to her moneyed world. They dined with renowned conductor Toscanini and film star Eddie Albert, who thought she was an attractive little dish. When the Americans joined the war, some even knew where to find New Zealand on the map!

In San Francisco Mum received a telegram: 'Regret news about your husband. Letter following.'

Most would've gnashed their teeth and fallen into spasms of despair.

Not Mother.

She'd had a dream about Dad.

He wasn't dead, just wounded. No need to worry. She boarded a ship to England to reunite with her husband. And to check out which part of his anatomy was damaged.

Since she hadn't seen him for several years, she was nervous about the meeting. Her old Nelson College school friend, who'd married a brave Kiwi Spitfire pilot, Jim Hayter, accompanied her. Dad had his arm in a sling, recovering from two bullet wounds where a sniper took a pot shot. He was proud of the dents in his forearm, and later we children would prod our podgy fingers into the loose skin covering the holes.

Years on, though at a tender age, my brother showed entrepreneurial skills. Always keen to make a fast buck, he told his school friends they could witness gunshot wounds from a real soldier but it would cost them a penny. I helped him to soften up Dad.

This was the 50s when small boys charged around backyards firing popguns—toy guns, which had corks tied to string—crying, "Put yer hands up. Yer money or yer life?" They capitulated immediately if someone's mum called out, "Lay down your weapons and come and have afternoon tea."

Mothers who offered piping hot scones saturated in butter, raspberry jam and cream lived in the most visited houses on the block. Lads of that decade squatted on bedroom floors, marching their miniature metal collection of army infantry in combat positions, making whooping rat-a-tat-tat boy noises.

Games ended when mothers sung out, "Tea time, dear. Tell your little friends they have to go home. It's getting late and I don't want their mothers worried."

The cryptic message meant your dad will be home soon and you'd better be at the dinner table with your hair slicked back and face scrubbed. And remember to use your knife and fork correctly. Your father's had a hard day.

Dad became suspicious when abnormally polite small boys lined up to inspect his battle wounds, asking, "How are you, sir?"

It seemed brother Jasper was pocketing the loot and spending it on strips of bullet caps for a silver pistol that fired short loud bangs and sulphuric fumes. The word 'rip off' now comes to mind for I never got a share of the spoils.

I expect it was an awkward, somewhat tender reunion, back then when Dad was finally reunited with Mother after he'd been shipped home to recover in an army hospital. He'd been used to obeying commands from senior ranks before being promoted to Captain and bellowing out his own orders. He'd witnessed comrades blown-up while Mum was safe on an eternal holiday somewhere in the West Indies.

Dad remained patriotic. According to him you couldn't improve on anything British—the Rolls Royce, the Royal Family, the Union Jack, kippers, Shakespeare, Yorkshire pudding, lardy cake and steak and kidney pies. Add to that Stonehenge, crumbling castles with moats, and a quiet country pub filled with scholarly men and chic women. Those women who laughed at your wit but otherwise kept their mouths shut. He admired Sir Winston Churchill's stirring battle cry, which roused a nation to eventual victory:

> "We shall fight on the beaches
> We shall fight on the landing grounds
> We shall fight in the fields and in the streets
> We shall fight in the hills
> We shall never surrender."

While my father might have been meek at work, in the shower he was not. He was a closet actor, roaring impassioned Shakespearian speeches and epithets such as 'Death, where is thy sting?' interspersed with throat and nasal clearings. Also furious cursing if someone turned on a tap and reduced the water pressure.

He liked Vera Lynn but ignored busty pin-ups of American movie stars, which he thought crass and un-British. He remained devoted and faithful to Mother all his life.

Mum could have happily spent her life drifting around the world, attending cocktail parties, visiting art galleries, painting coastal scenes in Italy and sketching charcoal portraits of interesting-looking people. She had fanciful ideas but Dad kept her grounded and pregnant for the first years.

They acquired a German Shepherd puppy called Tiki, named after the Maori ancient god of fertility, once greenstone, now mass-produced in China from plastic.

The puppy reminded Mum of her homeland. German Shepherds were usually called Alsatians because of ill feeling towards Hitler's country. By the time I was born after the war, Tiki was fully grown. With me in my large English perambulator and my proud mother in her fitch fur coat, Tiki accompanied us in spring peregrinations around leafy parks.

Mum remained in contact with the socialite who had an adult daughter called Anina, my second given name. The old lady posted an exquisite baby layette on my arrival, but soon after Mum received a short sad letter from the daughter. Her mother had fallen down some steps and fatally broken her neck.

Britain was still on rations for some years post war and initially families were allotted two eggs a week; Mum said she always saved the yolks for me. Many people were war-weary and hungered for a life that offered opportunities.

One day, my father returned to the tiny flat in Hampton Court with news from his London office. Mum was ready for another sea voyage, and it didn't matter where.

Chapter 3
Little Aussie Battlers

Dad accepted a job offer in Australia working as a cost accountant for one of Lord Vestey's meat-works firms. The lure of a sunny country on the other side of the world convinced Mum that was the right decision with the proviso they could return to London at regular intervals to renew the contract. Without a backward glance, Mum donned her fur coat, strapped up the leather suitcases, and the three of us, with the dog, boarded the Trojan Star.

The voyage took seven weeks with Mum confined to her bunk, pregnant again, and suffering severe seasickness. She only rose when the ship berthed at exotic ports, unloading and loading cargo. Dad marched the frisky Tiki around sea-sprayed decks in howling gales, clocking himself on each lap for he'd studied time and motion in the army. He had an extraordinary constitution Mum said was not normal.

The seas were so choppy the dining room was often empty, but Dad found tweedy gentlemen in the Smoking Lounge puffing on pipes and reminiscing about war experiences. I expect I was confined to a bunk cot with Mum, for she often said, "Your father's not good with children."

I learned to crawl on all fours, my chubby knees refusing to contact the rough planks of the ship's deck, and uttered my first word. I'd thrown my little white shoes into a lavatory bowl and, as they were bobbing around, excitedly exclaimed, "Boats. Boats."

When the *Trojan Star* berthed in Sydney, a gracious British couple connected to The Firm helped my parents settle into a country of perpetual sunshine. They found the mosquitoes and blowflies as charming as the lantern-jawed wharfies with protruding hairy bellies, pores reeking of Bushells Tea and a Capstan ciggie held between sun-blistered lips. They had arms like granite boulders and rough nasal voices, which made Mother wince, but they were cheerful and hard working.

Penniless but hopeful, my parents found a two-bedroom fibrolite cottage in North Curl Curl, a northern suburb about 40 minutes from the Sydney city centre, and a bank manager willing to give them a loan.

Mum had a wily streak in her, a cunningness and charm, when it came to money matters.

Pointing to the vacant adjacent section, she told the estate agent in a la-de-da voice, "My husband and I *might* consider buying this run-down place if you throw in the block next door."

It never occurred to my father to negotiate but, when the agent got back to them, it was a done deal. And that left Mum wondering what was wrong with the cottage.

Dad was pleased to own his first home, however humble, and Tiki was happy to run about in the vacant block once it had been fenced off.

Sadly Tiki died from a tick, and was buried next to a gum tree. The faithful hound had survived a war and crossing the Indian Ocean, but had succumbed to a blood-sucking insect.

My parents were happy when my brother was born. He was a sturdy blonde blue-eyed baby with an easy-going disposition. They hoped he would follow in his uncle's footsteps. Mum's oldest brother Richard, a Rear Admiral, was a gunner on board the *Achilles* in the war that saw the scuttling of the *Graf Spee*. A photograph of him beaming beneath bloodied bandages from a head injury stood on the walnut veneer sideboard as a reminder of his bravery and family connection.

My baby brother was so appealing a nuggetty Australian neighbour in a bush singlet commented what a good-looker the kid was, a real little Strine. Fair dinkum. My parents were appalled. They wanted him to be a proper little English boy with a brilliant sea-faring career ahead of him.

The baby was christened Richard Jasper after his uncle and an army colleague called Jasper who was 'a splendid chap. Damn good major. They don't make them like that nowadays.' My parents never dreamed their sunny-natured lad, named after military heroes, would rail against authority and disappoint them, but neither did other parents of the 60s.

At dawn when warm sunlight made flickering patterns on the fly-screen back door Mother became the military sergeant. Dressed in a floral frock and frilly apron, she'd order my father to a three-course breakfast because that was the way to start the day—porridge, bacon and eggs, and two pieces of toast with English marmalade.

Dad said a man couldn't live on coffee and prissy bits of bread. That was for pansies, weaklings and the French. And he was suspicious about any evening meal that didn't consist of meat and three vegetables.

"You're not serving me foreign muck, are you, Dot?" he'd ask my mother, who'd stretched the budget and spent precious time sweating in a hot airless kitchen to give her man variety.

Real men, Dad insisted, arose at first light, jogged around the block, took a two-minute cold shower before a one-minute hot shower. He'd be awakened by the noise of the milkmen at dawn—those fit young males, usually new immigrants—scampering up flowery paths to deliver pints of milk to the front porch. We'd hear the tinkling of coins, the cheerful cries of 'Milko!' and the graunching of gears as the truck rolled on to the next house. People who let their milk and half pints of cream sour in the morning sun were lazy bastards. They didn't know what a joy it was to greet the day doing God's duty.

Dressed for the office, he'd open *The Sydney Morning Herald* and prop it against the glass condiments. First he'd scan news from Britain, then the cricket and the weather. While he gulped down his cup of tea, Mum flicked his shoulders for bits of fluff, straightened his tie and ensured his triangular-shaped handkerchief in his breast pocket pointed upwards.

"Don't fuss with me, woman," Dad would say.

Sometimes her maternal touch put him in a splendid mood, and he'd pull the hanky out, blow violently into it, and say, "Elephants trumpeting through the woods."

We'd giggle at this vulgar eruption.

"Do it again, Daddy. More elephants, puleeeze."

"No, children," he'd say. "You can't repeat a good thing."

"Oh, Fairley!"

Mum would totter to the chest of drawers to look for another perfectly folded nose napkin.

He had a playful wit, and if he left us kids giggling, it was an excellent start to the day. His final ritual was to blow dust off his felt hat, batter it into shape, grab his leather briefcase, pipe, matches and tobacco, and tweak our noses.

"Be good for your mother. She will tell me *everything* when I get home."

He'd plant a kiss on her powdered cheeks, and march briskly down the parched brown hill to catch the bus.

Mum's days were spent scrubbing cloth nappies and popping them into the agitator washing machine with its wringer attachment. Then she'd tend vegetables and grub paspalum, sort out scuffles in the chook house, bake and take us walking after a lunchtime nap.

If we weren't sleepy she gave us colouring-in books, stencils, and Little Golden books like *The Little Fat Policeman*, or stories about brave firemen rescuing fat ladies, and children helping their parents around the house. Fathers were portrayed as thoughtful, somewhat detached, lean and lanky, with a moustache and pipe.

Mothers in picture books reeked of maternal pride, bright red lipstick and wore their short brown hair in bangs, which was an American term not used in Australia. She was often in the kitchen in a pristine white frilly apron—you could practically smell the baking from the pages—with her chubby dutiful children, usually a boy in a tartan shirt and bow tie and a girl with barrettes (another Americanism which annoyed me at a tender age.)

"I hope you don't turn out like your dad," Mum said, "getting upset over trivial things."

One afternoon I woke Mum from her nap.

"Mummy, there's a mistake in this silly book."

It was an aerial view of city buildings of all shapes and sizes painted in fascinating detail. My eyes had zoomed in to a sign reading To Let.

Mum couldn't see anything amiss.

"But it's wrong," I insisted. "They left out the 'i.' It should be toilet!"

Afternoon North Curl Curl sunshine with its exhausting strands of yellow heat and buzzing cicadas in the bushes caused a peaceful drowsiness. Every weekend, Mum said after lunch, "Your father and I need a lie-down," and the pattern continued for years. It put Dad in a good mood for he read stories to us in the small porch while Mother knitted. We relaxed around her sucking our thumbs.

Dad had a strange reaction to my brother's favourite story, *Little Pee Wee*, about a spotted dog that grew too big for the family and had to join a circus. Jasper, aged two, sobbed, "Why did they get rid of Pee Wee?"

My father looked aghast. "For godsakes, it's only a story. What's wrong with the boy?"

"Fairley!" Mum said. "Be glad you have a son with feelings. He's only a baby. How would you like to grow so big no one wanted you?"

Dad had hoped Jasper would grow into a man who obeyed orders from his seniors, not a softie who cried over sad stories. After all, weren't biological sons supposed to be successful replicas of their fathers?

Dad didn't understand about bonding for he was brought up fatherless. Most fathers back then were remote towards their sons, fearing they'd become 'sissies' if they became too close. Sadly, that aloofness caused many lads to turn to elements that thrilled and challenged them, and thus my brother became a child of the wild surfing 60s.

When Mum arose, fresh as a daisy, she dressed us in clean clothes and took us for a walk. She read *Home Beautiful* and hoped to be inspired by other people's bungalows. She pushed my brother in his stroller down Jocelyn Street and up the winding Headland Road. Some dwellings were a bit common, like their inhabitants, she thought, especially those with garden gnomes and soaring ceramic ducks arcing across doorways.

And Mother didn't expect to 'carry again' so soon.

Well-bred people in the 50s didn't use the word pregnant for it was considered vulgar.

Tired looking women with tummy protrusions were either in the family way, expecting or carrying. The benign choice of words glossed over the fact that there had been nocturnal hanky-panky between two consenting adults, because a woman often announced her condition with wide-eyed surprise.

"I'm sure I don't know how it happened. My husband is not that pleased, but I expect he'll get around to the idea."

These days, women wouldn't put up with such nonsense. Some might even say, "Don't you remember getting drunk, you low-life. I told you I had a headache, but no, you wanted your way. Now you have to support the kid for the rest of your working life so face up to your responsibilities, and, God, I hope it doesn't look like you."

What a difference fifty years made! Thanks, Germaine Greer.

Pent-up feelings of isolation, missing her family in New Zealand and the daily grind of trying to make ends meet, and bearing two children in two years with a third on the way, was the straw that broke the camel's back. Mum was fed up. And it had nothing to do with being hormonal or irrational.

"I hate this country," she cried, "I hate living here!" before committing the unforgivable.

She sat in Dad's chair at breakfast time—the only chair in the house. The master's seat!

Dad was flabbergasted at seeing his contrary wife tucking into cornflakes one morning when he'd dressed for the office. Normally, she was in the kitchen frying up bacon and eggs.

"Your breakfast is ready," she said sweetly. "Sit down."

"Why are you sitting in my seat?" he asked.

"Because I'm tired of sitting in the camp chair," said Mother coolly. "I'd like a change."

Dad's face turned from pale to crimson; anything unplanned put him in a panic.

"Why should you get the only decent bit of furniture in the house?" Mum added, rising to fetch his breakfast. "You can have the camp chair for a change and see how you like it."

Enraged, my father picked up the flimsy chair and flung it against the wall, shaking the foundations of the small fibrolite cottage. He always swore in Spanish when he'd run out of colourful English. The camp chair dented a hole in the wall and photographs of Mum's brothers shuddered on the sideboard. Mother feigned calmness.

"I'm sick of being poor," she said. "No decent furniture, a bad-tempered husband, so what's the point of it all? Let's pack up and leave."

This was the first noisy argument I remember and, although infrequent, Mum wanted to make a stand and Dad wanted respect.

He was the breadwinner, the head of the house. He was the one going off to slave at his office job and the family should be grateful he was providing for them. He wasn't staying at home, having a holiday.

In the 50s men had no idea how long it took to do housework without the invention of appliances we take for granted, such as pop-up toasters, electric jugs, automatic washing machines, convenient fast foods and, more importantly, transport. A car was a luxury.

Women were resourceful for they bottled and baked and embroidered smocked frocks for their little daughters. They knitted, gardened and told the kids to 'run outside and play in the nice fresh air' since there was no TV.

Dad calmed down, as he usually did after an angry spat, and handed over his chequebook.

"All right. You can go to David Jones and buy a chair. But I'm not made of money."

A day later a new dining suite was installed. I don't know how Mum had the gumption to tell Dad she'd bought a little extra.

When my father came home from the office about lunchtime on Saturdays, he got to fixing up the house. He was an accountant, not a handyman, and swore with frustration if nails he hammered curved in the wrong direction. Mum flapped around like a protective mother hen, deflecting frustrated dramas when Dad yelled from the ladder, "Dot, keep those blasted kids out of the way. Can't you see I'm trying to do a bit of spackling?"

She grabbed the stroller and took us for a fast walk up Headland Road to watch as steamrollers flattened the ground for new roads and a subdivision. Often she chatted to neighbours who were similarly pushing baby carriages.

When we got home, licking penny ice creams, Dad, from up the ladder, would cheerfully call out for a cup of tea. His balding head was caked in plaster from the ceiling.

Over a sherry, Mum talked about a real builder down the road. The wife was a good sort and they needed the money so he would be cheap to hire.

Sure enough, Mr Dudley was just the man for the job. Tall and nimble, his face prematurely lined from the Craven A ciggies he inhaled regularly, he pointed nicotine-stained digits at building plans, joists and carpentry. Mum thought he looked decent. His missus was also expecting their third. Little Bruce's arrival coincided with my sister's birth.

Happily, it cemented a relationship between a working-class man and a British gentleman working for a Lord. But when Mrs Dudley trundled up to proudly show off her new son with two chubby daughters in tow, Mum had nothing to offer.

Dad was painting the front door a bright orange when my toddler brother and I escaped through a hole in the fence. A truck lumbered over the rise, bearing down on us before we were snatched out of harm's way. Mum was so horrified when a woman with a hooked nose and black hair appeared at our gate clutching our hands that she went into premature labour.

Dad was annoyed he couldn't finish painting the door.

My sister was born out of fright and whisked away at birth.

"What's happened to my baby?" cried Mum. "Why can't I nurse her?"

It was days before she learned her baby was jaundiced and needed a blood transfusion. My parents' blood types were not compatible being Rh Negative and Rh Positive. It was a fortnight before Mum cradled her. Mum was exhausted and felt guilty, and sadly it caused bonding difficulties for them both.

My sister was bright but tended towards a liverish disposition. Some might argue she was at the lowest pecking order, but years later when I adopted children from overseas orphanages, I realised babies are scarred if they miss out on vital bonding. My sister wasn't breast-fed which contributed towards her feelings, while my brother and I had months of sucking at the trough, so to speak.

When it came to choosing names, Mum asked Mrs Dudley for suggestions.

"How about Nita?" she offered.

"I don't think so. I'm not fond of that name."

"Oh," said Mrs Dudley. "That's my name."

And Mum blushed at her *faux pas*. In the 50s it was common for neighbours and friends to address each other by their married status and not Christian names. It was called manners.

"Manners maketh the man!" Dad would thump on the table.

"That's not good manners, dear," Mum chided. "Can't we eat our dinner in peace?"

On the way to the suburban Births and Deaths registry office, they agreed on Joanna (a family name) and Juliet (since she was born in July.) Now they had three children in three years—Jonquil, Jasper and Joanna—often referred to as the three Js.

Mum was pleased when her doctor said it was dangerous to have more children. The pill wasn't invented so she solved the problem by buying twin beds and joining them together.

As the years rolled by they slept in the same room but their beds drifted further apart until they each hugged a wall, separated by a long dressing table. Mum filled her side with cut roses on linen doilies, tubs of face powder, hand lotions, rolled-up tissues which she clamped onto her teeth to even out the lipstick, mascara (in a tub and applied with a lick to the tiny brush), bobby pins, lavender talcum powder, tweezers, rouge, lipsticks (all bright red), rows of miniature sample perfumes and headache tablets—Aspro or Vincent's APCs for Mum and Bex powders for Dad.

Dad's side of the dressing table held nasal spray, cotton buds for ear wax, an engraved golden ashtray bought in Aden filled with tobacco dregs and dead matches, a carved wooden elephant with a tusk missing to rest his pipe on, screwed-up tissues, a patterned saucer to rest his spectacles on, and newspapers sent from England by his sister, all tied with string and brown paper. He didn't care if they were months old. It was a touch of home.

About the time my sister thought about crawling, Dad came home whistling.

He uttered the magic words Mum longed to hear.

Chapter 4
North Curl Curl

"The Head called me in to talk about leave. I said I'd ask the wife. When do you want to go?"

Lord Vestey's firm appreciated Dad. By offering carrots like a free passage on one of their company Blue Star ships back to his homeland for several months, he might agree to renew his contract for another five years. And return to Australia where he was clearly needed in the accounts' department.

He loved Mum and needed her support; if she were miserable in Australia he would negotiate a deal. It might mean staying with relatives until they could make their own way.

"Up to you, Dot," he said. "We've got a house here; it's warm, good for the kids."

"Let's see what happens when we get there," said Mum. She hated being pinned down.

They were keen to celebrate Christmas with Mum's naval brother and family in Wiltshire and Dad's family in Colchester, but unaware they were to experience blizzard conditions so severe there was almost a fatal outcome.

In the 50s and 60s it was cheaper to travel by ship than fly, and more relaxing. Sea voyages created a whiff of illusion, a chance to meet interesting people, taste exotic food from foreign ports, and live in a temporary bubble.

"I love a man in uniform," Mum murmured as handsome ship's officers, in bleached-white uniforms and brass buttons, welcomed our little family. We five clambered up the gangplank of the Rhodesia Star. The passenger list consisted of only twelve.

If there were delays loading cargo at ports along the Australian coast or across other oceans my parents didn't care. They weren't on a time schedule and would have been glad if the ship developed a major engine problem and was holed up for months in a foreign port.

Mum didn't have to cook or make beds. She didn't have to use an outside lavatory, and use small squares of *The Sydney Morning Herald*, which she'd cut to stretch the budget. And she didn't need to shake out our tiny gumboots for sleepy funnel-web or red-back spiders, or swat slithering reptiles in the chook house.

Her only concern was to ingest seasick pills when the vessel began lurching, and ensure she put reins on us if we toddled around the windy deck. These little harnesses saved us from harm. She sewed tingly golden bells on the thin leather straps and we pretended we were galloping horses.

Life on the ocean waves in a cargo ship was homely, comfortable and orderly. Though we were on holiday the crew were not. It wasn't their job to entertain us.

The Library and Smoking Room were dark and gloomy with their salt-sprayed windows, thick drapes and large rolled armchairs. Circular tables with coasters bearing the ship's name were nailed to the floor, while books with unappealing titles were stacked on floor-to-ceiling mahogany shelves behind heavy glass panels. There were board games, and many hours were passed pondering on a next move in chess. Stewards in starched white uniforms and cockney accents attended us, asking, "Care for a drink, sir?"

Duty-free drinks encouraged some passengers to be thirsty and cheerful. And an order of a Scotch on the rocks and a Dubonnet for the lady, my good sir, gave an ingratiating steward every chance of a handsome tip.

Women considered beer caveman's water, which needed to be drunk in copious quantities to get the same effect as a couple of short sharp aperitifs. Guzzling men thought they were real blokes who could down a few pints and remain upright and masculine. Women thought they were mad, and still do.

Ladies were useful accoutrements to men. They added decorative femininity sitting side saddle on a bar stool in high heels, a billowing organza skirt or a frock with a scooped neck, real pearls, expensive perfume, kiss-curls swished to the side of the face, and a smile of fake joy. Most men were nervous of women whose voices were slightly high-pitched and snappy with shades of hidden intelligence.

Days at sea were passed pleasantly playing deck quoits and avoiding the likes of the author of obscure books, a pontificating poet and the ruddy-faced ex-serviceman with the orange moustache. Dad said those types spoilt the exercise regime, creating in him a dilemma. Should one make eye contact or just nod at him on each deck lap?

Dad would mutter, "I'll have to get up earlier now or wait for that frisky bastard to finish his rounds."

And Mum would remind him he was on holiday and there was plenty of room on the ship for everyone.

More often than not Mum was sprawled in a deckchair feeling wretched while the ship lurched and albatrosses screeched overhead. She rallied if the dowager with thick ankles encased in leather brogues approached her, nodded and said, "Lovely day, we should hit some islands soon," then trot off in that dismissive superior way afforded titled countrywomen.

Mum looked forward to dining at night, the chance to dress up and be tempted by fare she'd never cook, food with French names that were basically 'tarted up Ocker meals' swimming in sauces you couldn't pronounce.

It was like the honeymoon she never had.

Dad relaxed. He showed his caring side and became the dapper gentleman he wished to portray. He lathered his remaining strands of hair with Brylcreem, donned a tuxedo or pair of wide-legged trousers, shirt, waistcoat and cravat, and sang fragments of operettas off key.

After feeding, bathing, and soothing us, Mum would put on a flouncy nylon frock, clasp a string of fat white pearls around her neck and unleash her hair. She curled it by bobbing her fingers in water and twisting her hair around her digits, then fastened it with bobby pins.

The gentle rocking of the ship, the soft swish of her pretty dress, and the lingering fragrance as she kissed us goodnight. We kids drifted into a sound sleep while Mum and Dad became a Hollywood couple who'd glide down the wide circular staircase to the lounge for cocktails prior to being summoned to the dining room.

What to choose from the menu?

As the voyage progressed, waiters remembered each passenger's food preference. If my parents decided to taste something different, they would point to the choice on the menu and, if it was not what the steward brought, Mum would say, "Oh, since you brought it, that will be perfectly lovely, thank you, won't it, dear?" giving Dad the beady eye.

Dad would reply, "Thank you, old chap. How's the family back in Goa?"

The Goanese waiter would smile, bow and scuttle back to the hot galley.

"So far from home," said Mum. "I wonder if he's missing his family?"

Pampered passengers gave stewards a rich tip in a sealed envelope when they berthed at their destination. Cabin boys were similarly rewarded. Cargo ship passengers had a certain amount of freedom. But they weren't allowed to see the cramped crew quarters below, or enter the galley that was so hot stewards were brushing off beads of perspiration from their forehead as they served meals.

"Waiters," my father said, "don't speak the Queen's English, but they can't help it, poor chaps."

Dad would try to guess what part of Britain they hailed from. On the Blue Star Line all the crew were from the Commonwealth, including cheap labour from India. They were reserved, polite and courteous. If they didn't obey orders, or passengers complained, they were not signed on for the next voyage.

This trip took us around the Cape of Good Hope and up to the Canary Islands.

When the ship berthed, the dock was alive with brown people with wide grins and black hair. They lined up rows of child-sized walking dolls in open cardboard boxes; gorgeous dolls with eyes that opened and shut wearing straw bonnets, white socks, plastic shoes and detailed costumes. They were so cheap Mum bought me one, and two more for her nieces in England. Photos were taken on deck so passengers could display their dolls. Some were taller than me.

We arrived in England in misty weather and a warm welcome from Mum's naval brother and family who lived in Lacock, Wiltshire. Their home was a magnificent three-storey rambling dwelling called Rey Bridge House. Snowflakes covered the quaint farming village where church bells pealed and streets were cobbled.

We children were bundled up in real fur coats Mum made from unpicking old ones, and Dad's little family from the tropics breathed in 'good old English air' to build up an appetite before the next meal at the dining table complete with silver candelabra.

Sunday nights we had a traditional light English supper served in the chintzy lounge, with a roaring fire, and our first glimpse of television, which hadn't arrived in Australia yet.

Sister Joanna learned to totter; chocolates were set at intervals, like bait, on the carpet in Aunt Olive's semi-detached in Colchester.

Ollie was a permed bottle-blonde; wrinkled, ditzy, funny, gushing. Dad said she had verbal diarrhoea. But she was given to irrational outbursts, which left Mum open-mouthed and the house under a dark mood from her fusses.

Whenever Dad had a blow-up, Mum would say, "Careful, Fairley! I hope you're not getting like your sister," and whisper to us, "I think the madness comes from your father's side of the family. Ollie should have had children—that would have quietened her down."

Ollie's husband was almost mute, spending his days reading the *Daily Express* from cover to cover, chewing over crosswords or crouched by an electric fire.

"Don't go in there, children," we were warned. "Uncle Lewis is a busy man. He's thinking."

He was an aloof gentle soul, a living cadaver, who wore a buttoned-up cardigan and scarf, and had a perpetual cup of tea at hand.

Ollie never indulged in a refrigerator or washing machine; it was seen as frippery. She preferred village friends, a nightly glug of sherry and cheap cigarettes. In good moods she was extremely likeable, in dark moods she caused your stomach to churn. She enjoyed her parochial existence, and informed friends, "My baby brother from Australia is visiting with his family. Do you know where Australia is, dear?"

Mum found herself in an embarrassing situation when I flatly refused to eat Ollie's stew.

"I don't like it," I cried. "It's dirty. I can't see the food."

"There's nothing dirty about my food, child," said Ollie haughtily.

"Don't make a fuss, darling," begged Mum, "or I'll have to send you to bed hungry."

"I'd rather be hungry," I whimpered.

Ollie said, "In my day a child was seen and not heard. Make her sit until she eats it."

Mum would glance at Dad but he'd shrug and join the mute brother-in-law in case he'd thought of anything interesting to say. So I spent hours sitting at the tiny table, my arms folded, face tearstained until my aunt came back into the kitchen.

"Why haven't they sent you to bed yet? What is she doing up at this time of night?"

Then the next day the same food was brought out until I eventually ate it over several days.

It was a relief to get back to the less strict parenting at Rey Bridge, to Nanny, our two cousins and Mamar, their grandmother, who made up thrilling imaginary stories about her life in Africa. She had a gravelly voice, wore lots of make-up and purple clothes, and adored children.

Though snow crippled many roads in England that year I wondered about the kindness of Santa. For Christmas he'd given both Jasper and me elongated cardboard boxes. Little Jasper squealed in delight, retrieving a fiery red train, and Mum said the other one was for me, the green box. Inside the box was a mountain of train tracks, signals, sentry boxes and switches.

"Call them Mary and John," she said. "Isn't Father Christmas kind?"

I thought, no, he got me mixed up with some other kid, probably a boy. I never wanted that sort of present. A plastic doll that pees, yes, but not this.

"We'll help you set it up," said Mum, and from Christmas until we returned to Australia the grown-ups acted like excited kids. Clutching glasses of home-brew, they watched Mary and John charge along the tracks with a clickety-clack and blowing whistles, while our tiny heads barely reached up to the top of the long table.

"I think Nanny's calling you for dinner," an adult warned if we fretted.

"It's mine, Mummy," I pleaded. "I want to play with Mary."

"I know, darling, but don't you want Mummy and Daddy to have fun? Father Christmas said you had to share."

Around this time my aunt nearly had her neck severed. Driving home from London, the vehicle slid on black ice. Rey Bridge House was hushed until she was brought home. She remained in bed with a scarf around her neck, whispering in short gasps and making sure the Teasmade was plugged in. (A machine that whistled at a set time to tell you tea was ready to pour.)

Nanny was always first up to attend to my cousins. My uncle went off to Bath or Admiralty House in London. The farmer's mother from next door, with her heavy gait and wispy white hair, planted herself at the table to clean the silver. During the day the butcher, the baker, the milkman and postie called. But when the clergyman made a spectacular entrance slipping on the freshly-scrubbed tiled hall, my aunt said it served him right and laughed heartily for days.

My aunt and uncle were well connected not only to naval staff, but people in the film industry, so sometimes 'Dear Charles from Belgium—we are so fond of him' visited and offered hospitality in his country.

Perhaps the cold English winter after sunny Australia, Ollie's little turns, and not being in our own home gave Mum pause for thought. When Dad went to the London office to renew his contract with Lord Vestey, she said, "Tell them we'll go back to Australia for another stint if they get us on a passenger liner. Tell them it's not fair for a family to dominate half the passenger list on a cargo ship. Make sure we travel an interesting route. Panama or Suez."

Dad booked us on the P & O liner *Strathmore*, and rattled off the exciting ports of call. But while the leather and tin luggage was being sorted on the day of departure, Mum said, "Where's Joanna?"

Everyone fled in different directions calling her name. She'd locked herself in the upstairs lavatory. Dad had to crawl through the attic window and out onto the shingled roof, then he broke the icy toilet window to retrieve his little girl.

"Horsey!" squealed Joanna, pointing at a large silver fox darting between a copse of snow-laden trees, a lasting picture before we set sail to Australia in time for me to start school.

I expect Mum found it hard to settle when we arrived back in North Curl Curl, back into the blazing heat. She was furious to find the people who had rented our house had reneged on payments and vanished. Then she saw the couple's four-year old son spinning around on his tricycle.

"Little boy," she said, sternly, "where's your father?"

Head down, he cycled off.

I didn't want to go to school but Mum said it was the law. "Do you want the police to put me in jail?" she said as I tugged tearfully at her skirt while she wheeled Joanna down the steep hill to the primary school. Jasper, on the other hand, begged to go.

"You'll love it, darling. I promise," she said.

I didn't. It was noisy and chaotic in the playground and I felt utterly alone.

Outside the classroom was a plump rosy-cheeked girl called Anne who resembled one of those walking-dolls from Tenerife. She was buckled into a wheelchair, her legs encased in iron and leather shoes, a polio victim. Another new entrant was so traumatised she was screaming and thrashing as a teacher and her mother carried her into the classroom.

"Don't go, Mummy," I wept.

"I have to," she said. "Mothers aren't allowed at school. Ah, look up there, you've got company."

Our duck, Esmeralda, had flown all the way from home and settled herself on a telegraph pole in the paddock next to the school.

My first glimpse of a classroom was row upon row of twinned wooden desks crammed with boys in grey flannels, hair slicked back, freckle-faced and grinning. Two little louts leered at me with pencils up their nostrils. They had names like John, Peter, Gary, Kenny, Philip, Barry, Stephen, Brian or Tony.

The girls wore smocked or printed frocks, their hair plaited or short with large ribbons, and had names like Susan, Judy, Carol, Patricia, Jennifer, Pamela, Vicky, Roslyn, Robyn, Diane, Wendy plus the 'ettes'—Nanette, Jeanette, Annette, Lynette. I had the most unusual name and, if it wasn't for a new girl who lived up the road with another uncommon name, I'd have been utterly miserable.

Ingrad lived on the hilly side of Headland Road with her parents and a brother Jasper's age in a ranch-style wooden home with a panoramic vista designed by her architect father. She was shy like me, with strawberry-blonde hair, and we became best friends, unaware our lives would entwine in extraordinary ways over the next few decades.

One day in singing class I nodded off to sleep and was removed by the teacher when a stream of liquid oozed onto the floor.

"Ooh, that new girl's wet her pants!"

Deeply embarrassed, I cried, "I didn't. She did," and pointed to Ingrad.

"No, Jonquil. You did," scolded the teacher, waggling her finger at the puddle I'd made. "Tell your mother to change your panties when you get home and, next time, relieve yourself before you come into the classroom. That's what the toilet blocks are for."

It wasn't long before Mum said she needed a change.

"You've just had a long holiday, woman," said Dad.

"Yes, but we need to better our circumstances."

Mum's next project was looking for a bigger house.

When Jasper, me and the new dog, Nikki, got badly stung by hornets in our vacant block, despite repeated warnings not to poke the nest with long sticks, Mum was even more determined.

She found a house at Collaroy, several miles north of North Curl Curl. It was a two-bedroom villa with a separate lounge and dining room and front and back verandah on the main Pittwater Road of a sleepy beach town. We children were told to sit on the front verandah and not move an inch while the adults negotiated over a cup of tea.

The talk went on forever but we stayed put until the owner's horrible daughter came out with a plate of biscuits.

"I don't like you," she said, glaring at me, "so you can't have any."

She gave them to my siblings. In the 50s, if parents told you not to interrupt then you didn't. Inwardly I cried about the injustice.

My parents were desperate to sell up to secure the Collaroy house. A man returned several times to view it but remained uncommitted, putting my parents on edge.

Late one afternoon the potential buyer, wearing a long overcoat and baggy pants, turned up with his family in a fawn Humber. His wife seemed keen and liked the rose garden and they agreed to buy it. Dad arrived home weary from the office as they were leaving. He was so relieved to find a buyer he said he'd throw in the block next door.

Mum was horrified!

The men shook hands and the deal was done. She ripped into Dad once they'd driven off.

"You bloody fool! The couple agreed to buy the house before you got home. How could you? You gave away the vacant section."

Dad was contrite.

"But you've got what you want now—a house near the sea. I thought I was making you happy."

In those days a handshake was a gentleman's agreement, a contract more honourable than a signed piece of paper. And since my father considered himself a gentleman, he was not going to break his promise.

That's just how it was in the 50s.

Chapter 5
Moving to Collaroy

"Have you got what you want now, Dot?" Dad asked as the removal truck backed down the driveway. I saw him slip ten shillings to the driver to buy himself some beer. Our new house was stacked with cardboard boxes tied in string and partially wrapped-up furniture.

"Well, it's not Buck Palace," Mum said, referring to the Queen's residence, "but it'll do us for now. Close to the beach so we save on holidays."

"That's the spirit, Dot."

Dad planted a fat kiss on her face, and patted her backside.

"Careful, Fairley," Mum warned coquettishly. "The children."

The wooden-gabled villa faced Pittwater Road, where green double-decker buses, trucks and cars rattled by at leisurely intervals.

"Is that a palace, Mummy?"

I was pointing to an elongated building with a verandah opposite our house. The imposing building sprawled imperiously on a rise across the four-lane highway.

"That's the Darby and Joan Home where old war vets live. Keep away from there. Some of the men got gassed in the war. They might be a bit funny."

The shell-shocked men resembled prisoners in their blue striped pyjamas and leather slip-ons. They were slumped in deckchairs on the deck encircling the Salvation Army. White-coated nurses strutted in and out of doors; they opened with promise, but shut with finality.

"Your father could end up there if you kids drive him round the bend."

Our new home looked seedy compared to other houses in the same street. Mum said once we painted the fence and added a splash of colour inside we'd be as smart as anyone.

"We've got a new place, a new house," I cried, opening doors, inspecting rooms.

"In polite circles we say *home*," cautioned Mum. "We invite people to our home, not place. It stamps you saying house or place. A house is someone else's home. A place is a public convenience."

The villa was surrounded by high wooden fences on three sides and flanked by a mulberry, loquat and weeping willow trees. The front lawn was wide enough to do cartwheels on and the back section spacious enough to play cricket. A narrow cracked path led to a garage covered in ivy and thorny rose bushes where Dad stored our tin trunks and battered suitcases.

"Are we getting a car?"

"Not now. We can't afford it."

In those days a car cost three years' wages.

"Are we poor, Mummy?"

Mother flicked her pageboy bob.

"We'll get a car one day. One should never live beyond one's station. Now you and Joanna can sleep in the front bedroom, Daddy and I will be across the hallway in this room and Jasper can sleep on the back verandah."

My designated bedroom, complete with high ceiling and a frieze around the walls, had panes of stained glass and side-hinged windows. In the gathering darkness I could see people reading newspapers in the passing buses. From the old soldiers' home, bare light bulbs threw shafts of yellow onto the street. I could see the inmates having supper.

"Can't we swap rooms? This one would be much better for grown-ups."

"No, darling," said Mum. "Your father needs peace. He has to get up early in the morning, so we need the quiet side of the house."

"But, Mummy, I'm scared."

"What on earth for?"

"Those old men across the road. What if they climb in here to kill me?"

"Don't be silly. You're only six. Who'd be bothered climbing over the prickly bush? Some of those men don't have legs. The only thing coming through the window will be mozzies. Anyway your sister's got a loud voice—she'd scare the devil away. We'll leave the door open and a light on in the hallway."

I remained fearful.

The shadows of passing traffic cast eerie patterns on the walls. It became a nightly ritual looking for old men lurking beneath the ruffles of the bedspread as I screeched, "I know you're under there. Come on out. I'm not scared."

Mum put a tin potty under our beds.

"No prowler would want to put his face up against that."

The potty saved us having to paddle through the darkened house onto the back verandah where Jasper slept and out the screen door to the outhouse.

When Joanna was younger Mum crept in before going to her bed and lifted her so she could pee into a pot.

"Good girl, you will have a nice dry night tonight."

This was somehow comforting and chased the boogiemen away.

"Why do you call them boogiemen?" Mum said. "In New Zealand we say bogeymen."

This further reinforced the idea that there were imaginary evils skulking around.

We had a small wooden shed with a corrugated roof at the bottom of our garden. Mum named it the lavatory and planted nasturtiums around the side, to make it more welcoming and smell better. She said ordinary people use the word toilet. The night-cart men knew which homes had septic tanks and those who needed a replacement tin bucket.

The shuddering lumbering sound of the lavvy truck with its noisy pistons was a weekly dawn event jolting neighbours from their sleep. Muscular men, usually Lebanese, Italians, Greeks and Slavs called foreigners, thudded down driveways hollering amid the clanging of cans. Their cheerful countenance was in sharp contrast to Mum's warning, "If you don't do well at school you might end up being a lavatory person."

One hot morning the dunny truck was late. Mum and I were in the chook yard tossing scraps of batter she'd let me whisk up in my toy tea set for a treat. Some hens were producing yolks with blood traces. Although Mum said it wasn't a good idea to feed animals what they produced, she made an exception this time.

"The lavatory man is late," she said, "and the can is full. I wonder if there's been a breakdown?"

Suddenly a burly man appeared with an empty toilet can slung over his shoulder.

"Quickly, inside, darling," she said, grabbing my arm. "We mustn't get in the way of the man's business."

As we dashed up the concrete steps clasping hankies to our nose the unfortunate night-cart man stumbled and lurched sideways. He corrected his balance but some of the bucket contents had splattered on his shoulders.

"Top of the morning to ye," he said, doffing his cap, then bounded off to his truck.

"What lovely manners that man has," said Mum. "Remind me to put out a bottle of beer for him at Christmas."

Why did people want to do disgusting jobs? Mum wasn't sure, but thought they were happier doing that than staying in their own country. Besides, she said, they probably got better paid than my poor father who sat on a crowded bus and slaved all day in the office.

"Mummy, do lampity (sic) men get married? Do they have special soap so they don't smell? Do they have friends?"

Mum thought they could be the cleanest people on earth. They'd have to be or no one would want them.

"Fairley," Mum said as Dad walked in the door that evening. "She's done it again. Your daughter's done another malaprop."

"Let me change out of these clothes first, Dot," he called down the hallway, "and get me a drink. I want to savour the moment."

In those days parents revelled in delayed gratification. He cleaned his pipe, lit it, and then sat back while Mum hovered over him, smiling.

"Now, what did our daughter say, Dot? This better be good."

"Jonquil said lampity for lavatory."

Dad chuckled.

"Lampity, eh? That's a good one."

So the moniker stuck.

"I think we'll keep this kid, Dot," he said cuddling me. "She's good for a laugh at least once a day."

"She takes after your sister, Olive," Mother reminded him. "She's always getting words mixed up."

On arrival at Collaroy, Mum didn't expect a neighbourhood welcome when we began unpacking, but she was surprised by a lack of inquisitiveness. On the first night at home, with suitcases and boxes and kids getting underfoot, Mum said, "Can you duck over to the house next door and ask to borrow half a cup of sugar? The shops are closed and I forgot to pack any. You know your father. He'll blow up if he hasn't got sugar for his tea."

I clutched my young brother's hand as we apprehensively trotted over to the brick house, which looked unfriendly in the nightlight. I lifted Jasper up and he pressed his dimpled finger onto the chimer.

A dog began yapping its blood-curdling warnings.

We stood nervously in the arched porch where blasts from the radiogram intermingled with the barking. "Shuddup, Bully," boomed a man's voice, and a large shadow emerged behind bubbled frosted glass.

"Yeah?" asked the man clasping a glass of beer. His drooling white bulldog panted heavily, baring its fangs. I timidly related my mother's request.

"Berry," the big man called out. "The new people have moved in."

He shut the door, leaving us sugarless and unsure.

Although it was an ominous start, the neighbour couldn't contain her distance. She became a chatty suburban fixture and an inveterate borrower. Mum thought Berry was a good sort. She might be 'a bit Australian' but she meant well and she was good for a laugh.

Berry said word had spread that a low-quality family had bought in Pittwater Road. They had strange kids and a mad dog. Mum was upset by the reference to our dog.

"How could they?" she said. "Nikki wouldn't hurt a flea. She's a lot nicer than most people. What an odd thing to say."

The neighbours liked Mum for she was friendly with a wide smile. She was not stuck up; despite nagging suspicions she might be a bit of old country, meaning England, since 'no Aussie wants bloody Poms making them feel inferior.' They warmed to her when she said she was from New Zealand and felt sorry she was so far from home.

"Yer poor love. Oi couldn't handle being away from me family. Strewth, that's crook. If yer feelin' lonely, ducks, you come an' have a nice cuppa with me, orright?"

Shortly after we settled in our new home, Dad said an important man from the office and his wife would be calling in next Sunday.

"Invite them in for tea," said Mum.

To make a good impression she feverishly cleaned the house, cooked pikelets (giving us the burnt ones to keep us quiet), laid out teacups and saucers on a trolley, and dressed us in our best clothes. After the clock ticked past five, Mum wondered if Dad had got the wrong weekend. When the older couple turned up but lingered on, Mum thought them thoughtless for she had three young children to feed and put to bed.

As darkness gathered and no one arose from the couch, Mum realised with horror the couple were expecting a meal.

What to do?

Shops closed over the weekend and she'd never embarrass Dad by telling his colleague there was not enough food in the house. But like many 50s housewives she was resourceful. After pouring sherry for the guests, she raced out to the chook yard in her rose-patterned frock and high heels, wrung the neck of a hen, plucked and cooked it.

By the time dinner was ready the guests were red-faced and laughing like hyenas at Dad's wit and the sherry decanter was empty.

Next day, Mum said, "In our home we have breakfast, lunch and dinner. It's slummy calling a perfectly nice evening meal tea. Tea is an afternoon snack. Once you open your mouth, people can tell if you're educated or not. Remember that, children. You'll never marry a nice person if you can't speak the Queen's English!"

Hearing the postman's whistle was a festive occasion on Pittwater Road.

Women with floury hands, bibbed aprons and large curlers flung open their front doors to stand outside in small groups catching up with the latest gossip. They'd dress up for walking to the corner grocery store by covering their pin-cushioned heads with a satin scarf emblazoned with a patriotic theme—

perhaps a koala resting on a sprig of greenery, bounding kangaroos or native birds of Australia with a Made in Britain tag sewn on.

In the 50s some women kept their hair in curlers all day so they could look presentable for their husband in the evening. Books on etiquette reminded women men did not like sleeping with head armoury; they had enough of that in the war.

"I hear the postie," Mum would call, causing us youngsters to shriek excitedly and clamber onto the fence to peer down the footpath.

Our postman was not typical. He wore his blue serge uniform with one sleeve neatly pinned back. His opposite hand manoeuvred a bike with a bulging leather pouch. Letters and magazines were cylindrically bound.

"Don't say anything about his arm missing," warned Mum. "We don't want to remind him and hurt his feelings."

Other one-armed jobs were given to wrinkled and fatigued-looking lift operators in department stores who squatted on a wooden stool in the crowded confines of elevators. If only these men knew what mums were telling their children about missing limbs.

Instead of explaining how that man fought for our country and part of his body got blown away, they used it as a warning.

"Remember to swim between the flags. Do you want to get bitten by a shark and end up like Mr Postie?"

Our mailman seemed ancient with a tiny crimsoned face and bulging cheeks. Mum said she wouldn't mind his job if she didn't have to look after naughty kids. She'd love the fresh air, chatting to people, and thought the postie was so good at whistling he must be a member of the Salvation Army band, playing the trumpet or bugle. Mum's remark put me off learning a brass instrument. I was not going to have inflated cheeks like Mr Postie.

When you're six you believe in the tooth fairy, Santa Claus, monsters and eating crusts to make your hair curl. You take for granted mothers are telling the truth when they say rain is caused by two clouds bumping into each other. Or, if you go cross-eyed, a wind will blow in another direction and you'll be left looking like that forever.

"If you start digging here you might get to China and find buried treasure," said Mum, when she needed help in the garden.

One evening we walked around the block with the dog on a lead since she was in season. Mum said only farm people said on heat. The neighbourhood hounds could sniff Nikki a mile away as she strained at the leash causing us to do little gallops. Mum was disgusted with inquisitive fox terriers, kelpies and mongrels half Nikki's size, darting down driveways, yapping into the still night while their owners parted curtains yelling, "Who's out there?" Come inside, Bluey, Rex, Bullet, Neville or whatever names people gave their dogs.

"Get a stick," Mum said. "I'm not having any low-life dog sniffing around Nikki. She's purebred. Shoo! Go away, you mongrels."

Passing the plumber's house, Mum had a rare insight. This plumber and his apple-cheeked wife had two bonny zinc-nosed toddlers who spent their days sifting sand into painted tin buckets. But he also had a magnificent pedigree German Shepherd.

"Perhaps if I tell him we'll be needing a septic tank sometime he'll lend us Rufus."

Sure enough, when Nikki was in season, Mum made a deal with the man. Panting Rufus was like a great bear, black and yellow, with pricked ears and uncontrollable excitement.

"Get inside, kids," ordered Mum, "and close the curtains."

"Do what your mother says," yelled the plumber, barely holding onto his lunging hound.

We scampered inside and knelt on the back verandah settee, lifting up a corner of the curtain.

"Action, Rufus," shouted the plumber.

"Good girl, Nikki," soothed Mum.

We were shocked when that big dog attacked our Nikki and bailed her up against the garage wall so violently that fragments of plaster fell off.

"Don't worry about the wall," shouted Mum. "My husband can fix it when he gets home. Take his mind off the office."

"Don't let that big doggie hurt Nikki," whimpered my little brother, clambering down the back steps.

"All over, Rover," said the plumber. "Good boy, Rufus." He patted him proudly.

"He's a *hobble* dog," I sniffed.

"Does Nikki look unhappy?" Mum said. "Look, she's smiling."

She didn't explain what happened. It was grown-up's business. And Nikki seemed to somehow glow.

That night, Mum said to Dad, "Oh, by the way, the plumber called today and the deed is done. If it works out we can afford to send the children to private schools."

Nikki became bloated and swollen and refused to run after sticks.

Mum said, "We're going to have some little surprises soon."

She made a bed from old blankets and sheets on the back verandah and told Jasper to keep an eye on Nikki, especially if she started groaning in the night. He was so excited by all the mystery he spent the night flashing his little torch at the dog.

I asked Mum, "When Nikki gets up, do the little puppies inside her get up and walk, too?"

When Nikki was about due, we returned from the shops and she'd disappeared.

We frantically searched, calling for her.

"She's here," yelled Jasper, shining his little torch under the house.

Mum, in her afternoon frock, scrambled under the floorboards pushing aside cobwebs, to find Nikki lying like a beached whale, panting and exhausted. She'd given birth in the dirt to a dozen puppies.

"Oh, she's smothered two of them," said Mum as she pulled the litter out one by one.

When we got Nikki inside to the clean bedding on the back verandah, we stroked her clever head and helped pop the puppies on milky teats. Mum said to leave her alone as she needed time to bond. But we wanted to watch so Mum set up a sofa at a distance. She served dinner on our laps while we sat like movie goers, squealing excitedly if a puppy urinated, discussing names that appealed to us.

"That puppy done a little jobbie," I cried. "Oh, you sweet little thing."

"I can't believe what I've just heard!"

Mum came roaring out of the kitchen.

"Did I hear correctly? Did I hear you say done instead of did?"

I couldn't remember.

"Have you ever heard me say that—or your father? Can you imagine the Queen saying that?"

I shook my head.

"Your teacher wouldn't use that language. I wonder where you picked it up? Only a kid from the slums would say that, or new migrants who don't know any better. No nice man will want you if you don't speak properly."

And for good measure, she added what every parent told their kids, "I'm only saying this for your own good. You'll thank me one day."

Nikki had several litters over the years. She paid for our schooling.

Chapter 6
School Life in the 50s

Conformity and conservatism ruled the 50s when children obeyed their parents and the days rumbled along like the rolling of the surf.

Daily Mum took us for swims at the Collaroy pool where a swimming instructor gave lessons in dog-paddling. She perched on the concrete steps. We were told to keep away from a gurgling pipe that sucked in surf water and sometimes flooded the pool. Later a local girl ended up miles away at another beach, battered but alive.

The Basin was a few minutes' walk from home. When the tide was out little boys wearing sun hats and clutching fishing rods perched on a rocky outlet. Their mothers in one-piece bathers, straw hats and sunglasses propped their elbows up on the coarse golden sands blinking against the fierce sunlight.

Our dads wore togs with a modesty flap. Overseas people with hairy torsos pranced on the sand tossing a large plastic beach ball; they were considered low-quality imports. Their scant bathers flaunting lively bulges nowadays called 'budgie smugglers' shocked the average Australian women. They didn't want their pristine beaches and sunburnt children exposed to such riff-raff. It was a case of 'do what you like in your own country, not ours.'

Aussie men didn't notice. If they did, their beach trip would have been spoilt by Freudian envy.

Lifesavers in tight Speedos and thin rubber caps were exempt from disapproving looks. These brawny strapping Aussies, so sun-tanned the hair on their arms glistened gold, were objects of desire especially when the song Please Don't Talk to the Lifeguard hit the pop charts. They perched high on towers, smoking and peering out for sharks, shouting through loudhailers ordering bathers to swim between the flags, and giving first aid to weeping kiddies who'd been stung by blue bottles.

A disconcerting episode occurred when Mum took us to The Basin with our buckets and spades, towels, zinc cream and plastic surf rings. A casual acquaintance was basking on an expansive beach towel and beckoned us over. She was a keen golfer, had a car and lived in a yellowy sandstone house in a nicer part of Collaroy. She could have afforded a packet of Gillette razor blades. As she dozed off, flat on her back, with a newspaper draped over her face, I glanced at her brown legs and green and pink rose-patterned togs. I was alarmed to see a black tendril poking from the top of her thighs. These days you call it pubic hair; those days it was too rude to mention. I had no idea what it was.

I whispered in Mum's ear, "What's coming out of her togs?"

Mum blushed. She said it might be a spider. When I gasped, she said, "Don't worry, it's probably dead. It'll drop off when she goes for a swim."

Eventually the woman nipped down for a quick dip to cool off before slumping on her back and exposing her beautiful long legs to the inviting sun. Her togs began to ride up after the immersion to expose a cluster of spiders.

"Mummy, there's more. Do you think her husband knows?"

For once Mum couldn't think of an answer.

"Go and build a lovely sandcastle," she said.

From then on I shook out my little cozzies for creepy crawlies before going for swims.

While parents were protective of their offspring, we enjoyed a freedom that was universal and these days can only be compared to a child growing up in the country. Doors might be locked but windows were left open, milk money was put on the porch and it wasn't stolen. Keys were left in cars and windows wound down. Children were told to play outside and we made our own fun.

We looked for fairies in shrubs, lay on our backs gazing at clouds and imagining people and animals, and, since most neighbourhoods had a run-down house and overgrown garden, we fantasised about wicked witches grabbing children.

Nikki, when she wasn't having puppies, was our playmate—we'd dress her in tutus, hats and sandshoes, and wheel her around in a pram. She'd happily comply until the urge to bark and chase tyres on Pittwater Road became irresistible.

Mum said, "Perhaps we'll invite Rufus to come around and calm her down."

We'd sneak Nikki bits of chewy meat under the table and the grateful dog licked our knees. If Nikki wasn't in season, Mum tied a note to her collar and sent her up the road. 'Children, be home by 5 o'clock' or 'Lunch is ready.' Nikki always found us.

The closest school to Collaroy was the next suburb on, Narrabeen, where the surfing beach continued in an endless golden stretch along Pittwater Road. It was a twenty minute walk past the shopping area, surf club, houses with small porches, past a block of flats where it was thought poor people who couldn't afford to buy a house lived—or people with mental problems—before a left turn to the primary school.

School days were regimented. When bells gonged we ran for assembly and formed queues on the hot asphalt. Classes were divided into 'houses' named after prominent Australians. We sang Advance Australia Fair and pledged allegiance to the Queen. Some schools had strict rules banning hair touching the shoulders, and the proper length of tunics. We marched to a military record blasting from loudspeakers while teachers blew whistles to herd us like sheep.

Classes were large with up to fifty pupils. High on a wall might be a picture of the Queen in her coronation gown and wide blue sash.

The primary school was divided into two sections: boys and girls. If we crossed the white demarcation line, our legs were slapped. Boys had male teachers, we had female. They were feared, sometimes admired and usually respected. Non-compliant girls had to stand in the corner facing the wall or wait outside the classroom. Recalcitrant boys got their hands whacked with a strap or were sent to the headmaster for caning. Several boasted about their bravado. It was another notch, a boy's rite to manhood.

When it came to folk dancing lessons, boys were marched into the girls' playground and teachers sized you up for partners of similar height. I was short and blonde and Harley, an angelic-looking boy with black hair, was chosen for me. Whew! I hadn't been paired up with the redhead with sleep in the corners of his eyes. When we danced for our parents, mothers dolled up in hats and billowy frocks and wore proud smiles.

Mum said, "Harley looks like he comes from a good home."

It was important to come from 'the right side of the track.'

Mother wasn't so happy at the annual school play. I told her she didn't need to come since she'd be doing housework.

"Of course I'm coming," she said. "I made your costume and it's nice to get out of the house. Now tell me your lines and I'll help you practice them."

I was a lyre bird and I had to flutter my draped-crepe-winged arms. And say, "I am a lyre bird. I can dance."

"No!" gasped Mother. "You can't say *dahnse*. You say *darnse*."

"But that's how they talk at school. Everyone says dahnse."

"No, they don't. We'll speak to your father about this when he gets home."

Dad said he'd had a bad day at the office.

"Dot, can this wait?"

Mum said it was urgent, and when he heard he agreed.

"By Jove. I don't want Americanisms creeping into this house. The Queen would roll over in her grave if she heard you speaking like that. Listen to your mother. It's darnse."

I compromised. When it was my turn I pranced across the stage and cried out, "I am a lyre bird. I can dunce."

With the advent of television and music American culture soon took over Australia.

Dad, like a lot of Commonwealth soldiers, was sour about American forces turning up late in the war. He said they seduced the women with stockings, perfume and chocolates while their loved ones were fighting in another war zone. Over-paid, over-sexed and over here was a popular saying.

After the war, as families migrated to Australia in a government scheme, sprinklings of foreign-looking children entered the classrooms and became New Australians. They adapted quicker than their parents who clung to their home culture. But through employment and learning a new language they began to assimilate in a safe large country still trying to find its own cultural identity.

Emphasis in the classroom was given to the three Rs—reading, writing and arithmetic. From pencils and learning running writing we graduated to pens with nibs and ink poured into slots on desks. Fountain pens were used at high school, a prized status symbol. Teaching was done on a green wall-length blackboard. Pupils had to sit up straight and pay attention.

"Hands on head! Hands behind your back!" shouted the teacher who scribbled sums on the board for children to fill in the answers.

It was a squirming moment to be selected, standing miserably in front of the blackboard under the gaze of the teacher and a roomful of peers, and be told, "No. That is not correct. Why haven't you learnt your tables? See me after school."

Classrooms throughout Australia were filled with children chanting their times table and singing, "12 pence one shilling; 20 shillings one pound; 240 pence one pound; one pound one shilling, one guinea."

We were shamed at spelling bees if we hadn't learnt our list of words. Emphasis was put on the apostrophe and never starting a sentence with 'and' or 'but' in composition. I excelled at art but was confused when the teacher insisted blue and green should never be seen. What colour should I paint the sky and grass?

Geometry was beyond me. Mum said I was a bit dim at times. I had trouble reading the clock at arithmetic lessons. I understood the 'past' hand, not the 'to' hand. Dad would turn down the radio and I'd sit on his lap while he showed me how the hands worked on his big watch. Sometimes he'd tease, "You wouldn't know if a lavatory fell on your head," and I'd retort indignantly, "Would so. Do you want me to get a complex and die of a coronary conclusion?"

He'd call to Mother in the kitchen, "Your daughter's done it again. Another malaprop."

Brighter children with exercise books filled with pencilled ticks and purple ink reward stamps were seated at the back while those who needed extra attention sat in the front rows. It was a sense of pride and achievement to progress towards the middle of the class by learning your spelling and tables.

We sat at our desks during singing class chirping rounds of Kookaburra Sits in the Old Gum Tree while the teacher tapped her ruler on the desk or prowled the aisles jamming her ear against your face to make sure you were singing in tune. I was tone deaf and dreaded the matron glaring over her spectacles as I silently formed the words.

"I can't hear much coming out of your mouth, Jonquil," she'd say.

A teacher of religion came every Wednesday for an hour.

"Church of England stay seated," ordered the teacher. "Catholics down the corridor."

I had two best friends, one from Dutch migrants and the other English.

"What am I?" asked my little Dutch friend Ineke, with the white hair.

"Be Church of England with us," I said, grabbing her hand and that of Melody, the pretty English girl. "We're best friends."

The teacher thought otherwise and told Ineke she could be Methodist since the Presbyterian was off sick.

"Ask your parents what you are when you get home," she said to the confused little girl.

Everyone was expected to have a religion and if you didn't have one, your parents had to explain why before an exemption was made. Irreligious people were treated like conscientious objectors.

Children brought cut lunches in leather schoolbags that smelt fusty by the end of term. They'd carried homemade lemon drinks, orange peel, mushy bananas, apple cores, egg and lettuce sandwiches, soggy tomato ones, Marmite and limp lettuce, and peanut butter. Rich kids had ham sandwiches and traded them for jam. My worst memory is being forced to drink third-pints of warm milk that were stacked in metal crates and soured in the sun by morning break. Baby boomers needed to build up good bones to produce future healthy Australians.

Children skipped to swaying ropes in the playground and, to stop a bossy kid demanding 'bags be first', the ringleader pointing a finger at a huddled group crying 'Ink, pink, pen and ink, I smell a dirty stink, and it comes from Y O U.' The rudest retort was pointing to our body parts, chanting, 'Milk, milk, lemonade, around the corner chocolate's made!'

The hula-hoop, hopscotch, yo-yos, French knitting, swapping cicadas and raising silkworms were the rage. We had a mulberry tree and I traded leaves for friendship. I discovered early on if someone wants something they have to be nice to you. The fat white slugs crawled in shoeboxes dotted with pinholes, greedily eating fresh leaves, and when they spun a yellow cocoon I was fascinated. But not when emerging moths fluttered and banged against the sides of the box and left little yellow specks.

"Ma," I wailed. "Those ugly moths have done number two."

Mum peered in the box.

"They're eggs, not little jobbies. And please don't say number two because it's coarse, darling. Don't copy those school children. We have standards."

As usual I didn't argue the toss—an expression that came into vogue later—but did jobbies compared to number two sound better?

1950s parents were keenly interested in their offspring's bowel habits and thought their darlings would succumb to worms by mixing with children from less affluent areas. Some children wiped their runny nose on their wrists, didn't wear socks or were shoeless, lived in caravan parks and said 'youse' and 'I done it' and 'me dad.' Mum gave us worm tablets; small chocolate squares called Laxettes. The jingle *Boys and girls come out to play, happy and gay the Laxette way* on the radio was a reminder for mothers to check their children's temperament.

"Just pinch your nose and swallow it," she insisted, rattling the sides of our cheeks. When we whimpered and gagged, she said, "You know I'm doing this for your own good. Believe me, it hurts me more than it hurts you."

Children dressed their cats in doll's clothes. Fathers muttered the kittens had gone to the country. Children from impoverished families had tadpoles and frogs for pets. We had budgies and canaries until a butcherbird pecked them to death. Mothers became hysterical about her offspring patting strange dogs, screeching, "You'll get mange!"

Raising silkworms could have given Mum the opportunity to talk about the mysteries of life. She said the moths were noisy because they were happy to be out of their little homes. She also felt like that at times. But a classmate said, "They're doing it."

"Doing what?"

"You know, playing mothers and fathers."

Sometimes it was called playing doctors and nurses.

"Jeez, you're rude," we said. "We're gunna tell on you."

Ineke must have discussed it with her mother for the next day she put her arm around me and Melody in the playground and decided it was all right to play with the silkworm informer. Her sensible Dutch mum said the moths were a bit like married grown-ups and it was all to do with instinct.

"One day we'll get 'stincted, too," she said knowledgeably.

When black worms hatched from the minute eggs like repulsive flyspecks I decided to give my shoebox collection to an Aboriginal girl who lived in a caravan.

We lived happily on the main road in a weatherboard villa with an outside dunny, a washing line strung across two posts, and a cat that regularly popped out cute kittens. Perhaps we were happier than some families on the hill in their brick veneer bungalows, manicured lawns, rose gardens and pop-up garage doors housing a new Holden car.

Their children asked to come and play at our place, and Mum welcomed them. Apparently it was more fun at ours than theirs for some had 'an atmosphere.' Their mothers looked outwardly smart, but behind closed doors lurked a husband who drank excessively, or who bullied and roughed up the missus. Women defended their men and home because it was deeply shameful to admit there was a problem, for what would the neighbours think?

Many men suffered post-traumatic war stress and sought companionship at RSL clubs, reminiscing and drinking. It was drummed into children that what happens inside home stays inside. Telling tales was injurious to the family unit.

If Mum were talking to a friend with a bruised eye, she'd tell us to run outside and play. There were no women's refuge centres to run to, no benefit and no place to go unless you had supportive relatives who would probably say, "Go back to your husband. You've made your choice. Live with it."

Dad was a family man, not a man's man. He never sought pleasure quaffing pints after work or becoming a victim to the six o'clock swill. But one night Mum was worried; Dad hadn't returned home at the usual time.

After the office Christmas do, he caught a train going west, singing Away in the Manger.

And Mum was upset he caught a train to the western suburbs where the poorer people and new immigrants lived.

"I bet he didn't even sing in tune," she said.

We lived on the northern shores and it was a matter of class and being seen as respectable to be living in the right part of Sydney. It was so imbued in me as a teen that I rejected advances from decent boys my age living in a part of Sydney I didn't want to embrace. You took on what your parents said during your vulnerable teenage years.

Christine was a popular girls' name in the late 40s and 50s. It was considered one of the sexiest names, although somewhat tainted after the Profumo Affair involving Christine Keeler. I became a Christine victim before that high-profile fiasco.

The little Christine in the brick house around the corner used to come round to play after school. She wore a large bow in her curly hair, a tartan skirt and embroidered twin-set, and a small smug grin. We caught the school bus outside the Salvation Army where an inmate called Willie, who was mentally unwell, sat at the bus stop jotting down bus numbers all day.

One morning, in a hurry, I forgot my penny bus fare. Christine had a spare penny and lent it to me. If I'd known the eventual hurt, I would have walked to school and risked being told off for being late. The next day she asked for her penny back. I put my hand to my mouth, gasping. I'd forgotten.

"Pay you back after school," I promised.

Christine couldn't wait. During class she vigorously waved her arm in the air to gain the teacher's attention.

"Jonquil's stolen my penny and won't give it back," she cried, and then glowed with satisfaction.

"Stand up, Jonquil," said the teacher, and she gave me a lecture in front of fifty pupils on the sins of stealing. Being small and timid, I didn't talk back but my face reddened with shame.

Mum gave me two pennies to keep Christine quiet and let me weep into the nape of her neck.

"Come and help me whip the cream for pudding and you can lick the egg beater."

Dad said at the dinner table, "Neither a lender nor a borrower be."

There are remnants of vacuous grown-up Christines working in tourist bureaus in Australia or behind perfume counters. They are snooty, bony, dark-haired, and thin-lipped, immaculately dressed with noses as sharp as their silent sting of superiority. Their voices betray them for my parents taught me what a good vowel sounds like.

I expect this little Christine married and divorced well several times.

Chapter 7
Child Models and Little Film Stars

The British Royal Family was big in the 50s. The Queen Mother represented decency and love of country, for with the war she and her family did not flee for safety during the blitz. The royals were loved and respected and many parents in Australia and New Zealand called their children Elizabeth and Margaret after the princesses. The current Queen came into her own when her father George VI died, and throughout the decades she remained dignified despite embarrassing royal scandals.

Australian youngsters cut pictures of royals from magazines and pasted them in scrapbooks. And when the Queen arrived in Australia in 1954, all school children assembled in paddocks, streets—anywhere where the royal cavalcade swept by, frantically waving flags. The Queen was a status symbol, now reserved for pop stars, but did she realise tiny tots in best frocks, fancy hair bows and party shoes stood for hours to catch a glimpse of her? Some fainted in the exhausting Australian heat.

"Where's her crown, teacher?" we asked.

We were told it was too hot to wear it that day, and there was a tinge of disappointment for she looked ordinary, like a well-dressed aunt.

Mum subscribed to the odd magazine including the glossy American *McCalls*, which came out of her housekeeping. Dad didn't care, as long as she kept the household running smoothly, gave him a three-course breakfast, a hot dinner and pudding at night, and had the kids in bed by six. What more could a man ask?

Mum enjoyed articles and advertisements on the latest overseas appliances. The bonus was inserts of the Betsy McCall paper doll, which absorbed little Australian girls who enjoyed cutting out costumes and bending the tiny tabs around her. Barbie and Ken plastic dolls were the craze at the end of the 50s.

The magazine had pictures of celebrities: Pat Boone, the singer, and Danny Kaye, the comedian, who were hugely popular on the radio. I wondered what it would be like to be

Pat Boone's kid and share him with his four daughters whose names were cute: Cherry, Debby, Laury and Lindy. Or perhaps Danny Kaye's kid? Did his daughter sit on his knee and laugh at his funnies? I wanted a dad who made me chuckle and didn't cause tension in the house by letting off steam.

Mum would have liked him to father Jasper more, allowing him to help paint the side of the house, or bang a nail into a bit of wood. Dad said his time at home was short and he could do the job faster himself.

"Take the kids to the beach, Dot, then a man can get a bit of peace around here."

In summer since mosquitoes were rampant we crawled under green netting draped over beds and read Enid Blyton books, forbidden comics, giggled over Coles Funny Picture Books and Boys' and Girls' Own Annuals. My horse-mad sister played with her collection of china ponies. I sat my dolls around the bed, chastising the beautifully-dressed dolls with their vacuous pretty look, cosseting a chocolate-coloured doll and gollywog. They looked displaced and forlorn. Even then I felt the white world was less kind to tan-coloured people.

One evening, walking the dog and squashing snails on the damp footpath, I said, "Hey, Mummy, if you didn't have Daddy and us ghastly kids, who would you want to be?"

"The Queen, then I'd have plenty of servants to do housework."

The private life of the royal family was mysterious. I wondered if the Queen had maids to carry her in a diamond-encrusted chair to the toilet to do the 'royal wee', but thought that too rude to ask Mum.

"Do you reckon the servants fill up the bath for her?"

"I expect so."

"So do they wash her?"

"Probably."

The Queen sounded lazy.

"But they'll see her bottom. Do you think she has a bottom?"

Mum replied, "What do you want to be when you grow up?"

"A ballerina," I sighed. I had pop-out books on ballet, which turned into a cardboard theatre if covers were stretched back to back. It was a popular little girl's dream.

Our first acquisition was a radiogram and a 78rpm record of David Oistrakh, the Jewish-Soviet violinist, playing haunting ballet music. We were warned to keep several feet away to stop the expensive record getting scratched, or to run outside and find something to do. When they could afford it, the collection of 78s grew slowly, always treasured and often played in the evening when we were sent to bed. At night, on the way to the dunny, we'd glimpse Dad smoking his pipe and Mum knitting in the lounge by the coal fire.

Joanna and I joined the Hazel Meldrum dancing class at Manly. Every Saturday morning we caught a bus to the dance studio, wearing coats over thin black tunics and leotards, and clutching pink ballet shoes. Mum gave me some paper bags since I was prone to travel sickness. I'd leave the damp bag somewhere before entering the large hall.

When you're little, all grown-ups seem old. Miss Meldrum looked ancient, but it's obvious she'd been a wonderful dancer. She was extremely strict and authoritative. Even our mothers, draped around the walled benches, shivered under her sternness. She had eyes at the back of her head and if you didn't do your demi-plie properly, she bawled at you.

One night we were offered a lift to a performance of Alice Blue Gown. We were to dance and sing in it. It was a squash in the sedan with both mothers wearing fur coats and fur stoles.

"Prudence," said the other mother to her four-year old. "You've forgotten your panties!"

"It won't matter," Mum murmured. "She's wearing a long outfit."

Little Prue panicked.

"Marmee! Go back home now! I have to wear panties!"

Mum said, "We'll be late for the concert."

Prudence became hysterical and threatened not to dance.

"My daughters can take theirs off," offered Mum to console her; she'd no intention of us doing so. "They're in the same dance in long frocks. Nobody will notice. It's not as if they're kicking up their legs and doing the tarantella."

Miss Meldrum was not happy when a breathless carload of tiny dancers in crushed frocks barely made it. Mum thought the turning back ridiculous. I wondered why Prue's mother's hand slid inside her daughter's frock.

Mum took Jasper to dance class and kept him occupied if Dad was at the office on Saturday mornings. If he was home, she said, "Look after your son and make sure he doesn't get up to mischief."

Arriving home after one class, I found my moneybox had been sabotaged.

Banks in those days issued fancy coloured tins to children, and the banks kept the key. Once the tin was filled with coins, you took it along where it was ceremoniously opened, the pennies counted and the sum recorded in a bankbook. The teller would smile at you indulgently.

"You must have been a good little girl and helped your mother with the dishes, so what are you saving for, dear?"

A new tin was issued while our bank accounts grew.

Mum found Jasper in the yard with a pair of scissors. She was more upset he'd cut off the cat's whiskers than stabbed my moneybox.

"I don't know why your father couldn't keep an eye on you. This drives me to murder."

'I could murder you' was a popular expression in the 50s uttered by exasperated mothers.

Mum thought of a way to increase our bank account with enough for pocket money to spend on cat's eye marbles, strips of bullets for toy guns, Disney comics, 2/6penny Golden books, fizzy sherbet and jelly babies.

We would be child models.

She enrolled us with agents who took photographs and put us on their books. Periodically she'd get a phone call asking for one of us to come in for a modelling assignment. Joanna with her fringe and pigtails was popular and modelled anything from hats to nightwear, frocks and school uniforms.

We posed for knitting patterns, swimsuits, toys, and coats—even the latest electrical device. The fee was about 17/6. Mum had no qualms about pulling us out of school, even if the teacher did. Since we were car-less, Mum had to catch a bus north to collect us from school, wipe a cloth over our hands and face, and give us a banana each. Then we'd catch the bus south into Sydney centre and hail a taxi to the photographers.

This led on to fashion parades at department stores like Anthony Horderns where reporters from newspapers flashed cameras and made notes.

Dana Wilson, child star in the movie The Shiralee who played Buster, the swagman's daughter, looked out of place in the stunning tiered frocks we modelled. She had her own dressing room while we others hastily changed in a cramped fitting room with helpers. Party frocks for children had layers of stiff petticoat underneath, topped off with lacy socks and black patent shoes. We resembled beautiful lampshades.

Some mothers were pushy, turning their little darlings into demanding toads who eyed other child models with a competitive disdainful look. Mum didn't care. She was glad she'd produced three kids who were marketable.

When television arrived in 1956, we modelled clothes for a daytime programme and the odd advertisement. No archives of the ads were kept but Joanna licked a Streets ice cream and I was on a Cadbury's drinking chocolate ad that flashed between breaks of the popular comedy series Father Knows Best. Mum pursed her lips when she saw me rehearsing. I was instructed to quaff the drink, turn to my actor brother and say, "Jeez, this tastes beaut." And we'd grin with chocolate-coated lips.

"Bit c-o-m-m-o-n," she muttered. "Couldn't they have thought of something else to say?"

"How'd you like to be in a movie?" asked Mum one day, putting down the telephone. "Don't get too excited, but the producer said you three are the sort of children he's looking for. They want to do a screen test tomorrow."

"I've got a test at school," I wailed. "I'll get into trouble."

"Don't worry. I'll write a note and say you're indisposed. Bugga school, this is more educational. How many other children your age get this opportunity?"

The film The Way We Live was an hour-long promotional documentary depicting the lives of a migrant family arriving in Australia on the assisted passage. It was aimed at Europeans and is now considered historically important, for snippets appear in flashbacks of Australian migration. Since we were blue-eyed and blonde, we represented typical children from Germany, Scandinavia, Holland and Britain; the kind of immigrants Australia wanted. Italians and Greeks came in thousands.

The opening scenes showed new arrivals embarking off the Castel Felice in Melbourne. Dining cafeteria-style at the Nunawadding hostel and accommodation were offered.

Jasper and Joanna played the initial role of migrant children of veteran actors Deryck Barnes and Margaret Roberts before the film flashed forward to explain how the new Australians settled. I then morphed into Joanna, and a Latvian teenager with a striking resemblance to Jasper played the part of my big brother. The grip from the camera crew had a blonde two-year old son who became the new addition—a real dinky-di Aussie kid!

Mum bleached Joanna's hair to match mine and told the school we were away on family business with our parents. One night when my siblings were tired after filming and were kicking each other under the table, Deryck suggested they make words out of countries. Mum loved word games and joined in. The result caused much hilarity.

Are ye Hungary?

Ye' Siam.

Then Russia to the table and I'll Fiji.

Sweden my coffee.

Denmark my bill.

Get it, India!

Back in Sydney, scenes were shot of my actor parents choosing the proverbial quarter-acre section, talking to a helpful bank manager, building a new home, applying for the child endowment, father working at a factory, mum shopping, and schooling. French's Forest primary school was in a state of excitement when the camera crew rolled in. The teachers opened the staffroom me for to dress in a school uniform and, after filming, a row of children lined up for my autograph. There's a scene of my platinum blonde actress mother in a summer frock, frying bacon and eggs in oodles of fat.

Breakfast is the most important meal of the day, was drummed into us as we tucked into bowls of steaming porridge, brown sugar and a sprinkling of Kellogg's cornflakes. The first to the table got the top off the milk, the creamy part.

We met movie actor friends of Deryck Barnes for they were filming Summer of the Seventeenth Doll at the same time. Guy Doleman, another well-known actor, wrote in my autograph book, 'I think you'll be a good actress—but don't!'

Autograph books were the rage.

Entries included 'By hook or by crook I'll be last (or first') in this book, with opportunists cramming in 'By eggs or by bacon, I think you're mistaken.' Popular were 'If all the boys lived over the sea, what a good swimmer Jonquil would be', or 'A little bit of powder, a little bit of paint, makes an old lady think what she ain't' and 'When you slide down the banister of life may you never meet a splinter.'

One day Jasper came home from scouting around the Collaroy golf links collecting rogue golf balls which he could sell back to the caddies, and he said American movie stars were sitting up there in deck chairs. I grabbed my autograph book and ran all the way up Pittwater Road to see two ordinary looking people signing their names on bits of paper for barefoot local kids in shorts. Peter Graves (Mission Impossible) and British co-actress Jennifer Jayne Jones had come to Australia to film Whiplash. Their fame would promote local television viewing. 'Happiness always,' signed Jennifer Jones in bold handwriting.

I walked home with some kids. One said, "Me Mum'll kill me if oi'm not home by five for me tea."

Another child came to tell Mum, "We seen real movie stars."

"Seen?" said Mum at dinner. "Seen? Where did you meet that little girl? What does her father do for a living? Don't spend too much time in her company. People judge you by your friends. It stamps you."

"But, Mummy, lots of people talk like that."

"And you are not lots of people. We have standards. You might be referring to the Italians at the greengrocers. Well, they can't help it. They don't know any better, but you do."

Mum walked to the shops every day with her string bag.

"Ah, senora," the Italian fruit shop man would greet. "Izza bewdifool day, no? Anda whata can I do for da bewdifool senora?"

For a few minutes while choosing produce the feeling of Italy throbbed through Mum and she could pretend she was in Venice or La Spezia. What she was probably experiencing was people from the slums of Naples.

"How many bambini do you have now?" she'd ask, and he'd almost genuflect hearing a foreigner speak his language, even if it was only one word.

"Comma down here," he'd call to his family who were in a small room above the shop. The smiling wife would appear from behind a curtain holding a newborn while several barefoot children with dark liquid eyes, a tangle of ringlets, gold earrings and traces of caterpillar discharge from their noses smiled coyly, clutching her skirt.

The greengrocer performed trickery of the scales, grabbing a handful of beans, talking nineteen to the dozen and distracting her before snatching some back. We didn't have scales at home, but Mum knew she was being cheated. She liked the little man, although there was too much breeding going on above the shop.

After we made the movie Mum took Jasper to audition for Smiley with a line of other hopefuls, but the agents thought him too angelic-looking. They were after a typical Aussie boy—skinny, freckled and plain, with acting ability.

I auditioned for The Sundowners and was told I was perfect for the part if I'd been a bit older. Perhaps it was a polite way of saying unsuitable but Mum was glad I didn't get the role.

"I heard you reading the script in the next room," she said, "and frankly it was rather risqué. I don't think we'll bother seeing it."

Before television came into the living room of Australian homes, we looked forward to going to the flicks, unsupervised, to see Hopalong Cassidy and other Westerns, a Walt Disney film or anything our parents deemed suitable. The Collaroy Odeon erupted in gasps, laughter, wriggling on seats while an usherette with a flashlight paraded up and down the aisles remonstrating with us if there was any untoward behaviour.

"If you wanna neck go outside and while you're about it give me your parent's phone number."

Teenagers became furtive and some boasted on a score of one to ten of 'making out.' After the movie the floor was littered with sweet and chocolate wrappers, popcorn, chips, shoes, cardigans and occasionally a pair of briefs.

"Gee, it was a bonzer movie. You shoulda seen all the blood and guts," we'd tell Mum.

I told her Joanna sobbed a lot in The Littlest Outlaw when a prancing horse, Conquistador, cut its leg.

"But I gave her a lolly and said they use tomato sauce for pretend blood."

"Mmm," said Mum. "Can you say 'sweetie' instead of 'lolly'? It sounds nicer. And if anyone offers you a sweet, say no, thank you, sweets are bad for my teeth. No nice man will want you if you end up with false teeth."

Chapter 8
Voyage to England

Parents are viewed in different hues and some give you a lasting legacy that costs nothing. I was nine-years old when Dad came home from work and said he had a surprise for me.

"What about us?" asked my siblings, who'd been playing cowboys and Indians and had the dog saddled up like a horse, tethered to the kitchen table.

"It's special," he said, removing his tie and jacket.

But a neighbour came to the door in a distressed state so Mum popped on the kettle. The woman blurted that she was up the creek. My Kiwi mum translated it from up the duff, a euphemism for being pregnant then.

"I don't know how it happened," the neighbour wept. "My husband will be furious."

Mum couldn't say how it happened either. She was up to her eyeballs with us kids, and against procreation.

"Don't worry. I'm sure you will have quite a nice child."

The saga had a happy ending. The husband built a bar in his lounge and when the healthy baby boy was born he was the proudest man on Pittwater Road! The beer flowed for weeks but Dad didn't attend for he didn't think that brawny crass Aussie was a gentleman.

"What's my surprise, Daddy?"

"Patience," he said. "A thing of beauty is worth waiting for."

He settled into his chair, huffing mouth steam into his glasses, wiping and adjusting them on his nose.

"Now, where's my confounded pipe and matches?" he teased. "And what are you doing here?"

"You've got a present for me."

"Ah, correct. I've brought this back from the office because I think you'll appreciate it."

He handed me a small brown leather pocket book with a thin pencil inserted into the spine. There were sepia photographs of the Queen, races of the world, the halfpenny bus fare, Latin verbs, facts on Winston Churchill, and weights and measures in French.

It was a diary.

"What shall I write?" I perched on his knee while he wrote, 'Daddy went to work and got wet on his bald head.' Decades later it tells me I had an employed father, it was raining that day and he had a hair deficiency.

That year we boarded the refrigerated cargo liner MV Raeburn on a trip back to England for Dad to renew his contract. The diary became my companion and I felt a day not recorded was a day lost. Later I wrote in excruciating detail about boozy parties and the birth and demise of teenage boyfriends, for it was a source of solace and insight into soured relationships. A word, a name, a place evoked memories, some bittersweet, some regrettable; moments of exquisite happiness, and many that were mundane.

'I broke my arm' reminds me how a playmate and I held hands twirling around in her backyard, but she let go and I fell heavily. Mum took me to a doctor who told her to bring me back later because he was listening to the races. It was a satterdie arvo (Saturday afternoon.) He smelt of drink when he thumbed through his medical journal to confirm the difference between the ulna and the radius. I cried all night from the throbbing pain.

"Why are you making such a fuss?" Dad said. "I knew a man who stuck his head out of a bus window and it got chopped off when a big truck went by."

"What happened?" I sobbed.

"What do you think? He got off the bus, put his head back on and continued reading the paper. He was brave."

"I'm not shamming, Mummy. Cross m' heart and spit to death."

"I know, darling, but do you have to use coarse playground language?"

Mum said since Dad had no feelings he could jolly well sleep in another room and I'd sleep in his bed. After the weekend Mum took me into the X-ray department in Manly and my arm was set in plaster for indeed it was broken. At school, children crowded around me like I was a celebrity, and I offered my cast for them to sign.

"Just don't write anything rude."

The trip to England took seven weeks.

"People seem to be excited about us leaving," said Mum, who was packing for the voyage. She wanted to look trim but lamingtons, butterfly cakes and buttery scones were offered at farewell tea parties on Pittwater Road. I was surprised when classmates gave me gifts of thimble-size scent, soap and hankies.

After catching the train The Spirit of Progress to Melbourne, we boarded the MV Raeburn and Dad invited a work colleague for dinner. He was raising a child on his own and still in the throes of grief since his beloved wife died. He was a dignified man and spoke thoughtfully through his pipe. I wondered how it felt to be his motherless daughter with the waist-length hair. Did he brush and plait her hair, and was he embarrassed going to department stores to buy her undies? I couldn't imagine life without my mother. She might criticise and say outrageous things but she was caring and supportive. She was our universe.

"What's the matter?" Dad asked when I began hopping awkwardly. He was in the Smoking Lounge ordering duty-free drinks.

"Daddy, I wanta go to the toilet."

"Go," he said.

"I can't."

"Why not?"

"Coz the doors are shut and I've been waiting for someone to come out."

"Just knock and ask if anyone's in."

"I have. But it's always engaged or vay-sant."

Dad cackled, "Vacant!"

He laughed so hard he ordered another round of drinks. When the waiter appeared, he asked me what I would like.

"Lemonade on the rocks." I tried to sound sophisticated.

Even though the ship lurched violently and china was being tossed around the dining room, our white-faced mother still had the presence to say, when rounding the Great Australian Bight, "Isn't this wonderful? Aren't we having fun? I don't want to go back to reality."

We felt the same way. Dad was behaving like an involved parent. He was not swearing or upset. He was the dad we missed at home, for now he had time to enjoy us and challenge our thinking. While the school had provided a correspondence course, what we learnt was far more. Back at sea after visiting a port, Dad said, "We'll have a memory test. When you got off the ship, describe the buildings starting at the terminal."

We had to write compositions on the countries we visited and illustrate them.

At one Australian port we met delightful friends connected to The Firm who offered a meal, and we played with their daughters, who were about our age.

"Mummy," I said later. "Did you notice a funny smell, like kaka?"

"What do you mean, darling? They were nice clean people, I think."

"But, Mummy, I smelt jobbies."

"Big or little?"

"Big—and they didn't have a dog so it wasn't a doggy do-do."

"That's strange," she mused. "It might have been their sullage pit. I don't think it was coming from those people, although redheads are prone to a bit of B.O. Something to do with their sweat glands."

As the vessel steamed towards Singapore, Malaysia, Sri Lanka (then called Ceylon), Bombay (now Mumbai) and through the Suez Canal, Dad took the three of us up to the bow daily and read adventure books—*The Bafut Beagles* by Gerald Durrell, *Tom Sawyer* and *Huckleberry Finn*, *The Wind in the Willows* and other classics.

"Read another chapter, Daddy," we'd beg, and he'd clear his throat and narrate in a dramatic and enthralling voice while Mum slumped in a deck chair staring at islands, or played quoits and deck golf with a fellow passenger.

"Learn *If* by Rudyard Kipling," he said, "and you'll earn spending money in ports."

While the ship swayed and rolled in a blue-grey ocean and albatrosses and squawking seagulls circled overhead, we paced the deck and recited the words off by heart:

'If you can keep your head when all about you
    Are losing theirs and blaming it on you,
    If you can trust yourself when all men doubt you,

But make allowance for their doubting too...'

In Singapore Dad was given red-carpet treatment while making contact with The Firm agents.

At ten-years old, I felt a sense of shame for being a white privileged child. Brown-skinned adults working for The Firm were grinning, bowing and ordering lower ranks to fetch bottles of Coca-Cola for us. It seemed extraordinary that people Dad's age worked like slaves. I felt as a child we hadn't earned the right to make older people subservient simply because they were economically disadvantaged.

I was disturbed by the begging homeless in Bombay living on the streets, women with withered breasts feeding scraps of babies, and wizened men in rickshaws jogging like donkeys taking plump tourists from shop to shop where they'd bargain. I began to understand and dislike the upper class privileged system. In those short weeks I absorbed more than any social study lesson at school.

"You can't write that," Mum said, when I wrote in my diary 'a nigger waved at me.'

We were gliding through the Suez Canal. I was mesmerised by the barren desert landscape dotted with date palms, skeletons of rusted burnt out hulls half-submerged, occasional clusters of flat roofed huts and children running in playgrounds of sand. A black boy frantically waved as our ship slid past and we kept waving to each other until he was a mere grinning speck.

"We don't use that word now," she said. "It's offensive. Rub it out."

"But we say 'Eenie meenie miney mo, catch a nigger by his toe' when we do skipping at school. And it's in the Coles Funny Picture books, too."

Ten Little Nigger Boys was a nursery rhyme and *Little Black Sambo* was a favourite. Now *he* was brave fighting a tiger and I loved the picture of his big mama making pancakes.

"Times have changed now," said Mum. "Just write you saw a nice little native boy."

Nice was a popular 50s word for it was bland, inoffensive.

"You used to be nice once," parents would say a decade later. "What happened?"

They'd receive a shoulder jerk from a zinc-nosed surfie son who'd reply, "Dunno. Search me. What's your prob?"

I became more secretive with my diary. "Don't look," I'd caution diary peepers. "This is privet (sic.)"

Mum was smart enough not to correct the spelling. My sister wasn't. She got annoyed if I wrote derogatory comments about her, like 'Joanna is being a spiteful little girl today and driving Mummy mad.' She'd cross out her name in red biro and write 'Am not.'

In the tropics we got boils. A nurse passenger said it was salt deficiency and lanced our infection. Mum thought we contracted sweat droplets from the foreheads of cabin boys or kitchen staff.

"Please, children, don't go down to the galley or get familiar with the stewards. They have a job to do and they're not here to entertain you."

At Port Said, the gully-gully man, a magician and illusionist, came aboard and enthralled passengers with live fluffy yellow chickens. "Gully, gully, gully," he gurgled as chickens appeared in our pockets and up our sleeves. Then he'd pass his red fez around and we put coins into it.

Haggling was done from the side of the ship where, way below, trade boats called 'bumboats' were filled with leather bags, ivory and wooden trinkets, carved elephants, hubble-bubble pipes and flowing Egyptian gowns and hats. The seller would yell up to you after he caught your attention and when his hand touched the object you fancied, a noisy negotiation ensued. Another selling the same object called out, "Allo, nice laydee, I give better price."

"Mummy," I cried, patting her arm. "They make me sad, those poor people. They look desperate. Can you buy something from everyone?"

Mum said it was business, they enjoyed trading and not to feel sorry for them. Some were scoundrels. She'd been ripped off in Aden buying a diamond ring when the seller switched it for glass. Several came on board to sell and pocketed some of the ship's fittings.

"It's a lesson to you kids. Nice smiling people selling goods might woo you, but there could be a hidden agenda."

Her words resonate today.

After pounding seas in the Bay of Biscay, we arrived in England where our Kiwi naval uncle took us back to Rey Bridge House in Wiltshire to stay with his family. Dad visited The Firm's London office to decide the future for his wife and three kids.

We loved the rambling country manor that also housed Mamar (grandmother) and nanny. This time our parents huddled over the kitchen table planning a trip to the continent.

"You kids are too young to appreciate the richness and beauty of Europe," they said, "but we'll bring you back a present. What do you want?"

"A horse," said Joanna. "A real one."

She got a china horse.

"A gun," said Jasper.

He got a Tyrolean hat and lederhosen.

"A watch," I said, "and I'll be good for the rest of my life."

I got my watch.

Now the market is flooded with cheap imports from Asia making watches, toys and books affordable. Today's children are bombarded with throwaways and so much choice. Any gift given to 50s kids was treasured and we were made to write thank you notes. For birthdays and Christmases we wrote lists of what we'd like, and one or two items might be selected, and we were grateful.

When I was given a white leather Bible, I was the proudest little girl at Sunday school. Jasper got a Davy Crockett hat for his birthday, which Mum fashioned out of a moth-eaten fur coat. He wore it all day for weeks, running about in the hot Australian sun.

When Mum bought a Singer sewing machine she sat on the front verandah and whipped up pyjamas, frilly A-line party frocks, Bermuda shorts, muumuus, curtains, quilted bedspreads and furniture coverings.

"Bugga," she'd mutter. "I hate sewing."

She made cute outfits for all my dolls but in those days most women learned to sew and even draft their own patterns.

I unwittingly upset her one Christmas morning, for in the pillowcase at the end of my bed was a small cane basket beautifully lined with pale blue satin, housing cotton reels, buttons, material remnants, needles and tiny scissors.

"Mummy," I cried, running into her room. "Santa's made a mistake. He's given me a sewing basket. He meant it for you."

"It's five o'clock in the morning," she yawned. "Go back to bed. Father Christmas doesn't make mistakes."

"But, Mummy, I'm like you. I hate sewing, so you can have it."

My sister wouldn't trade for she was perfectly happy with her colouring-in books and metal toy ponies.

The next trip coincided with English summer holidays and I was told I'd spend a few weeks with an older cousin while my siblings stayed at Rey Bridge House.

"It's too much for nanny to look after you all," explained Mum. "Be a big girl, wipe your eyes and treat this as an experience. They'll be nice to you. Don't you want Mummy and Daddy to have a nice camping trip in Europe?"

I didn't care. I felt abandoned.

"I promise we'll come back, and we'll buy you a nice little watch in Switzerland."

Dad accompanied me on a train to Colchester to initially stay with Aunt Ollie until I was handed over to his sister and family in a nearby village. I'd never spent much time alone with Dad and felt shy and awkward on the train. He must have felt the same way for he coughed a lot, offered a piece of chocolate and bought me a girlie comic.

I was upset over being separated from my siblings since I was extremely shy. We walked into a time-warp as my elderly uncle was still upright in the same chintzy armchair reading the *Daily Express* and my ditzy aunt was still cooking stew, quaffing sherry and talking nineteen to the dozen. Her skinny legs sprawled even further apart where her long Johns met her brown wrinkly stockings. She fussed over Dad, her baby brother, and tolerated us.

She and my uncle lived in a semi-detached on Mile End Road. It felt foreign to me. Back home people had their own stand-alone houses with a good size garden and, if they could afford it, a rotary clothes line to hang the washing. This garden was small and narrow but she was proud of it. Uncle didn't fight in the war for he worked in the post office and was on Home Guard. Aunt Ollie said a bomb once landed in a garden two doors away in the war and left twin baby girls orphaned. She would have liked to adopt them.

Aunt Marjorie, Dad's second sister, was the opposite of childless Aunt Ollie. She was tall and stooped, lived in a thatch-roofed cottage twenty minutes away by bicycle, with a husband who'd served in the army in India. My cousin, nicknamed Popsy, was their only child, adored by doting parents and Ollie.

During the idyllic holiday, Pops and I cycled miles down country lanes, ringing our bells. We had midnight feasts, ate massive strawberries from their garden, took hens for a stroll in a nearby forest and wondered why rain fell over half the thatched cottage while sunshine prevailed on the other side.

My parents returned refreshed from soaking in art galleries and churches across Europe, then spent hours in a dark room at Rey Bridge House developing their holiday films. Some evenings we gathered in the bowels of the house drinking cider to watch flickering family movies. Playfully, Uncle Richard turned segments backwards so instead of eating a banana, my cousins were disgorging them. Mum didn't say much about Dad renewing his contract back to Australia until he said we were returning on the Tasmania Star.

"Another cargo ship," she cried. "And it's going on a boring route. How many times have we done Africa? Couldn't The Firm put us on a passenger liner and go via Panama?"

My father hated fusses and challenging authority.

"Woman, be grateful! You're all my baggage. I'm not going to dictate to The Firm what we travel on."

Mum sighed, packed our bags and memories, and we boarded the twelve-passenger ship. It was a thirty-seven-day voyage with stopovers at Tenerife, Cape Town and the Australian ports. I was shocked by apartheid in Cape Town with signs saying Whites, Coloureds and Blacks. The Indian taxi drivers greased up to us, the black people shuffled in the dirt and were barred from some shopping areas, and the white inhabitants seemed indifferent.

Now the odd hormone was lurking, I asked my seven-year old sister, "Who do you like on this ship?"

Since we weren't allowed to like stewards she said the Chief Engineer. He was a silver-haired single man and took a shine

74

to our family. He invited us to visit the engine room and whenever his ship sailed into Sydney, Mum would bring him home for a meal. I preferred the rotund Chief Officer with his black captain's beard who had six kids waiting for him at home.

One morning, while doing our correspondence in the ship's lounge, we waved to a young cadet cleaning the salty windows outside. He was balanced on a tall ladder. One minute he was smiling at us, the next minute he disappeared. The Chief Engineer arranged for us to visit him in the ship's hospital with our elaborately drawn Get Better Soon cards.

"Another five years you're asked to serve in Australia!" Mum complained as soon as we arrived home. Our house looked seedy and small. "There's going to be some changes here."

While Dad didn't like subtle threats, he complied. In the late 50s, society was changing from male-dominated to being respectful of women who were bored at home and demanding voice and choice.

Chapter 9
Mod Cons and Music Lessons

Australia enjoyed relative prosperity in the 1950s with infrastructure projects such as the Snowy Mountains scheme, absorbing tens of thousands of migrant workers from thirty countries. Elsewhere jobs were plentiful. The Korean War and the Cold War with the threat of Communism hung over us.

Once television entered suburbia, we swung from total allegiance to England to embracing American culture. Mum boned up on magazine ads, keen to improve our situation. She hired the local plumber whose dog had mated ours. When we came home from school, a concrete mausoleum was being erected outside the kitchen. We were going modern—an inside toilet! The dunny man would no longer scamper down our driveway at dawn.

Mum was thrilled with the burly men in bush singlets and steaming armpits pouring the concrete. Donny's family next door in the brick house had a toilet with a chain you yanked, but it was at the bottom of a set of steep steps and looked like a cell.

"You won't know yourself," she told Dad as he muttered about the expense ending us up in the poor house. "Don't be silly, dear."

She reminded him about Jimmy, an English teen, who had been sent to the colonies to toughen up. Mum took him in because she felt sorry for a youngster so far from home, and hoped we'd copy his upmarket English accent. But Jimmy was not used to the feral bucket dunny system down behind our garage. He left the lid up, an invitation to flies and maggots.

Mum left messages. 'Please close the lid after use.' Then she wondered if Jimmy's mental incapacity was the reason he was sent to Australia so her messages became bolder. 'Please understand that if you don't close the lavatory lid, you are exposing my children to filthy diseases.'

Daily she wrote a new note to no avail, culminating in her angrily scrawling 'Close this lid, you bloody fool. Do you want to give us dysentery, cholera, smallpox, gastric fever, typhoid and worms? Stop being so thoughtless, you selfish bastard!'

Once the new toilet was installed in the bathroom and the large above-ground concrete septic tank was erected between the back door steps and the loquat tree, my father was a happy man.

"It's a beauty," he said, patting the monolith. "Run inside, one of you kids, and push the lavatory button."

A grinding whirring sound thundered through the cavern as gurgling water cascaded through the pipes.

"Sounds like the surf," said Jasper. "Can I invite my friends for a look?"

Dad didn't care if he invited the neighbourhood. For days the septic tank was a novelty. We had picnics on the back lawn, gazing at it. Mum said she liked the sound of rushing water and on sunny days she'd perch on the doorstep sipping tea from a china cup, listening to the symphonic rumblings. The tall ugly slab, like the new rotary clothesline, symbolised progress.

Joanna and I clambered onto it with beach towels and peered into neighbour's backyards.

"Don't be sticky beaks," Mum called through the kitchen window. "What can you see?"

We gave a commentary on women in hairnets hanging out washing, Mr So-and-So burning something in the incinerator, another mowing lawns with a push mower, a baby in a large pram and someone's kid getting told off.

Our bathroom window faced directly opposite a neighbouring weatherboard house, with an eye level window. A tall fence separated us but we were perilously close to each other. I complained it wasn't private anymore. I worried the neighbours would hear me flush the la-la-pongo (toilet.)

"For heaven's sake, they're religious," Mum said. "Too busy praying and singing."

Dad would fling open the windows to bellow at the pair and the war vets from across the road. In slippers, they'd arrive to sing uplifting hymns like Onward Christian Soldiers.

"Cut out that noise," Dad hollered. "A man can't think with that infernal racket."

Ingrad's family, off Pittwater Road, had their dunny next to a chicken coop. One day their corgi chased their prize layer, called Henny Penny. A scuffle ensued and the hen dived into the open toilet, or thunder-box, as they called it.

"Get her out," screeched Ingrad's mum, handing her daughter a long stick.

When Henny Penny popped up from the mire, Ingrad flipped the hen to safety.

This became my children's favourite bedtime story.

"What happened to Henny Penny?" they wanted to know.

"She was never the same again. She got brain damage and went off the lay."

One evening Dad came home and wondered why the house was so quiet.

"You didn't," he gasped. "I don't want that contraption in my house or the kids' heads filled with American rubbish."

Mum had hired a 17-inch Pye Technico TV set with the option to buy if satisfied. Bob Dyer, the Pick-a-Box host of the enormously popular quiz show, recommended it—"Pye's really something out of the box, customers!"

"Shhh," said Mum. "The news is on. He's reading with a cultured accent. There might be some cricket later."

"Those kids should be in bed by now," said Dad. "And where's my dinner?"

"In the oven. Look how happy the kids are. Not fighting, are they?"

Dad flapped an evening paper in the dining room as he tucked into his gravy-laced meat and veggies, but we caught him peeping through the hatch into the lounge.

"Balderdash and bunkum," he sneered.

"It's really good, Daddy," we called out. "There's a programme coming on. I think it's English."

He felt usurped. It was an intrusion in his house. He enjoyed the radio when we all sat around listening to Take it from Here and The Goon Show. If a test match was on, he took over the lounge listening to the cricket scores, crying excitedly, "An over!"

Mum thought, thank God it's over, but he said, "You don't understand, woman. Cricket is a gentleman's sport and there's a lot of skill and intelligence."

"If it makes your father happy," Mum said. "I don't understand him sometimes. Put your togs on, kids, and we'll go to the beach."

When Dad said we should return the TV, Mum put her foot down.

"It's good for your children's education. Besides, I want to watch I Love Lucy. Don't you want to enjoy some decent British drama? Do you want to be like those people up the road not knowing what's going on in the rest of the world?"

So the walnut veneer box on spindly legs stayed like an unwelcome relative.

When a salesman came to the door selling encyclopaedias Dad bought them and, while useful for school projects, he was dismayed we weren't reading them. Watching too much of 'that idiot box.' He packed an encyclopaedia into his briefcase and read every page while on the bus. It took him years to wade through the whole set.

We loved Lassie, sang along with the Mouseketeers in the Mickey Mouse Club and during school holidays watched the midday matinee. It opened to the Elizabethan Serenade and featured American westerns, poignant dramas, The Little Rascals, Shirley Temple and dashing stars like Cary Grant and Cornel Wilde, wacky Bob Hope, Bing Crosby and Dorothy Lamour movies, and the odd Alfred Hitchcock horror movie. Film stars kissed with closed mouths and there was never a scene that made parents cringe or switch off the set.

Rather than have us look like boiled lobsters, Mum sent the dog down to the beach to fetch us at noon. Life couldn't get better than munching hot crusty white bread with Devon sausage, tomatoes and lettuce as cicadas croaked outside and exhausted mothers had a catnap knowing the box was a safe babysitter.

Dad became a selective victim when it came to the News and English period pieces like David Copperfield, Jane Eyre, and The Forsyte Saga. He was charmed by the coquettish demureness of the female of yesteryear in stark contrast to some Pittwater Road women who spoke like fishmonger's wives.

"Women land themselves in trouble when they open their mouths and forget to shut it," he said. "What's the beauty in that? A man can't think listening to verbal diarrhoea."

But television had some positive spin-offs when used as a threat if we were belligerent.

"You can't stop me watching Fury," Joanna shouted. "You know I love horses. What sort of mother are you to do that to your child?"

"Go next door," Mum said. "See if they like your behaviour and will let you watch Fury."

When Fury coincided with Liberace on the other channel I became hysterical.

"Mummy, I'll die if I don't watch Libby. I love him. He's the only person who makes my life worthwhile!"

I'd become infatuated with a screen idol—a flamboyant glitzy pianist with chubby good looks, wavy hair and fingers dripping with diamonds. His charm, his cherubic smile and deep dimples sent middle-aged women and grannies swooning. He was one of the most highly paid entertainers in show biz in the 50s.

Mum sorted it out with the neighbour. While she had a sherry in the kitchen I closed the lounge drapes and perched on a pile of cushions, gazing at Libby through binoculars. Occasionally Mum would call, "Has he winked yet, darling?" and I'd yell back, "Shoosh, Mummy. You're spoiling the loveliness of the moment."

Once Dad came into the lounge, looking for his pipe. "Why are you watching that greasy ol' Pole? Pretend I'm Libby!"

He began mincing, his hands on his hips, puckering his lips.

"Go away," I screamed. "This is *my* time. You have no idea what it's like to be in love."

Mum bought me a second-hand piano for £60 from my modelling money, and found a teacher on Pittwater Road, ten minutes' walk away.

Miss Johnson charged 2/6 for a half-hour lesson. She taught several instruments and, since we enjoyed Florian Zabach (1918-2006), a virtuoso violinist who hosted a half-hour TV show, Mum bought Jasper a violin for £10. Joanna began the ukulele before graduating to the piano. Our teacher was like many unmarried women in those times—the dutiful daughter expected to care for a parent. She was fairly deaf but she loved us, and never rapped our knuckles if we played too many wrong notes.

Her home was small and dark, cluttered with ornaments, plastic flowers and sepia portraits. Her senile mother slumped in a rocking chair, dribbling and muttering. If she became too noisy, Miss Johnson said, "Excuse me, dear, while I attend to Mother. Keep playing."

She'd wheel her out to the kitchen, shouting, "It's all right, Mother. I'm popping on a cuppa."

What an excuse to dash over the hard parts of a tune, which hadn't been practised properly since she couldn't hear. And tell her one of her kittens had done something behind the couch.

We didn't mind her mopping up feline or Mother messes. But her gargantuan breasts resting on the piano keys like dormant puppies perturbed me. Halfway through my scales I'd panic. She'd urge me to continue, leaning perilously close, pointing to the music sheet.

"I just bash into her tits," Joanna said. "She shouldn't leave them on the piano."

For Christmas we practiced a piece to impress our parents who were invited to a concert at her home. We needed to show them their hard-earned money was well spent. On the concert day a large group of us crammed into Miss Johnson's tiny lounge. Our mothers were in their best frocks with their new hair dos. At one recital I froze and had an out-of-body experience. I felt I was dead, looking down onto my racing fingers, wildly praying for correct notes.

"Very nice, dear," said the teacher kindly, "though it's quite a lot faster than the composer intended."

Everyone clapped politely.

By the end of the 50s we had acquired a new clothesline, a septic tank which dad called La Bomba, a TV set and a Kelvinator refrigerator with a tiny freezing compartment often filled with custard squares and experimental ice cream. Mum shopped daily at the corner grocery store for items like biscuits, sugar, flour, sultanas, rice and other dried goods. They were weighed, put into a brown paper bag, and then totted up by the grocer with a thick pencil he retrieved from behind his ear. Later there were cash registers. But Mum still preferred we mix with children whose parents owned sheep stations or were white-collar workers.

"We have to upgrade," she said. "The kids need a room of their own. Let's turn all that attic space into bedrooms. You can ask that nice Mr Dudley to do the job. You can help at weekends."

Dad agreed since he'd screwed it up at North Curl Curl by giving away our land. So now we were officially a two-storey. Similar gabled weatherboard villas had an enormous unused space for marauding mice while we had our own rooms, an office space, and Mum had won money in *House and Garden* for her futuristic design. She let Joanna paint prancing ponies on the walls and I covered mine with Liberace pictures. The push-out windows overlooked the Salvation Army and the main road, offering glimpses of downtown Collaroy and the surf.

When we became teenagers we would nip out onto the sloping roof for a smoke or to discuss boyfriends, and scramble down the drainpipe if we heard Dad's footsteps. On cold dark nights we were scared going upstairs since there was no landing switch.

"There might be a boogie monster up there," whimpered Joanna.

I tramped ahead, crying out, "We know you're there. Come out, you disgusting old man."

After checking under the beds, we'd titter nervously with relief and chat between the connecting doors. Instead of getting an electrician to fix the problem, Mum sent the dog ahead. The job was to sniff out any limbless war vets who'd climbed a two-storey house, squeezed through a tiny window and hid under our messy beds.

On July 8th 1960 an 8-year old Sydney schoolboy, Graeme Thorne, whose father had won a hundred thousand pounds in the Opera House lottery, was kidnapped. A massive search for the lad continued for weeks, scouring the bush in our neck of the woods. This shocking crime was the first known kidnapping for ransom in Australia, and if children weren't home by 5 o'clock parents panicked and prowled the streets with long sticks.

On August 16th the boy's body was found, his face, hands and legs bound. A frantic search continued for the murderer. The following night, as my sister was going to bed, she began shrieking hysterically; she'd seen a face at the window. Mum said it wouldn't be the murderer, possibly a 'possum, but Joanna was inconsolable. She slept the night in Mum and Dad's bed and had the following day off school as the screaming had given her a sore throat and fever. Other children were terrified a man would snatch them from their parents. The killer was extradited from Colombo, Ceylon, on 10th October that year. The kidnapping changed an innocence and sense of safety we'd once enjoyed.

Enid Blyton's Famous Five books appealed to vivid imaginations for most kids were scared of any derelict house with ivy and an overgrown garden. The owner was probably a lonely pensioner abandoned by her family but gossip was rife among children. For a dare, some kids would rush up a path to ring the bell and then rush back, hearts racing.

Mum began dropping hints, like, "We need a car. It will save us in the end. Instead of shopping daily I can go to the mall and get bargains."

Mum loved driving for she'd driven army tanks in the war. One evening Dad drove home in a dark green Wolseley.

"It's better than a Holden," said my brother, "coz it's got more gadgets."

"It's British," Dad said. "Look at the walnut trim. Respect it. We'll call it Greensleeves."

We sat around the dinner table in an excitable state. I was just relieved the car didn't have an embarrassing number plate. It was CBB 234.

"Where do you want to go?" asked Dad, thinking about our first family trip.

"Take me to a villa with a sunken Italian garden, preferably for sale," said Mum.

"I wanta go to French's Forest and ride horses," begged my sister, Joanna.

Jasper said, "Anywhere where the surf's good."

I wanted to see where poor people lived.

"Take me to the slums, please."

Dad gear-graunched around Kings Cross and the outskirts of Redfern while Mum questioned his driving skills. The three of us in the back seat nervously cupped our hands over our mouths, stifling giggles. Busty prostitutes lurked around alleyways looking like oversexed dolls. Mum called them streetwalkers and told us they were hanging around to soak up the nice sun. Dad doffed his hat at one wearing crimson lips and a pleading countenance.

Telling him to keep his hands on the steering wheel, Mum turned to us.

"Your father has lovely manners, doesn't he? Are you enjoying the outing children?"

Well, yes, apart from the naughty words Dad blurted while changing lanes. Or apart from when he was annoyed by louts hanging their arms out of beat-up Zephyrs, swigging bottles of Fosters and shouting, "Go, Daddio. Wanna tow?"

"God help this country," Dad said, and Mum replied, "If you want your kids brought up decently we'll have to move to England, or New Zealand."

"I need a smoke," he'd say. "Where's my confounded pipe?"

It was too big a gamble uprooting from a safe sunny country where his job was secure to the lands of their birth. Dad erred on the side of caution as Mum tested his patience.

Chapter 10
Growing Pains

"I'm not having this rot invading our house," exploded Dad, as he glimpsed the beginnings of rock 'n' roll. "Turn off the TV. He's a greasy-haired farm lout."

"But, Dad, he's fun," we whined, watching Elvis with his snarling pouting lips gyrate on a guest show. He was different, a thrilling bad boy with a good voice.

Dad said it wasn't singing. It was rebellious bunkum with no lasting value.

When a thirteen-year old girl came to stay she asked if we had a gramophone. Mum perhaps expected Perry Como who soothed her, or a bright little number from Rosemary Clooney. But Janet from Melbourne popped on her 45rpm by Crash Craddock called Boom Boom Baby. We hung around the large upright radiogram in happy disbelief while she blew out fluff from the stylus, and put the tiny record on repeat.

"It's a bit noisy in there, children," Mum called from the kitchen. "Your father will be home from the office soon. He likes his peace and quiet."

Janet didn't care. She didn't have a father so didn't know what that meant. I suggested we'd better turn it down.

"Why?" she said. "Don't you like it?"

I thought of Mum in the kitchen. I didn't know how to resolve potential conflict, for I was fearful of domestic fusses.

"You just want everything to be perfect," Dad once growled. "Well, life is not like that. You live, you eat, you die. No mystery. Accept it."

"What's that appalling racket?" he demanded as he walked in the door and hung up his hat.

"I'll get you a drink," Mum soothed. "And Kath's daughter's here for a few days. Kath was nice to you in the war so be nice to her daughter. She's R.C. So watch your Ps and Qs."

"What day is it today, Auntie?" asked Janet at breakfast after she'd eaten a plate of bacon and eggs with the family.

"Friday. We'll go to the beach later."

Janet clasped her fingers to her head.

"No," she gasped. "I'll have to go to confession."

"You haven't done anything wrong," said Mum. "Have you?"

"I ate bacon. Catholics aren't allowed to eat meat on Fridays. Only fish."

"Pretend it's another day," said Mum. "It doesn't matter."

"It does! Oh, Auntie, I'll go to hell!"

"No, you won't. You're a child."

But Janet was distressed. We stared at her with the same confusion as when she'd brought Crash Craddock into our home.

"Only murderers go to hell," said Joanna. "And parents who won't buy their daughter a horse when they know that's the only thing that'll make her happy."

"Be Australian Catholic," said Jasper. "Different rules here. It's all bullshit, anyway."

I said the Pope wouldn't know.

Mum suggested we go to the beach while Janet was at church confessing.

"Jonquil, I suppose you should go and support Janet. I'll buy you both a nice cream bun afterwards."

"You have to cover your head," said Janet, so Mum dug around for hats and netting.

"A scarf will do," Janet said when I scowled. I didn't want to look like a Russian peasant with a rag around my head. "And you have to cover your shoulders," she added.

Since Sydney was suffering a massive heat wave with the death rate climbing daily, my new sleeveless frock with its fashionable keyhole-neck was out of the question.

The service was held in a quaint stone church filled with flickering candles. Nearby the pounding surf rose and fell rhythmically, and the priest droned on in Latin. As Janet disappeared behind drapes to confess, I reflected on the power of a religion to cause grievance to some when the rest of us didn't care.

I was bothered when the offering box came around again after I'd given my sixpence. Why second helpings?

Splashing in the surf was a happy release, despite being bowled over by dumpers. A smiling mother rubbed zinc cream onto our noses and backs.

When Janet left clutching her precious record, the house returned to normal. Mum took us to pantomimes, concerts and shows in Sydney to enrich our cultural awakening. She gave Jasper a transistor radio to listen to the adventures of Superman, and allowed comics into the house. She enrolled Joanna in Charm School with Mrs Horner-Smith where she learnt to fold her legs elegantly and sip tea with a finger curled just so, and let her go and brush ponies when visiting circuses came to town, or nuzzle the long furry faces of horses at the War Vets.

Since I liked painting and writing, Mum encouraged me to enter competitions. Receiving a letter in the post was a thrill, especially when ATN Channel 7 wrote I'd won a special mention for a play and Captain Fortune would be handing out prizes at the studio. This was a popular children's TV programme with the benevolent compere in a captain's uniform and a fluffy black beard. He was known for his voice on the Smokey Dawson radio serial.

"When you go to get your prize," said Mum, "give a little curtsy."

"Why? He's not the Queen."

"Well," said Mum, struggling for words. "It'll make you stand out, be a bit different. And it's a nice polite thing to do, don't you think?"

"No. I'll look silly."

"No. You'll look special."

And, because she was my mum, I had to trust her instinct. I gave a token bob.

"Did you see those other children?" said Mum later. "They just walked up to Captain Fortune and grabbed their present without smiling. You looked lovely, darling."

When an art competition encouraged youngsters to submit paintings about our locality, Mum splashed out on acrylic paints and art paper. While I sketched she sat in the car reading *House and Garden*.

"You've won a cup," she cried and dashed off to tell the neighbours. I'd come second out of a thousand entries. "I'll make you a special dinner to celebrate. What do you want?"

"Anything," I said, "as long as it's not stew or broccoli."

"Hard work and persistence pays off," said Dad, and he let Mum pour me a thimble of sherry. "She's a plodder. Slow to start, but by Jove, when she grasps something she won't give up. The other two pick up things quickly, but..."

"So," I snapped, "you don't think I'm very bright, then?"

"Daddy's not meaning that, darling," said Mum, glaring at Dad who looked perplexed.

Tears pricked my eyes.

"You're spoiling my moment. I'm not a plodder. I can't help my brain. You made me."

"Don't be so sensitive, darling."

"So that's another thing wrong with me! What *do* you like about me?"

I left the room.

"You can be quite helpful," Mum called, "and you've got nice hair."

"I'll show them," I sobbed into my pillow. "I'm going to work so hard at school and then they'll be sorry at my funeral when I'm dead from studying."

I reached for the picture of Liberace, which he'd personally autographed—'To my new little friend Jonquil, who is as lovely and pretty as her name implies. Sincerely, Liberace.'

I kissed his sweet face.

Mum said Dad was a tactless fool. He insisted he didn't know what he'd done, and when was dinner? Joanna came to fetch me. I vowed I'd never eat for the rest of my life.

"Jonquil's on a diet," shouted Joanna from the staircase. "She's not hungry."

While they tucked into a happy family dinner I clutched my photo, and whispered, "Now they think I'm fat, Libby. It's just you and me against this cruel world, my darling."

I came home from school and yanked the bottom drawer open, to receive a nasty shock. Feminine products weren't advertised on TV but I knew what they were—those growing up things—Modess. The square green packet came with a tiny booklet. I flicked through it with a mixture of curiosity and revulsion. There were sketches of hens and eggs and a woman's swollen belly with words like 'fertilisation' and 'embryos.'

What a rude little pamphlet, I thought. I'm not going to grow up.

What was on Mother's mind to sneakily put this in my drawer? Obviously she knew I was hormonal, but people didn't use that expression then.

"Change out of your uniform," said Mum next day. "There's a little surprise on your bed."

A Liberace LP? I thought excitedly, but when I opened the brown paper bag on my floral attic bedspread, I recoiled in horror. Two white pristine teenage bras!

"How dare you get me such a horrible present?" I cried. "I hate you."

"Darling," said Mum, sipping a cup of tea, "you can't be a Peter Pan all your life."

"Why's Jonquil crying?" asked Joanna.

When Mum explained, Joanna said it wasn't fair. She wanted a bra, and when told she was too young she padded her front with cotton wool and socks. She even dressed our German Shepherd Nikki in a pink tutu, tennis shoes and put golf balls into strips of sheets in the bosom area. Then opened the back door.

Nikki took off up the driveway chasing a cat. The cat tore up the street to the corner grocery store and jumped onto a shelf of boxed tins of biscuits. Nikki, in a tangle of tennis shoes and tutu, discharged the golf balls on the shop's floor, glaring at the hissing cat.

Mum made us write a note of apology so she could still buy her groceries there.

Since we lived on the main road, children flocked to our house like hornets. Despite Mum saying she was allergic to children she was warm and welcoming. She whipped up pikelets and took us for drives at the drop of a hat. But first we'd have to clean up the back verandah, or she'd wax the hall linoleum and hand out Dad's old woollen socks, telling us to skate. School friends loved the novel idea of slithering on the floor to buff it up as we all held hands.

"Crikey," they said. "Ya got a noyce mother."

A man's best friend is his dog and Dad had a soft spot for Nikki. Sometimes the large hound jumped onto his lap while he smoked his pipe and watched cricket on the box. And Dad had his fun moments at midday Sunday roast dinners. He did the carving since he was the head of the house. While salivating and watching steam rise from the chook's back, he'd asked, "Have you been good, kids?"

"Yes," we cried in unison. "Oh, please, Daddy. Can you say it?"

"Humph. No. Not this time. It's too special."

"Oh, puleeeze," we'd beg. "Daddy, we'll do the dishes if you say it."

"All right, just this once, kids."

And he'd look at Mum while we suppressed smiles and squirmed on our chairs in anticipation.

"Are you sure you're ready for this?"

"Yes. Say it, Daddy!"

Like an actor delivering a dramatic earth-shattering speech, he rose from his chair and, with a poker face, bellowed, "Monkey's bottom!"

It never failed. We laughed so hard we'd fall off our seats clutching our stomachs.

Once he brought home a Dictaphone from the office.

"You can speak into it," he said, "and hear your voice."

It seemed the most amazing technology.

"Say something," he said, and Jasper burped. Then Joanna topped it with a double one, Mum emitted a small squeak and we played it back.

"Let's have a burping contest," said Dad. "Is that all right with you, Dot?"

Mum said she didn't mind and the five of us found novel ways to cause vulgar mouth eruptions, laughing hysterically when I played The Blue Danube waltz on the piano with my beloved family belching at the end of each stanza.

Guy Fawkes Night was thrilling. Most Collaroy families walked their kids in pyjamas and coats to the Crippled Children's Home, a street away from ours, where the Salvation Army put on a spectacular display. Small polio victims with their legs strapped up had their beds wheeled onto the wide verandah. The Salvos played rollicking tunes while the surf rose and fell and made its own crashing sound.

It was scary for Nikki hearing fireworks because dogs have an acute sense of hearing. So Mum gave Nikki an aspirin, and said, "Just this once we'll let her up on the sofa."

We'd soothe and kiss her floppy ears and soulful brown eyes, cover her with Mum's best fur coat and turn on gentle music. We'd walk out into the starry night clutching our parents' hands and a packet of sparklers.

Despite our initial childish fear, the war vets at the Salvation Army were harmless and many were too incapacitated to shuffle along the pavement. After one unsettling incident, Dad bought a ping-pong table that took up most of the front verandah. Mum came home from shopping one day to find a disoriented old man sitting on a couch on the verandah.

Dad was busy at the back of the house, fixing a window that frequently got broken by back lawn cricket games. He never complained about shattered windows if cricket was involved. If Jasper couldn't be a naval cadet, he might have the makings of a cricketer. While poor Mum cleaned up shards of glass, Dad would joyfully shout, "Did you see the boy's over-arm bowling! Good shot, son," and Jasper would lap up Dad's praise.

"What's the matter, old chap?" asked Dad, shaking the shoulder of the slumbering man on the sofa. "You got a bit lost? I'll help you across the road."

Perhaps the feeble ex-soldier got a telling off from the matrons, for the next day he knocked on the front door.

"Sorry for yesterday, Ma'am. I didn't mean to frighten you and the kiddies."

He raised his hat and offered a string bag of groceries— Christmas pudding, tarts and other treats. Mum thanked him, accepted the tub of ice cream since it was melting and helped him back across the road telling him to share the goodies with his friends.

"I feel ashamed," she said. "That poor old man fought in the war and it's come to this."

Though I was still nervous about whiskery doddery men, I said, "Should we invite him for a cup of tea sometime?"

"I don't think so, dear. Your father wouldn't approve."

Every month, Dad said, "Fetch me the bills, Dot. I suppose I'll have to face the inevitable."

Mum would retrieve them from the kitchen drawer and he took them upstairs to his study while Mum warned us to keep quiet. His growl of disbelief turned into noisy mutterings and worked its way up to a full-blown tirade in Spanish.

"Don't listen to his filthy words, darlings," said Mum. "You kids are costing him a lot."

"Why'd ya bother having us then?" we'd ask.

"I don't know. Let's make some nice apple tarts. That'll sweeten him and then we'll go to the beach for the day."

At nightfall we returned apprehensively home. Cheques had been written ready to post, a dozen tarts were eaten and Dad was ready to receive his sunburnt family and a stiff drink.

"Once you know how to handle men, you're home and hosed," said Mum. "Feed them and leave them alone."

The cost of uniforms, textbooks, and sending three children to private schools would cripple most families today, but Mum thought it important to 'rise above our station.' It offered a chance for her children to marry well and release her into a world she'd once enjoyed.

At private schools, pupils sat a gruelling entrance exam (English, Comprehension, Maths and an IQ test) and were judged on academic ability as classes were streamed. Mum took me to SCEGGS (Sydney Church of England Grammar Girls School) in Cremorne; its austere brick buildings flanked by tennis courts and a concrete playground. She looked at dress shops to fill in time. I was crying after the ordeal.

"In English it said to parse," I sobbed. "What does that mean? I've failed. I hate it. Please, can I go to Narrabeen High and be with my friends."

Mum said she was doing this for my own good. She took me into David Jones to be outfitted in tunic uniforms. White shirts, a tie, Panama hat for summer and a navy beret for winter, gloves, black stockings and suspender belt and black shoes.

"My daughter's starting at SCEGGS, Redlands," said Mum grandly, and the shop assistants treated her like an affluent parent. "She'll need a school bag. What sort do children take to school there?"

The woman pointed Mum to another department selling small Globite suitcases with locks.

"You'll enjoy it once you get used to it," said Mum, "and you'll meet nice girls from nice families."

I hated my first day. I was in the bottom of four classes.

"I knew you weren't learning much at the public school," said Mum. "I'm taking you to meet the headmistress. Your father's not spending a fortune on your education for you to learn sewing."

Mrs Humphrey, the headmistress, tried to dissuade Mum but gracefully capitulated. I was put into the top class and told it was a privilege.

"I'll work very hard," I promised; Mum had said I wasn't feeling well on the exam day.

Subjects taught included Latin, French, Maths, Science, Biology, Geography, Ancient and Modern History, English and Divinity and singing. The female teachers wore black robes. The P.E. teacher, Mr Turner, wore white pants and made us bounce up and down until sweat oozed out of unshaven armpits. A surly caretaker shovelled leaves and stoked the incinerator.

I was the smallest and youngest in the class and became so stressed I got a rash.

"It's shingles," said the doctor. "I've never seen this in a child so young."

He said if the spots joined I could die.

"Relax!" Mum called out when she spied me walking around the garden swotting for a test.

"I'll get a detention at school if I fail the biology test!"

"It doesn't matter, we'll still love you."

"You don't understand. We have to pass our exams. Our parents are spending good money on our education. What does photo-synthesis mean?"

"Search me," said Mum. She'd learnt that expression from my brother.

The girls in my class said *darnse* instead of *dahnse*, ate dainty de-crusted sandwiches, poured coconut oil on their brown shaven legs projecting them sunwards at lunchtime, and adored Elvis, Fabian, Ricky Nelson and other heartthrobs. They had large foreheads so that meant good brains, and they lived in suburbs beyond my parents' reach. I felt small, blonde, inferior and ashamed of our home. I wanted my parents to be rich and affluent like theirs so I would be their equal, but I struggled, out of my depth.

Paradoxically my parents gave me a gift I didn't appreciate then—the chance to succeed. Often life doesn't give you what you desire. However, through determination, effort and being focused, you can achieve whatever you want. Besides, how many parents take their kids on world trips?

Perhaps we were rich after all.

Chapter 11
Liberace and Puberty Blues

"Was Canon Newth canonized by the Pope?"

Jasper was referring to the headmaster of St. Andrews Cathedral Anglican School. While Jasper didn't win a scholarship to be a choirboy who'd wear a purple surplice and sing like an angel, at least he was accepted into this prestigious school in the heart of Sydney.

Families who could afford it sent their boys to Sydney Grammar School, but Mum liked the sound of St Andrews and thought the headmaster was a dear, so Dad opened his cheque book.

Parents who sent their children to private schools thought they had a better chance of raising model children who'd soak up school values, stay tightly connected to the family and choose suitable friends.

The 60s changed attitudes.

"Why has that minister's daughter become a widgie? She was nice, once, and taught you at Sunday school. I can't understand why she wears such ghastly clothes and hangs out with a common crowd." Mum was aghast. "Her poor parents, pillars of society, don't deserve this."

Bodgies and widgies were an Australian and New Zealand teen cult, an offshoot of the Rockers in America and Teddy Boys in England who rebelled against staid attitudes. They caused moral panic with their Gothic look and confused gender identity.

Bodgies with duck-tailed hair wore satin shirts, black stovepipe pants, winkle-picker shoes and a James Dean sneer.

Surly widgies had short hair, lots of make-up and wore trashy jewellery over their dark clothing. They rode motorbikes and hung around milk bars, intimidating but harmless.

Parents worried their sons would end up in Borstal and their daughters would 'get into trouble' if they associated with this 'element.'

In the late 50s and early 60s, before the onslaught of the Beatles, cinemagoers rose to the stirring God Save the Queen anthem. It preceded a black and white grainy newsreel. A growling lion introduced the latest movie. Mothers baked

Anzac biscuits, embraced the Mix Master and new laundry products. Sundays were for mowing lawns and going to church.

Radio jingles sang We're happy little Vegemites as bright as bright can be... and I like Aeroplane jelly. Toilet rolls unravelled on TV as ads chanted What's the gentlest tissue in the bathroom you can issue, why, it's new, new, new Sorbent. Jokes sprang up. Q. What's 7 inches wide and 200 ft long? A. A toilet roll. Any bum knows that!

In the city rush hour, paperboys hawked newspapers, screeching, 'Extra! Extra! Read all about it!' while on street corners the deluded ranted religious mumbo-jumbo.

Mum said, "No one wants to be told they are sinners and the world is ending."

She thought they had head injuries and were disturbed, perhaps having an afternoon break from the mental asylum.

The worst whiffs came from underground urinals used by men needing to splash the boots. Women were more refined. They visited the powder room to spend a penny, where they popped a penny coin into the slot on the restroom door. Some places had sour-faced attendants handing out soap and small towels while ushering you to a vacant cubicle.

Fraught mothers wearing hats, gloves, high heels and a fashionable coat whipped down the knickers of their toddler and held the kid over a city gutter for an urgent pee.

Double-decker buses replaced trams, and horses with nosebags towed fruit and flower carts. A 50s city thing was a mother's quick clean up of her child's grubby face. She spat into a hanky and gave her darling a quick wipe.

School days were the best days of our life, or so we were told. We had no responsibilities. But it came at a cost; if we didn't pass our exams we had to repeat the year. If we misbehaved we were sent to the Head for a dressing down and our parents were phoned.

At school, teachers on duty paraded in black gowns like benign vultures and their presence gave a clear warning—behave! Intransigent students were expelled and pupils could leave after their third year at secondary school.

Most early leavers aspired to hairdressing, nursing or went to business college to learn shorthand and typing. No parent wanted a daughter to be a shop assistant. Boys were scooped up to become apprentice plumbers, electricians, bakers or builders. Jobs were plentiful and so were opportunities.

I couldn't cope with the stress in the A class. Once I was demoted to the second tier, I remained in the top ten and won art prizes, excelling at subjects like history which involved memorising more than understanding.

The Industrial Revolution was boring compared to the lives of dead artists who painted cherubic babies with meaty thighs and dimpled fingers resting on the laps of haloed Madonnas.

I was interested in the titillating side of Van Gogh going bonkers, cutting off his ear with a razor and wrapping it in tissue to give to a prostitute. Or his foe Paul Gaugin who fled to Tahiti and died of syphilis after painting fat local women. I wondered if madness went with creativity since both artists shared bouts of depression.

The art teacher had an acne problem, like half the school, but she married young, giving hope for the rest of us. She wanted me to think more about abstract art and Pointillism, and analysing the various brush strokes of famous deceased painters.

Apparently I wasn't going to score highly in exam results writing about the names, diseases and number of wives famous painters had, or their mental breakdowns and family alienation.

Mum was not happy. She put on her hat and gloves and marched me to the principal's office. The curriculum was wrong.

"Why should my daughter have to make a choice between French and Art?" she demanded. "They go together. Any fool knows that. Can't she do both and leave out sewing?"

The headmistress thought not, but compromised. I could learn French without tuition while the rest of the class flocked to the sewing room with pins, needles and material.

Sewing was taught in primary schools starting with oblongs of linen material. We learnt various stitches, and these oblongs were then pasted into exercise books. Then we'd graduate onto handkerchiefs, tablemats and aprons. These were given as Christmas gifts, though grubby or with bloodstains from pricked fingers. Mum fussed over the cost at the local haberdashery when my sister said she needed a yard of material to make shortie pyjamas.

"This is awful material, Joanna," said her sewing teacher. "Your mother mustn't think much of you."

"She doesn't," agreed Joanna.

But Mrs Armstrong, my sewing teacher, was a cross between an indulgent grandmother and a kindly Sallie (Salvation Army) woman. Fed up with being banished to the library to swot French on my own, I frittered time on sewing, and let the teacher do most of my drafting. She didn't mind since I was well behaved in class and passed the subject at Intermediate on the strength of illustrating costumes of the Elizabethan period.

Meanwhile, Mum was turning out patchwork quilted bed-covers, matador pants, flannelette nighties, cushion covers, curtains and the latest fashion on the Singer sewing machine. The art of sewing is not so popular now as shops are flooded with affordable clothing from China.

Punishment was noted on yellow cards attached to our tunics in little pouches. A student who got three notations on their card in a week got detention. They had to stay after school and write on a social topic.

I received my one and only for failing a biology test by half a mark. Ashamed, I wrote my essay on the Common Market.

It was nearly 6pm before the bus dropped me at home. The dog was howling because Joanna was teaching it to sing, my brother was immersed in *Goofy, Bumsteads* and *Dennis the Menace* comics, Mum was sipping Vermouth and pondering Dad's mood. He climbed from a later bus, and it was as though no one missed me. I was a school failure but at home no one cared.

"Libby, darling," I whimpered to the pianist in flashy clothes adorning my bedroom attic walls, "I know I'm thirty years younger than you, but I can make you happy. I adore your gorgeous smile and dimples. I will wait on you and take care of you. And we won't do anything yukky. And, oh, I'm sorry, my darling, I failed a biology test. It's a stupid rude subject talking about pistils and stamens. I don't know what plants get up to. Our love will be pure. I ask nothing of you, just to sit alongside you while you play your theme song I'll be

Seeing You or Chopsticks or whatever your diamond-studded fingers want to do on the keyboard. I'm yours, Libby, forever and forever."

And then I bawled into my pillow. My teacher was mean and the world was crass. I hated wearing a bra. The dog stole bloodstained knickers from under my bed and paraded them in front of Dad. I hated my parents' verbal eruptions when they were both tired. And my sister crossed out diary entries so it looked like I loathed myself instead of her and everyone else.

"Dash up to the chemist for me, darling," said Mother.

I'd just come home from school. She was entertaining our next-door neighbour from the brick house. Her Donny was under the table playing with my brother's lead soldiers and Meccano set.

"Just remembered. We're out of something."

"Okay," I offered. "What do you want?"

"A roll of toilet paper."

"No, I'll get you anything else but that."

"Why on earth not?"

"It's rude."

"Nothing rude about it, darling," she said. "We all use it."

And the neighbour nodded.

"Please don't make me go," I pleaded. "I'll give you my pocket money."

Mum rolled her eyes and the neighbour said, "Take little Donny with you. He uses toilet paper."

I primed little Donny on the way to the shops, a two-minute walk, but since he was three and lisped, he needed additional coaching.

When we reached the chemist shop the glass doors were closing for the night. It was run by two brothers in white coats and their ageing mum; she was keen for her young bachelor sons to find a nice local girl. She spied me from behind a counter laden with Cyclax, Charlie, Imprevu and other bottled scents. She urged her younger son to shove his pointed shoe between the closing doors to allow me in.

"It's that nice girl with the pretty hair from down the road," she squeaked.

"I don't want anything," I stammered, "but Donny does."

I pushed the tot forward. Little Donny mangled his words and for a minute it was a guessing game.

"Ask for toilet paper," I hissed into his tiny ears.

"Need poo poo paper," he blurted.

I was appalled.

"What did he say?" smiled the old mother while the son hovered, blushing. "Did you say powder puff? Is that what you want?"

"Yes," I said.

She rolled the powder puff in soft tissue to extend the occasion. The atmosphere was full of unspoken desire, yearning and virginal behaviour.

"Bring it back if your mother is not happy with it."

"She'll love it," I said, and hoped Mum never went there to buy Kotex or Modess sanitary pads. Those bachelor sons didn't need to know I was becoming a young woman.

Mum simply said, "It's not quite what I asked you to get. Your father will have to use bits of *The Sydney Morning Herald* tonight. And God help us if it blocks the lavatory system."

When my father came home one night and said The Firm was talking about holidays, as it was five years since we'd been to England, Mum went into overdrive. Weeks were spent talking about available ships and what to wear.

Dad thought it was just a matter of shoving a few clothes in a suitcase and finding someone to look after the dog for a few months. Mum said it was more complicated. We had to look decent on a long voyage since we were expected to dress up for dinner on board.

Our family had standards.

She shopped frantically at the Bargain Centre in Dee Why bringing home swimming togs, frocks, skirts and embroidered blouses for us, and marked-down evening gowns for herself.

"You're nearly fifteen, so I've bought you shoes with little heels."

When I protested they were too adult, she added, "You're growing up. You never know who you might meet."

Walking around in sling backs felt like hobbling on stilts.

Joanna wanted some, too. She was only twelve so she got riding boots, more to stop her complaining about her piano lessons. The music teacher's cats annoyed her. At one lesson she was playing the Colonel Bogey March and wriggling on her seat.

The teacher said, "It is a lively tune, isn't it, Joanna? I'm glad you're enjoying it."

My sister curled her lip and kept her countenance. She was squirming from the cats' fleas.

My horse-mad kid sister had been lent a Shetland pony for a day, which she tethered to the washing line. She and her excitable American friend brushed and lathered and kissed the cute animal.

When Mum nipped up to the shops, Joanna decided Pepper looked bored, so the girls led the pony up the back concrete steps, through the kitchen and into the dining room. He enjoyed spoils from the refrigerator and trotted around the house until the girls tried to lead him back down the steps. He wouldn't budge.

"Go next door for help before Mum comes home!"

"There's something big in the house and we can't get it out," drawled the little American girl.

Donny's mother, expecting a spider, grabbed a fly swat and sprinted over to find an astonishing scene. Joanna was seated at the piano playing Colonel Bogey with Pepper leaning over her shoulder. Underneath the swishing tail was a strategically placed plastic bucket.

Our parents were worried. We were beginning to draw out our vowels and speak in a flat lazy accent.

"Fair dinkum, the surf was grouse," said my brother, shivering, lips blue from staying in the sea so long. Mum wondered what he meant. Perhaps 'gross'?

"No, it was a gasser," Jasper explained. "You shoulda seen the waves out on the bommie (bombora.) Man, it was king."

The parents went into a huddle and Dad came up with a suggestion. He'd raise our pocket money if we did two things. The first was to jump out of bed and greet the day joyfully, addressing him, "Good morning, sir."

Joanna lasted two days. "I'm not saying that to him!"

Mum begged, "It's the only thing that makes him happy."

"Nah!" she said. "He doesn't deserve it."

But I said it to get the money, and Dad glowed if Jasper greeted him. Perhaps the boy was beginning to bend to authority.

The other thing was to repeat after him, three times daily, "Green beer."

Not green *be-are* but green *bare*, the English way. It felt silly and affected but the Queen's children spoke like that, he explained, and it would help us in the long run finding a good job or a decent partner.

My siblings scoffed. Joanna said the only thing she'd be marrying was a horse and Jasper asked why make one woman unhappy when you could make several happy?

"See what you've done, bringing our family out to this country, Fairley? Perhaps we'll have to look for schools in England."

"Don't! It's good living here. All right. We'll say *green bare*."

And our parents passed each other satisfied smiles.

Before we left on our next overseas trip Dad had another idea. He nailed a large sheet of blackboard onto the back verandah wall. The three of us slouched on a sofa, or curled up with a comic or forbidden book with saucy language, wrapped in brown paper and inside a *Girls' Annual.*

"We're taking you to the Continent this time, so let's learn some useful phrases."

Vo ich kann meine wagon parken? Where can I park my car? Daily he wrote new words and we chanted them, while Mum said she'd prefer to learn Italian.

"It's a much nicer language than German."

Dad looked peeved but drew a chalk line down the centre so we had two languages on the go.

"How do you ask what the surf's like?"

My father frowned at Jasper.

"I doubt you'll see any surf where we're taking you."

"There better be horses," said Joanna.

I wanted to see the Mona Lisa, and the wax figures at Madame Tussaud's. Maybe Libby was there with a wax piano.

Dad grunted.

"It's decent of your mother and me taking you lot overseas instead of shoving you in boarding schools, which we couldn't afford anyway."

"Oh, we're grateful," I said, speaking for us all.

Mum said she'd thought of something useful and got Dad to write it down. Where is the nearest toilet? That phrase got a flogging in every country and added to the richness of our latest cultural experience.

Chapter 12
Tea with the Queen

Just weeks before we were due to embark on Stratheden, a terrible event occurred three doors up the road. A neighbour's son and his best man returned from a bachelor night out, called a buck's turn, to celebrate his nuptials to a local girl the next day.

Jasper was a light sleeper and, just before dawn, peered out of his attic window to see smoke billowing out of a house.

"Brucie's house's on fire!"

. He thundered down the stairs.

Mum grabbed her dressing gown and charged up the street. We banged on the door next to the stricken house, which was a wedding present for the groom. His mother and her brother lived there and they were as deaf as posts.

"Wake them up," screamed Mum.

Horrified neighbours grabbed garden hoses. A passing taxi radioed for the fire brigade. Mum dropped on all fours at the back door; she'd heard scratching noises in the smoky confusion.

"I can't get in," she cried. "The door's locked. It's a furnace in there."

"Get that woman back from the door," shouted a man in pyjamas. "It's going to explode."

"Brucie! Are you in there?" wailed the distraught mother, and then she fainted.

An hour later it was evident two fine young men, lifeguards in their twenties, had been asphyxiated; a smouldering cigarette and a night at the club. Instead of a wedding, the local lads at Collaroy Surf Club organised a funeral.

In the following weeks, Mum comforted the weeping mother, the house was pulled down and the block lay charred and vacant for years. A memorial plaque was erected at the Collaroy children's playground.

Mum felt guilty going to England after what happened to poor Brucie.

"Don't be silly, Heather," his mother said. (Heather was Mum's real name.) "My life's ruined so don't ruin yours for the sake of a sad old woman."

The days leading up to our departure were a flurry of farewell parties, organising correspondence courses, scrubbing the house, and giving the dog to a family who'd loved her so much she ended up in bed with them. Gifts and telegrams poured into our cabins and, as the Stratheden blasted its horn, my sister began bawling. We'd thrown streamers to a sea of friends and the colourful tissue began snapping as the ship pulled out of Sydney harbour.

"I don't want to go," she cried, so Mum thought Joanna needed a sedative to calm her.

Joanna and I shared a cabin and fought over who'd sleep in the top bunk. But she cheered up when a Cockney cabin boy brought us a tray of tea and biscuits.

"We're going to the Continent!"

"Cor lummy, are ya, ducks?"

Joanna was a good mimic, though it wasn't the English accent Mum had in mind for us.

While the ship sailed around the ports of Australia, up to Singapore, Sri Lanka, India, and through the Suez Canal to Marseille, the days were peppered with activities leaving little time for schoolwork.

"Write about the places you've visited," Mum said. "I've got to play deck quoits with Lady (so and so), have my hair done and get ready for the Captain's cocktail party."

As soon as she disappeared, my siblings folded up their work and pretended they were seasick.

Our parents barely saw us for the whole voyage and were happy as long as we wrote the occasional composition with illustrations and had a stab at maths. Joanna spent her days riding up and down in the lift with the bellboys.

No one knew what Jasper got up to, although he intimated he'd been playing chess with an old titled man. It sounded safe enough to them.

"Joanna," I said one night from my bunk. "Do you like anyone on board?"

She named a dowdy widow, Mrs Horsburgh, because she had a horse name.

"Do you?"

"I'm in love with twenty-eight people," I sighed. "All of the officers, of course, but there's someone special. Promise you won't tell?"

She did, but later said it didn't count as she had her fingers crossed in the dark.

"Ma! Jonquil likes the drinks waiter."

"No, I don't," I hissed.

"Yes, you do! You told me last night!"

Mum and Dad are cross because I like Charlie, I wrote in my diary. I'd never spoken to him, just furtive glances before lowering my eyes and looking away. Mum was happily preoccupied and didn't mind me coming into her cabin, using her make-up. I said I was protecting my face from the sun.

The teenage lift boys thought I was Joanna's younger sister, much to my annoyance, but I perked up when she said, "Nah, she's older. She likes Liberace."

"That poof!" they said.

I didn't like bellboys after that.

"Is that the waiter you like?" asked Dad in a thunderously good mood. He called him over.

"Waiter! Glass of beer, old boy, and something for my daughter. What would you like, dear?"

"A Dubonnet would be nice," I suggested trying to appear older, but Dad thought not.

"A shandy," he compromised. "Where do you come from?" he asked the waiter whose brass buttons and starched uniform were making me heady.

"Naples, sir," he said.

"Family?"

"Yes, sir, a wife and one small boy back home. Will that be all, sir?"

Dad smirked.

"You're trying to ruin my life," I cried. "He's nice. I like him. What's wrong with that?"

"Nothing," chuckled Dad. "He's got a fish-face."

For the rest of the journey my fifteen-year old heart pounded for Charlie with his Latin looks and unavailability. I never spoke to him, but then I hadn't spoken to Liberace either.

Daily Dad teased, "How's Fish-face?"

Towards the end of the voyage Dad was clearly on edge. He was concerned about one passenger. I was in the near-empty ship lounge tinkling Beethoven's Moonlight Sonata on the grand piano when a tall stooped gentleman with silvery hair and an air of good breeding ambled up and sat on a chair and watched me.

"Good, good," he said. "Go ahead."

But my hands turned to jelly.

"Let me show you," he offered, and played the sonata with poise and elegance.

He was an author and concert pianist. When passengers heard us playing they demanded he put on a concert.

"Only if Blondie turns the pages for me," he said.

After the concert and my siblings had been banished to bed, he joined us for a drink. He seemed to be smitten by my mother. Dad and I weren't happy.

Mum said, "How could anything happen with a husband and kids spying on my every move. He's a clever man with a nice brain. I liked his writing."

The pianist/author obviously had cosy conversations with Mum because she emerged from her cabin one morning clutching a manuscript.

"What are you reading, Ma?"

I took the folder. The third sentence floored me. It was something about fondling a white breast.

"Mum! Why are you reading filth from a man you barely know?"

"It's a novel, darling. He's written other books. He's well-known. Don't you like him?"

"Not now! And Daddy and I are keeping our eyes on you."

The man seemed aloof, rich and famous, but my teenage eyes focussed on the bristling hairs on his wrist, his expensive gold watch, the eau de cologne he wore that Dad said was for 'pansies', and the unexplained arrogance that a wealthy Jewish bachelor could turn Mum's head.

Dad was decent and devoted to Mum. This interloper would never get a look in.

In Marseille, other passengers looked after my siblings while my parents and I, and 'that man' ambled around the balmy city.

We watched an open-air evening concert starring Petula Clark, with Dad and me sitting on either side of Mum. She behaved perfectly and so did the rest of us.

Perhaps Dad and I had misread smouldering desires? It was hard to tell when you're in a bubble world devoid of responsibilities and your only aim is to have fun. Usually whirlwind relationships fade just as fast but this was still glowing when we reached England.

Meanwhile the evenings were alive with the Mad Hatter's Parade where Jasper dressed up as a potato clutching a newspaper (Common Tater on the News.) I idled up to an officer and borrowed his cap, filling it with ciggie butts and debris (Officers Mess), and Joanna dressed as a hobo with Mum's red lipstick plastered on her nose, and wearing a bag (Got the Sack.)

We three won prizes and bought ashtrays at the ship's duty-free store. It seemed grown-up.

There were gala and quiz nights, frog race meetings, concerts, and dancing to an orchestra.

"Why won't you dance with charming Mr Scott?" asked Mum.

Despite having a brother a year younger, I'd never touched a man's hand.

"I'm biding my time and enjoying the scenery."

Cavorting on a dance floor with a man in uniform felt safer than shyly knocking against the protruding stomach of an older passenger.

Days before the ship docked, Mum came into my cabin and asked how I'd feel if someone adopted Joanna. I was surprised; who'd want her? Mum said it was someone who'd give her a good life in Africa with a big home and horses she could ride to school every day. She implied she'd go, too, and sought my opinion. That man had turned Mother's head.

"What about me? What about Daddy?" I cried.

"You can come too, of course."

"No!" I shouted. "Jasper wouldn't go—he likes the surf in Australia—and I need to finish my schooling. That man is creepy. You've made your bed, Mum, so you've got to lie in it."

Apparently as the ship berthed in England Mum was still undecided. Dad later admitted he didn't know what our mother saw in him, and he couldn't prevent her from doing what she wanted.

A surprising admission to make.

In the 60s few people separated, and in our Collaroy suburb we only heard whisperings of a divorced person, 'a scarlet woman.' When you married it was for life. If you chose the wrong partner, tough! You were grown up enough to accept responsibilities. If you made babies, don't expect the State to help you out. It is unheard of today because children are precious commodities and get government support.

Mum's brother Richard unwittingly saved the situation.

He'd sent a limousine from Admiralty House to collect us, and our twelve pieces of luggage. Mum obediently climbed in and, while her heart was elsewhere, good sense prevailed. After temporary shipboard insanity, my parents remained together like comfortable cushions and fell back into a pattern of commitment and raising the three of us.

"You made it by the skin of your teeth," said Aunt June when we alighted at the country estate, Rey Bridge House. "We have one day to get ready."

"What for, Auntie June?" I asked.

"Good gracious, child. Haven't your parents told you? You're going to Buckingham Palace to the Royal Garden Party."

"Am I, Ma? Is that the surprise?"

She'd hinted at something prior to our voyage.

Mum nodded. They hadn't mentioned it earlier because technically a child of fifteen is not invited. She and Dad had been approved to attend through Uncle Richard's connections in the navy and services to Queen and country.

I'd go on Daddy's ticket, but it would be so busy at that time they didn't want to disappoint me in case we couldn't make it. Daddy thought it would be a treat if I went in his place while he went to the London office and talked to Lord Vestey about his job.

Aunt June had another surprise. Mum's oldest sister Enga from New Zealand, whom she hadn't seen in years, had flown over. Not only would she be attending the garden party at

Buckingham Palace, but she'd come with us on a tour of Europe. Mum was thrilled.

Enga was a well-known New Zealand artist and, later, author of a book called *Courage and Camp Ovens*. She'd flown over earlier to poke around cemeteries in search of dead relatives for her book, hoping to find a scallywag who'd been shipped out to Australia on a convict ship, then stowed away to New Zealand.

Parents like the idea of genetic throwbacks for it takes the blame off their parenting.

We loved hearing about her life on a large sheep station out of Nelson, her endless ghost stories and the naughty things our cousins got up to.

"Jonquil has to look older," said Aunt June. "I'll take her shopping for something more sophisticated."

Enga, whose usual attire was tartan pants, gumboots and Fair Isle sweaters, said she needed tarting up, too. Mum said she could do with something more elegant. We piled into Susannah, the Combi van, a gaggle of excitable females and drove to Bath.

"Will this look all right for the Queen?" asked Enga, emerging from the dressing room in a shiny two-piece.

Mum had shop assistants rallying around her as if she were royalty, because she uttered words like having tea with the Queen.

I was embarrassed and covered my breasts each time Aunt June came into the room.

"We all have bosoms, nothing wrong with that. It's a woman's greatest asset. Men love them. You're a beautiful young lady. Flaunt it."

No one had ever said that to me.

My English godmother taught me more than all the schoolteachers who frowned if we didn't follow rules, failed at exams or sent us to detention if we danced across the schoolyard crossing our suspenders doing the can-can.

"Girls! You'll be mothers of the future generation. Act with decorum."

Mum and Enga gasped when they saw me in the outfit Aunt June chose. She'd taken me from my comfort zone of muumuus, serge box-pleated tunics, and pedal pushers (three-quarter pants), and put me into an autumn-patterned frock with a scooped neck, black vinyl belt and chisel-toed shoes with one and a half inch heels. Gloves, a perky hat and a white coat, called a dust jacket, completed the ensemble. She said I looked delightful, and Mum agreed.

While Aunt June's husband, my handsome naval Uncle Richard, had manned ships, his wife had a knack of launching relatives from Australia and New Zealand with the same panache.

We were so excited by now. And when we had afternoon tea at a posh café, Aunt June took it all in her stride.

At the Royal Garden Party we walked around Her Majesty's vast gardens, admiring the pink flamingos, enjoying delicacies from trestle tables.

"I think Prince Charles and Princess Anne are peeping out from an upstairs room," I babbled.

Amidst swishing frocks, wide hats and silk gloves, perfumed women with pencilled eyebrows and ruby red lipstick promenaded with partners in top hats and three-piece suits. Mum thought the royal children would be at boarding school but Aunt June said it was possible I saw them since it was the summer holidays in Britain.

We didn't get to shake hands with the Queen, who was wearing a nautical satin two-piece, and tell her we'd travelled across the high seas to attend her party. But we spied several members of the royal family, including Prince Philip grinning from his wheelchair; he'd broken a bone in his foot from playing polo.

"This has been a memorial day," I scribbled in my diary. "We went to the Queen's party in our new shoes. The sky was blue except for a suggestive cloud here and there. Mummy's asparagus (varicose) veins played up and I think I'm getting a bunion."

The next couple of weeks were a flurry of packing for our camping trip, buying lilos and sleeping bags. Cousin Liza took Jane Austen to read to her father while he was driving, and replaced the Bible with *Verse and Worse* and its quaint epitaphs.

'God took our flower, our little Nell, He thought He too, would like a smell.'

Dad was visiting frail Great Aunt May who lived in a grand family home but was being bullied. Despite a lavish afternoon tea, we were sickened to see the nefarious housekeeper fawning over Dad's aunt. When the harridan scuttled upstairs Aunt May whispered urgently to Dad, "Please, take these. I want you to have them, but don't say anything."

They were family heirlooms—silver candlesticks, silver salvers and other knick-knacks to share with his sisters. It was a link to England, igniting boyhood memories. Great Aunt May seemed charmed by Mum and we three well-behaved Aussie children, and was happy to remove such treasures from her housekeeper's clutches.

Every Christmas, she dutifully posted us a pound note which we banked. It never occurred to us to pull out our savings or moan for a toy. We'd gaze at our little bankbook with pride as the money grew. Dad explained about having a nest egg, or did we want to live in the gutter like some poor people who'd never saved?

"It's ghastly getting old," Mum said on our last visit to Great Aunt May. "Shoot me if I do."

Mum and Dad newly married

Daddy's girl

The family on Pittwater Road

Jonquil in Tenerife

Backyard drama at Collaroy

Little ballerinas, Jonquil & Joanna

Onboard the MV Raeburn, near Aden

Finest Qu
Coats pric
From
£5/18/-

From
5/5/-

Jonquil modelling a coat

Dad & the three J's in Singapore

Mum, Enga, Me, June & Cousin Liza dressed for Buckingham Palace

Camping with the Admiral, outside Rey Bridge House

With our Kiwi cousins outside Uncle Arty's, Onekaka, NZ

Jasper and Joanna as migrant children from "The Way we Live" (1959). Film Australia Stills Collection on Flickr

Screen grab of Jonquil as a schoolgirl from "The Way we Live" (1959).

Jasper

Indiaman trip across Asia.
A priest blessing shoppers.

Jonquil & Joanna in Monte Carlo

Hitching in France

Ingrad and Jonquil in Athens

Jonquil somewhere in Turkey (Indiaman trip).

Chapter 13
Camping with the Admiral

In the 60s camping was popular. Small cars laden with families and roof rack luggage drove across Europe. Freedom camping was opportunistic and possible while cities had established camping grounds.

Today the emphasis is on package trips and hired campervans. Caravans are popular now but were less affordable then. In Australia and New Zealand, children often spent holidays with grandparents who lived away from the family and were seen as special, indulgent and old-fashioned. Today, through necessity, some grandparents live nearby helping raise their children's youngsters, uncommon in the 60s.

Before we left Australia and commenced our six-week camping tour across Europe, Uncle Richard, although busy with naval duties in England, wrote asking us what we'd most like to see. There were no emails in those days, Trans-Atlantic telephone calls were expensive and aerogrammes took a week at least.

At the dinner table, Mum said, "Children, we're taking you on an expensive holiday. It'll just about kill us. What do you want to see?"

Joanna waved her arm in the air. "I wanna see horses."

So Mum told her about the Spanish dancing horses in Vienna, and how she probably wouldn't see them since it would cost an arm and a leg to get in.

"But there'll be plenty of old peasants and draught horses ploughing fields in Austria. You might even get to pat one."

Jasper said he'd like to see the surf. Mum wrote down Venice.

"Plenty of water there, son. And, darling, can't you rise above the Collaroy influence? There's more to life than surfboards and waves."

Jasper gave her a withered you'll-never-understand look.

I wanted to make my art teacher jealous by going to Milan and viewing The Last Supper. Mum thought that splendid and said my private school fees were exorbitant since sewing was included. She admitted she had a hankering to visit the Mad

King of Bavaria's castle with its Disneyland image and funny foreign royalty with long noses caused by inbreeding.

Dad said, "Drop me off at a Weinstube in Innsbruck and collect me later. Do we have to take the kids?"

"They're your kids, too, dear. Having a bit of culture might be the making of them, and would you like a little more roast beef and marrow?"

Back in England, Uncle Richard's wife, June, laid down the 'musts.' She adored Spain. Uncle, who'd spent his boyhood climbing New Zealand peaks, suggested the Alps and criss-crossing over mountain passes. Their two teenage children were used to European camping trips. Cousin Jo, aged thirteen, wanted to go sailing, and Liza, nearly seventeen, sided with her mum with a secular leaning towards Rome. She had a penchant for hairy men.

When it came to reciting the foreign words Dad had chalked up on the blackboard on the back verandah, none of us got much past 'Where can I park my car?' in German. I had too much homework and became annoyed learning languages where verbs were at the end.

"Think about your poor father. He'll have to learn to drive on the wrong side of the road and, God knows, he's not the best of drivers."

I'd had a smattering of French in the first year at school but the ill-tempered Parisian teacher put me off. She had flashing green eyes, brick-red hair and long fingernails that scraped on the blackboard as she shouted out past imperfect tenses. I couldn't remember which way the *grave* and *acute* on French words went and my exercise book was filled with red ink corrections.

Mum said learning German was too guttural, as she couldn't get her throat to cough up authentic sounds. Besides, she was furious about Hitler making poor Daddy go to war. Italian was prettier, she thought, as she could practice with the greengrocer when he was weighing (and cheating) on the vegetables. And, she added, she might be driven to living in Italy one day if Dad kept using that ghastly 'F' word when tinkering under the car, and if we children didn't stop bickering.

"Do you think I like being home all day cooking, cleaning and Hoovering the slummy back verandah? God, there's more to life. I could be living in a little *pensione*, eating scampi and studying art in Perugia with decent people."

I tried to humour Mum to stop her dashing off, so learnt a few words of Italian. While cooking dinner, she'd pop on a black vinyl LP of Italian Made Easy and turn it up loud, which was annoying if we were watching Lassie or Leave it to Beaver on the box.

My sister had a Dutch friend and remembered odd words and phrases like 'You are mad in the head,' but Mum said that and names of vulgar body parts weren't useful in the long run.

When our family arrived in England, once again, we got the good and bad news. The good news was we were still going camping. The bad news was none of us would get our wishes.

Uncle Richard said, "We've spent weeks in savage argument on an itinerary and I have to be brutal."

He had penned in a start in Belgium, circling through Holland, Germany, Austria and Switzerland if the car could make it, then a dash over to Italy before France. It was a comprehensive tour.

On the back paddock at Rey Bridge House Uncle Richard supervised tent pitching and pumping up Lilo bedding military style, while Dad got out his stopwatch.

"You might be in a howling gale when we camp for the night," Auntie June said. "Don't expect anyone to come and help. Grown-ups have other things to do like revving up the primus for din-din (dinner) and opening the bar for drinkies."

She was both practical, and experienced. She told Enga and Mum to pack a skirt. It was useful for urgent comfort stops when you're out in the wop-wops. She'd hop into a paddock and spread her skirt, pretending to pick wild flowers. She laughingly told us that Jo, her son, as a small boy took after his dad regarding nautical terms. In need of a loo he'd cry, "Daddy! My bilges are bulging."

In the early 60s women didn't wear trouser pants when visiting foreign cities for it was seen as disrespectful. So Mum and my aunts packed corsets and nylon stockings with a seam up the back. The bane of women's lives before the invention of panty hose was making sure the seam ran straight when putting them on.

"Darn, I've got a ladder," women cried, for stockings were expensive, and blobs of nail varnish or soap were put on miscreant holes to stop them getting larger.

Aunt June said she always travelled with a collection of silk scarves for it would be a dreadful shame to come upon a quaint Catholic church and be turned away simply because one wore a sleeveless blouse; it was considered vulgar showing upper arm flesh. Privately, I wondered if priests made that rule, disgusted by tourists with bushy armpits swaying over candles, but Mum said there was something in the Bible about modesty, and hadn't I learnt that at Sunday school?

In the 50s and 60s, Aussie kids were sent to Sunday school because parents said they needed a lie-in. Mothers feigned tiredness after dressing their darlings in party frocks, or rubbing Brylcreem into son's hair cooing, "A little dab'll do ya," and waving them out of the door saying, "Don't come back too soon."

Clutching little Bibles, baby boomers were content to walk long distances in the sunshine and return home with verses to learn for next Sunday. Our parents had made a remarkable recovery with an unexplained closeness in their demeanour, the table set and the kitchen wafting of roast mutton and vegetables, followed by desserts such as rhubarb and junket, rice puddings, jelly with fruit wobbling in it, apple tarts and custard squares.

Parents became ill-tempered if a neighbour started up the lawn mower just as the kids were being thrust out of the door.

"That blasted oaf with that infernal machine!" Dad would roar. "What a sewer. He's ruining the beauty on God's day. How can a man think around here?"

And Mum would make another cup of tea, and add an extra dollop of sugar to sweeten him.

If it hadn't been for Dad's job, we could never have afforded overseas trips. But if my parents were invited to a slide show, Dad would mutter, "Ring them back, Dot. I don't want to see any bastard's boring slides."

Mum, itching for a night out, said it was rude not to be nice about friends' continental trips.

Desperate to share their holiday memories, hosts always said to bring the kids. Wearing pyjamas and dressing gowns, we children tucked into a smorgasbord of curried chicken and Pavlova before squatting on a couch to peer at slides, often upside down, while hosts argued about what city they were in.

Some acted like university lecturers, inviting yawning guests to savour the rippling yellow and pink façade of renaissance buildings. If anyone politely asked a question, the slide slid back into reverse with a lengthy monologue no one cared about. Fed up, Dad would shout, "Next!" and Mum would poke him in the ribs, or he'd yawn noisily saying he had to be in bed by 10pm.

Intimating a burning smell from the projector always got the quickest reaction. No one wants holes in their precious slides. Tripping over the flex cord in the dark for a Chianti top-up or bathroom visit was also a novel way to shorten the viewing.

Mum would say, "I'll just check on the kids to see they haven't wet your bed."

At school our geography teacher thrust a stick at sketches of countries chalked on the blackboard, mostly on growing rice in China or the wheat belt in Australia. Privately, we students wondered if the teacher wore a mini skirt under her flowing black robes and if she had a boyfriend.

Knowing we were about to head off to England, Mum tried to make small savings like re-stewing tea (no teabags then), making our clothes, ripping sheets that had torn in the middle and sewing the outer edges together, growing vegetables and brewing ginger beer and wine. Sometimes we were awoken by loud pops in the linen cupboard.

We were fascinated when the pressure cooker exploded and bits of meat and carrot flew up to the ceiling.

"What a pity," Mum muttered. "Here's five shillings." (Five bob was considered slangy lower talk.) "Run up to the fish and chip shop and make sure they don't put in funny things."

She was referring to a mouse once found in a Friday night greasy paper. She'd sent us to the shop with a note because she hated to confront poor immigrants, but was upset by their lack of hygiene. They were only worried Mum might report them to the police.

My English aunt and uncle would have no such qualms. They tackled situations head-on with a healthy dose of jocularity.

Once the pressure cooker exploded in the Combi van and spat Aunt June's tasty ox kidneys, garlic, peppers, tomatoes, red wine and spices onto the mat. Undeterred, she scraped up every bit of it with a useful gadget called 'the bendy thing' and re-served it with rice and marrow.

We'd been imbibing Hungarian Bull's Blood and, since it was too dark to see what we were eating, the meal was appreciated. No one got the collywobbles.

Uncle Richard did most of the shopping, cooking and itinerary. He wrote a diary on a clunky typewriter while the rest of us slept off the effects of food, wine and travel. We travelled in convoy in two vehicles. Susannah, their Volkswagen microbus, took six family members and the camping gear. Dad drove four of us in their 8hp 1938 Ford, called Susie that had had five engines, been strengthened with fibreglass, and chalked up 150,000 miles.

We took cameras varying from my Box Brownie to 35mm slides. Digital cameras hadn't been invented. When we put our film in for processing later, the delayed gratification gave thrills, or despair if the negatives were blank, or the prints came out over-exposed, under-exposed, streaked or with black spots. Mum was perplexed as to why the Leaning Tower of Pisa remained perpendicular while the landscape tilted in her snaps. We blamed the chemist.

For the next six weeks as we looped around Europe, the days were filled with museums, churches, alpine villages, mediaeval castles, swimming, and eating strange food. Everyone, except us tough little Aussies, 'got the dog.' Aunt June said that was perfectly normal and dished out tablets. Dad tried the alcohol cure with success. We ate conger eels, pig trotters, fried squid, paella, all kinds of sausages and sauerkraut, cheeses and even toadstools. Uncle Richard remained at the helm, and dealt calmly with any hiccups.

Dad followed Susannah like a leech. He was visually comforted when glimpsing the family ahead waving, and Joanna flattening her face against the back window, poking her tongue out.

He panicked if Susannah squeezed between the yellow and red traffic lights, or nipped across heavy oncoming traffic. Uncle Richard said keeping Susie in his rear vision mirror was like towing a long trailer on an extendible tow-bar, for the scream of brakes, skidding tyres and the hooting and cursing of baulked drivers haunted him.

Once in view, Mum would pop a barley sugar into Dad's mouth, agree that all the other traffic on the road was a menace, and I could hear Enga breathing again.

"Oh, look at those darling petty-pies," she exclaimed over flocks of sheep. If Mum pointed things out Dad said not to distract him. I kept my head down, furiously writing my journal.

We camped by rivers, railway tracks, in forests, farms where entire families pitched hay together. Their children, in Tyrolean lederhosen, offered eggs and canisters of milk for sale. In Belgium, a couple with two small children who spoke four languages let us pitch our tents on their spacious lawns. They had a bull terrier called Pigale, named for his low taste.

In Amsterdam, the camping ground had been booked solid by a World Convention of Jehovah's Witnesses. They arrived by the thousands. We flinched at the sight of an ocean of tents and the roaring sea of buses.

"Vot der hell," said a charming Dutchman when we explained our predicament. "It's only for a night. Come and join us."

The washhouse was full of giggling Indonesian women thrusting their skinny brown legs into a long stone trough. The only words vaguely recognisable were 'Allo brudder, allo sista' blaring from loudspeakers.

Uncle Richard had a wicked sense of humour for he wrote at night: "We sip our demon alcohol with care and attention, that the shadow-graph on the tent walls shall not advertise our un-Jehovah-like depravity."

An incident shook us in Germany.

Dad was proceeding at 35mph on his side of the road at dusk when a car drew alongside and, once abreast, swerved twice into Susan. We lurched to a halt. Uncle Richard strode back along the autobahn when he lost sight of us and saw two youths screaming at Dad.

No one could understand the other, but money and the police were mentioned. One of the Hungarian youths swiped Uncle Richard's international licence, but Mum lunged forward and snatched it back, crying, "Smell their breath," while we five children cheered.

I grabbed my diary and wrote up the details, including the men's facial features and clothing.

Sympathetic lorry drivers joined in the circus and, when two unemotional German *polizei* noted the rusty dents on the Skoda, they established it was a try-on to get hush money out of the rich English. The men lost their bluster, the *polizei* were thrilled to meet Australians, and we all parted friends, having literally been at each other's throats for an hour.

"This is going to be the best day of my life," I cried as we entered Florence.

I was itching to see the paintings and art treasures we'd been studying at school. How my classmates would be envious especially seeing Michelangelo's nude statue of David! A giant replica stood outside the Palazzo della Signoria where camera-clicking tourists thronged and children licked gelatos.

"Gee, you're rude," said my sister. "I can see your eyes staring at David's doynker."

"Shut up, you little brat. I'm staring at the pigeons on his head."

"Were not! Hey, Ma, Jonquil's spending a long time looking at that statue's diddle."

"Joanna!" scolded Mum. "You must be hungry. Go find Uncle Richard and help him get something nice for lunch."

"I wasn't staring at his rudies, Ma. The statue's out of proportion. The hands are too large."

For an hour I raced from paintings to statues, free of a twelve-year old accusing me of lasciviousness, while Aunt June cooked squid in the broiling sun on the banks of River Arno.

A few years later a replica of David was brought to David Jones store in Sydney and planted by the perfumery department. Some prudes objected and refused to take their kiddies into the shop while papers screamed *Are we ready for this?* The art encyclopaedia at home had small photographs of nakedness but I always clamped the book shut if I heard Mum's footsteps.

Now, in David Jones, as a young working girl, I could feast upon this drawcard while nibbling on a sandwich in my lunch hour.

In Berchtesgaden, near Salzburg, it rained steadily, drearily, and unceasingly. We wanted to visit Hitler's Eagle's Nest high above our camp. So what do ten people do on a wet day when everything is sodden and the tourist shops are full of expensive souvenirs?

"Hairy men," shouted Jasper, who'd been exploring the campsite. "Liza, we've found some hairy men for you!"

A twenty-strong brass band in Bavarian costume oom-pah-pah-ing.

When we returned to camp in a deluge that threatened to wash our tents away, we found the grown-ups had opened the bar in Susannah and Uncle Richard was cooking up a feed.

He summed up the memorable evening, saying, "As dark fell, out came the bottles, to let us forget the prevailing moisture, the floods, and the drips. The evening culminated in song, but the sort of song that is not often heard in South Germany, the land of Schubert and Mozart. I blushed for the good name of our G.B. number plates.

"I especially remember my senior sister, Enga, wielding two Melaware soup bowls as percussion instruments, whilst the very mixed company sang bawdy, and sometimes other, songs with enthusiasm and abandon, but little, if any other, musical quality."

It was a moment of sweet fun and happiness where we blended as relatives and enjoyed each other, young and old. We slept like dogs while lightning flashed and thunder roared, and if we didn't get to see Hitler's hideout, *vot der hell?*

By the time we arrived in Paris towards the end of our trip, we'd bathed in the River Po (so we could boast to our school friends about that), tasted fare not available Down Under, and Aunt Enga had knocked up commendable watercolours of the Dolomites, with a cloth over her head between light showers.

At our own slide viewing back home, Mum remarked on the beauty of the Swiss Alps.

In Paris I slipped and broke a bone in my foot.

"I'll die if I don't see the Mona Lisa," I howled. "I've been learning about it at school—the lady with an enema smile."

129

"Enigmatic, I think you mean," laughed Aunt June, and, with her usual forthrightness, secured a wheelchair and wheeled me around the Louvre from floor to floor as tourists parted before us.

I came face to face with the famous painting. It was just me and the Mona Lisa staring at each other. Back in Susannah, while eating snails in garlic butter, Aunt June said the next time she went to Paris she'd arrive on crutches and demand a wheelchair so she could enjoy the paintings in comfort.

Chapter 14
Ship, Surf and Suburbia

"What do you mean, the dog's dead?"

Mum blew her nose into a lace hanky, and struggled to read the letter from Australia.

"Nikki had a growth under her tail. Cancerous. It was kinder to put her down."

Dad tightened his lips like a soldier and said we'd buy another dog. Joanna and I sobbed on Mum's shoulders.

"Don't you care about Nikki?" Joanna snapped at Jasper, who had a poker face.

But Mum said, "Shush, your brother does have feelings. Look, his lips are trembling, and for God's sake don't tease him. His voice is breaking."

She then said she couldn't face going home now because Nikki was the nicest person in our family, even if she was a dog.

Nikki had been a substitute pony, a surrogate mother to stray animals and a money-earner for Jasper ferreting golf balls on the Collaroy links. She was extremely devoted and howled when left on her own. Once she escaped out the bathroom window and sprinted down the road looking for us when we caught the bus to Sydney. A couple of stops on, Nikki boarded the double-decker and, sniffing us out upstairs, thumped her tail excitedly and licked our faces.

"Pretend we don't know her," said Mum. "Go away, bad dog. Where's your owner?"

When the conductor blew hard on his whistle we had to admit the dog was ours and Mum tottered all the way home in her high heels telling Nikki what an embarrassing disgrace she was, but since she was laughing the confused dog got mixed messages.

Retail therapy always eased Mum's worries and disappointments, and while Dad was at the London office she looked for bargains in Harrods. She knew he'd sign up for another five year stint in Australia and it was his job to find a passenger liner going back home via an interesting route. Hers was to make sure we children were well-dressed. The Firm always sent us first class. I didn't understand Dad's job except he had a furrowed brow, wrote pencilled figures in columns and brought home packets of ox tongue in brown paper which Mum tried to disguise at meal times, calling it bubble and squeak.

"We're poor," she said. "Just ram it down your throat. Here's the tomato sauce."

At school we'd been asked what our parents did for a living. Most said their dads were doctors, lawyers or architects even if they weren't. Pity the odd pupil who had an absent father. No one had parents who were tradespeople for they couldn't have afforded private school fees.

"What sticky beaks your teachers are!" Mum said. "What did you say?"

"I said Dad's a cost accountant and *a'costs* people."

Mum was shocked. "Accosts? You didn't, darling!"

Dad laughed so hard he later used that as a valedictory speech. It brought the house down.

He booked us on the *Orsova,* which travelled through the Suez Canal with ports of call at Gibraltar, Naples, Aden and Colombo before ducking down to Australia. Mum said she'd go because Italy was mentioned and there was a nip in the English air. During the weeks leading up to the voyage we did a frenzied educational tour from Stonehenge to the Chamber of Horrors, clambering over old ships, museums, parks, castles, spent a weekend in Wales and we also attended naval parties.

Enga had flown home, and sent a telegram *Arrived the right way up* begging us to come to New Zealand some time. Mum gave up trying to make us do school work. She was in grief mode having to return Down Under, although excited about being waited on and treated like Lady Muck on a ship.

We were kissed, hugged, given money and gifts from the English relatives before climbing aboard the train to the awaiting ship.

"Mummy says you're not to like the stewards," warned my sister running up the gangplank, her plaits flapping in the November wind, "and I'm having the top bunk."

The voyage took thirty days with the ship battling fifty-foot waves after Gibraltar. The dining room was empty, except for Dad who said everyone was neurotic not seasick. Mum found a titled lady companion whose skittle and deck quoit skills were as sharp as her crisp speech and the duo won prizes from the ship's shop.

Second class passengers weren't allowed to mix but the entertainment was the same. Peering over the railings they looked like a bunch of refugees in their cramped quarters and, since they were a younger crowd, I was disappointed handsome officers disappeared down there for evening dances.

One distinguished traveller was Leslie Hutchinson (1900-1969) known as Hutch, a cabaret star and popular entertainer. He agreed to put on a concert. The atmosphere was spoilt when some passengers, noting he was black, walked out at the start of the performance. Mum was horrified and said they were the lowest of the low. She said we better be nice to him, and that gave me an idea for the Mad Hatter's parade. I made a cage out of cardboard, filled it with food scraps and a china rabbit, and plonked it on my head.

"It's called Hutch," I told the perplexed entertainer, "and, gee, I liked your singing."

Hutch tossed his head back and roared with laughter and I won a special prize for teenagers. Dad wore a jockey hat and straddled a stick with a wooden horse head dragging on the ground. He went as Ors-ova, a play on our ship *Orsova*. My siblings were banned to their bunks for playing up.

"Psst, ladies. Wanta see da naughty pitchers (sic) in Pompeii?" asked a taxi driver, when the *Orsova* docked in Naples, referring to frescoes. Mum thought that remark uncouth and had the price dropped to £3 for a tour of the old ruins. Every Friday afternoon our Latin teacher had told us engaging stories of Ancient Rome and now we were peering at copulating couples frozen in time. Mum said, "Those poor people must have been as scared as heck with all that ash erupting out of Mount Vesuvius and were having a final cuddle."

We barely saw our parents as the ship steamed towards Sydney, except in port, for we were far too busy joining in activities, lounging by the pool and making friends. My heart flip-flopped from the dark-haired Irish drinks waiter to the rosy-cheeked bureau officer.

"He was staring at you," Dad teased. "Do you want me to lose something and you can ask him at the lost property department?"

Mum said I should talk to him about joining the WRENS.

"You'd look lovely in a uniform, darling," she said, "and you'd get to meet lots of nice men."

I didn't know if I'd want to live in England. But Mum assured me I would.

The first thing my brother did when we arrived in Sydney was to head for the surf. Joanna and I fought over the phone, informing school friends we were back. Mum nipped next door to catch up on gossip ranging from gall bladders to car accidents, and a neighbour who was found unconscious in a paddock but awoke, calling out, "Who's put grass in my lounge?"

Since it was nearly Christmas Mum let us roam wild over Collaroy, only railing us in for the frequent dinner parties and slide shows. "Stay away for the day," she'd say, and give us bottles of ginger beer, sausages and a coat hanger for prongs. "Have a barbecue but don't set fire to the beach and try not to get too sunburnt." The latter remark fell on deaf ears. We all wanted to be brown and wearing zinc cream was for *dweebs* and *dorks*.

Teenage girls envied long straight blonde hair. Some surfie girls bleached theirs, even using Harpic, and ironed it straight. Jasper grew tanned and blonder, which made his eyes bluer. Parents moaned about their sons wearing board shorts to a vulgar level.

"I'm ashamed of you, darling," said Mum as Jasper grabbed his surfboard. "It's not in the canons of good taste."

"It's the fashion, Ma," he'd reply.

Our world was relatively safe in the early 60s despite some high profile murders. There was the Bogle-Chandler case where Bogle, a former Rhodes scholar and brilliant scientist, and a married woman who'd attended the same New Year's Eve party at Chatswood left together. Their bodies were found at Lane Cove hours later on 1 January, 1963, with traces of poison. That baffling mystery has never been solved, and caused wild speculation and endless discussion in every Australian home. Mum was interested because it had a New

Zealand connection. Others tut-tutted over swingers and wife swapping.

Closer to home was the commercial artist, photographer and cartoon creator, Leonard Keith Lawson. He'd boarded with the mother of Jasper's friend in Anzac Avenue, Collaroy. After sexually assaulting and stabbing to death a young girl he burst into SCEGGS, Mossvale, the sister school to the one I attended.

The brave headmistress grappled with the gunman who'd taken schoolgirl hostages and, in the commotion, the gun went off, killing a fifteen-year old pupil. The murderer back in 1954 had raped and assaulted five June Dally-Watkins models and, although condemned to death, was released after serving half of a fourteen-year sentence. Jasper said his mate's mother, who'd provided lodgings for this fiend, was so traumatised she was seeing a mental specialist.

One thing which annoyed Dad were trade unionists marching through the city crying, "Waddabout the workers?" Dad said they should be shot, the whole lot of them. Our parents, as Liberal supporters, thought any Labour voter was suspect, perhaps harbouring communist tendencies, and should buzz off to Russia and see how they liked it. They thought Prime Minister Menzies was doing a good job. While I was a kid completing my final year at school, there was talk of *reds under the bed, the yellow peril invading our shores* and *beware of computers and robots taking over.* Yet Ingrad's dad was an architect who had a massive computer that occupied the lounge. The family had to walk around it to get to the kitchen.

Soon after we arrived back in Australia Mum was offered a job at Calabash, a clothing boutique in Spit Junction, bought by a lawyer to keep his spoilt wife occupied. We'd missed two terms of schooling and Mum couldn't stand staying home to make us catch up. After Christmas, she hired a headmistress from a country school who was holidaying with friends.

I spent the summer vacation frantically writing up notes from a school friend's books while my siblings yawned. Jasper's excuse was he'd become becalmed while sailing with his mates; otherwise he attacked algebra and served up milky cups of coffee and biscuits at regular intervals. Joanna said she

135

was needed to brush the sheltered ponies and feed six-legged sheep freaks when a circus came to town.

Between customer browsing at the exclusive boutique, Mum typed up my journal of our European trip on a Remington typewriter. "Don't be offended, darling. I know how sensitive you get, but it has quite a lot of adjectives."

"I can't help it," I said. "I have a very *abjective* mind."

By the time Calabash was forced to close because of opportunistic theft by men in hats and gabardine coats thrusting ball gowns under their clothing, Mum was bored with sitting all day waiting for people to come and buy an expensive frock. She got a job with Nestle doing market research. Housework was a thankless task she said compared to driving around, knocking on doors and handing out questionnaires. Some people liked Mum and gave her rose cuttings from their gardens. Others seemed offended to be asked their husband's occupation.

Sending three children to private schools was costly and Dad still threw his hands up in horror and swore in Spanish when the bills came in. There were no warehouses selling cheap clothing so blazers and tunics were bought on the large side and, when they became tight, hems were let down and seams let out.

Shopping for school shoes was a serious business because shop assistants crouched on the floor and x-rayed and measured a child's foot on a machine, and then added an inch for growth. We grinned as the leather shoes squeaked when we tested them under supervision and went to bed hugging them, sniffing in their newness. The prized shoebox with crinkly tissue was used for treasures like injured birds, locusts, a pretend doll's bed, shells, stamps, pet mice, or a rat's corpse to show the biology teacher.

Birthdays at home were celebrated with much fanfare. The golden rule was, be pleasant to that person, they choose the TV programme and they don't do dishes. On her own birthday, Mum would cut out the price tags from Grace Bros. or David Jones and wrap her own presents. "Ooh! Look what your kind father gave me." Dad got socks, hankies, a pot of putty, a spanner and an LP of the latest show airing in Sydney.

Chinese goods hadn't flooded the market in the early 60s but Japanese imports had. Some people refused to buy them, a hangover from the war, calling them cheap and nasty. But for two shillings and sixpence we could buy a gaudy glass brooch, a china ornament or wooden coasters from Woolies for our parents.

Mum said she didn't want presents for Mother's Day, just kids who didn't bicker and a nice cup of tea in bed.

One year I granted Mum's wish. I crept downstairs at dawn and fussed over a tea tray, which included a hydrangea swimming in a Mickey Mouse jar, a pot of tea and a plate of buttery toast turned cold.

Dad yawned, "For Chrissakes, what's the time?" as Mum sleepily said, "It's Mother's Day, you oaf. Your daughter's trying to be kind, and you never say no to a nice cuppa." When Dad had blown his nose, reached for his spectacles and pipe, yawned again, he said, "Pour the tea, Dot. Happy Mother's day, old girl." I beamed.

The hot water in the teapot trickled clear. "You forgot to put in the tea-leaves, darling." I stormed out of the room, saying, "Jeez, some people are fussy." Mum and Dad chuckled for weeks, asking if tea was being served with tea-leaves.

Mum gushed over gifts, especially homemade cards with poems she treasured, even if she had to ask Jasper to explain his ghoulish cartoon surfing characters. We usually got clothes, perhaps a school uniform. The fashion was desert or moofie boots, oversized fishermen's cabled jumpers and black mohair sweaters, sissy blouses, thongs (jandals), tight nylon patterned slacks, and straight skirts. I always received a Liberace LP. And I beamed with happiness as Mum basted a chicken in the oven and told the kids to set the table with the best silverware and light the candles.

"I'm special," I reminded them.

"Yeah, but not tomorrow," they replied.

Back in my attic bedroom, on my sixteenth birthday, I addressed the photograph on the wall.

"Libby, my darling. I had a wonderful birthday. Everyone was nice to me. And, by the way, I've forgiven you ever since you made me cry for a whole night when I thought you were going to marry Princess Margaret. How could you! Wait for me, my gorgeous sweetheart. I am growing up."

Mum was hanging over the fence telling Donny's mother the cake I'd baked was rock-hard. She turned to me. "You must have missed out something. There's no butter in it."

"The recipe said add butter or substitute with sugar, so I substituted with sugar, and I was going to make pastry but I couldn't find a scarf to put around my eyes coz it said bake blind. How dangerous is that! What a stupid cook book."

Donny's mum talked with pegs in her mouth when hanging white sheets on her rotary clothesline. Since patterned ones were not available, housewives were embarrassed if their sheets were a shade of grey for it meant you were poor or hadn't listened to the jingles about washing powder products. She said that at Donny's fifth birthday party, a fight nearly erupted and the little guests were threatening the birthday boy, saying they'd get their big brothers or dads onto him. The fight evaporated when Donny retorted, "Well, I'm going to get Jonquil onto you—coz she's nearly a lady!"

Despite missing so much schooling, I spent my final year cramming frantically and memorising pages of subjects without understanding anything just to pass the exams. I didn't care about the blood circulation of fish and amphibians and the strengths and weaknesses of the United Nations or the Colombo Plan, for soon I'd be launched into the real world and earning a living until the right man came along, preferably English in my parent's opinion. Teenagers worried that if they weren't engaged by twenty-one, they'd be left on the shelf. The late 60s changed that archaic thinking.

"You're heading for the gutter, son," said Dad when Jasper's peroxided hair turned orange and he bought himself purple pointed shoes called winkle-pickers and tight green jeans. He sold newspapers to the fish and chip shops.

"We don't know where we got you from," said Mum, as Joanna wrapped the cat around her head and snuggled her face into its furry belly. "You'll get ringworm and then nobody will want you."

She was in trouble for locking the cat in a parrot cage then bathing it to get rid of fleas, and for bringing home an Alsatian/mongrel puppy.

"Where did you get that yellow-faced bitzer bitch from?" asked Mum.

It was from the local greengrocer. Mum told her to return it. She was not going to have a pup that might end up mating indiscriminately. It could have hydatids.

Joanna snarled, "Gee, you're cruel. Bet I'm adopted," and since she brought up the subject, I wondered about my identity.

"Think about it," my sister whispered that night. "I'm nothing like them. Do you reckon they're our real parents? They won't even buy me a horse."

I reflected on the differences, too. I suspected my parents might be a tad common; they liked musicals. I preferred deeper things like stirring piano concertos. I was more religious for I had a crush on a prematurely balding curate at our Church of England parish.

"Jonquil's in love with a priest," teased my sister when my eyes filled with tears on hearing he was off to the jungles to preach the Good Word. Mum told her to be quiet until I said, "If I win the Sydney House Opera Lottery, I'm going to give the money to the church."

Mum said, "What a damn silly idea," so I confronted her at her most vulnerable—waxing the linoleum in the hallway on her hands and knees like a lowly domestic. "Ma, tell the truth," I said. "Did I spring from your loins?"

She looked up like a startled squirrel.

"What a peculiar thing for a child to say. No one in their right mind would take on other people's children."

To stop the silly talk she drove Joanna to Parramatta to buy a puppy.

"Prinky Poo, I love you," sang Joanna, her face in the golden hair of Princess, a miniature Shetland sheepdog, kissing her moist snout. She agreed to stop saying she was adopted.

Instead of warnings like *wait until your father gets home* or *if you don't do what you're told you'll go to bed with your lips quaking and your bottom aching*, our parents held formal meetings in the lounge. "We're having a blitz on your behaviour," they said.

Jasper was the main focus because surfing interfered with his homework.

"We're trying to work out what is going on in your brain," they said. "You've got a terrible school report and you're mixing with inferior people."

To Joanna, they said, "We're worried about your irritability. You must have worms." She said she couldn't go to church because she had to write one hundred lines after twanging a girl's suspender.

I'd be upstairs swotting and crying, "I'm going to fail my exams. I hate biology. Why did you have to make me! I'm no good to man or beast!"

"Have we bred lunatics?" Mum sighed.

Teachers were annoyed by end of year pranks. The year of my finals, students from Manly Boys High roared up to our prim Christian school in beat-up cars, rang the school bell and lumbered down corridors. "My humble apologies, dear Headmistress," said one miscreant kneeling before our astonished principal and squirting her with a water pistol.

"No more pencils, no more books, no more teacher's filthy looks," we sang on the school bus while throwing rolls of toilet paper out of the window onto passing cars.

"School days are the best days of your life," older people told us, but baby boomers couldn't wait to *get out of jail* and see what adventures lay ahead.

Chapter 15
Beginnings of Rebellion

Every January *The Sydney Morning Herald* published exam results for pupils who'd completed five years of secondary schooling, also known as the Leaving Certificate. It was a nail-biting time.

When the paper thudded onto our front porch at dawn, coinciding with the Milko doing his run, I woke my parents.

"Is my name there?" I cried. "Oh God, oh God, please make me pass. I'll be good for the rest of my life. I'll give my pocket money to the missions."

"We know you've worked hard, but you've missed a lot of schooling," said Mum, blinking in the morning light. "The world isn't going to stop if you've failed."

"It will! It will! I'll go into *perjury*!"

"Don't be silly," said Dad. "First, a nice cup of tea. Where's my jolly pipe and tobacco?"

When Dad read I'd passed every subject, I whooped with joy.

"Even biology," I kept repeating. "I can't believe it!"

"She's a stubborn little so and so," said Dad proudly to Mum who was taking bobby pins out of her hair and rubbing vanishing cream into her face.

"See, I'm not dim."

"We never thought you were, darling," said Mum, "did we, Fairley?"

Dad headed off for a quick swim at The Basin, our local beach. Fathers in those days were reluctant to lavish praise and display affection as they felt it would undermine their authority. Mum dipped into the housekeeping and bought me a pink chiffon frock.

"That's a present from your father."

I wore it to my first teenage party at Collaroy with my fifteen-year old brother as chaperone.

Once the punch had been imbibed, the lights were turned out. Someone's kid brother operated a turntable playing stacks of 45rpm rock 'n' roll records, while teenage boys with skin eruptions and wandering hands sprawled on the floor, stroking thighs of surfie chicks, nuzzling into their long hair.

I spent the night in the kitchen, chatting with the host's recently bereaved mother, hating the party. Mum was right, after all. I'd save myself for the right person and not let any opportunistic creep thrust his hormonal eruptions on me.

Girl pupils who completed school had limited choices in the 60s. Some went to Teachers College or Uni, became dental assistants or worked in banks. A friend from the next street said her ambition was to be a beatnik, draw nude figures, read Shakespeare and blob out on Dave Brubeck jazz.

Those from wealthy families became debs (debutantes) and were sent abroad to finishing school or did a Cordon Bleu course in France.

Art school was too bohemian, I decided, after seeing students with teased multi-coloured hair, batik-printed smocks, wearing Dr Scholl clogs and smoking. Mum said learning shorthand and typing would be a solid choice since it could take you anywhere in the world. For £120 a year, I became a pupil of the Lillian Smith Secretarial School in Dee Why, a suburb over by bus, or a long sunny walk home.

Mrs Smith had sent her twin daughters to a private school and treated me kindly. An extra two years' education was unusual as most of her pupils had left after Intermediate (three years of secondary education.) Other early school leavers became apprentice hairdressers and worked in department stores. The fifteen-year olds at Secretarial school were more interested in boys and how many friendship rings they'd scored.

We learnt touch-typing using a manual typewriter where a wooden box was placed over our hands so we couldn't peek at the keys, Pitman's shorthand with Friday speed tests, book-keeping and switchboard skills. Mrs Smith frowned on poor speech and pupils who wore short skirts, long boots and lots of black eye liner.

"Why aren't you concentrating on your book-keeping?" she demanded, walking up to our table. "What's so important you are distracted?"

I blushed deeply when a pupil two years my junior said, "We were telling Jonquil how to catch a boy."

Towns and beaches along the east coast of Australia began to pulsate in the early 60s with adrenalin from American pop culture and the surfing craze. Instead of the benign 50s daddio, teenagers referred to their father as the old man, mothers as the old lady, and collectively they were the oldies. They were viewed as authoritarian and out of touch, while despondent parents saw their fledgling teens as hedonistic by disregarding the ethics of hard work, doing the right thing, and playing by the rules.

"Rules are meant to be broken," said my brother glibly. "Get with it, Ma."

He never understood Dad's values of having backbone and commitment to a future career.

"Are you studying to be a halfwit?" Dad asked.

Jasper said, "You'll never understand our generation."

His thrills were riding monstrous curling waves and roaming beaches in his mates' panel vans, their sunburnt arms hanging out the windows, holding up surfboards wobbling on the roof rack.

Since we lived on the main road of Collaroy, minutes from the beach, our humble villa became a focal point for Jasper and his surfing mates. When the surf was shithouse, a term that made Mum cringe—Jasper invited them all home. Mum welcomed them and thought of them as nice boys but rather misguided in their enthusiasm for the waves.

"Aren't you afraid of sharks?" she asked.

Jasper's friends liked her for she invited some for dinner, but if they had problems with their parents she refused to let them stay the night. They were always respectful; some even wore a tie when Mum gave them a roast dinner and a tinkle of Sparkling Porphyry Pearl.

Our parents never drank beer at meals or garnished the table with pots of tea, slabs of bread and tomato sauce. That was for shearers and the working class. We had a tablecloth and placemats Mum made at evening woodwork classes at the Narrabeen primary school.

"Has anyone read a good book lately?" Mum would inquire to set the dinner tone. I didn't admit the wannabe beatnik around the corner had lent me two banned books—Lolita and Lady Chatterley's Lover!

One of Jasper's best mates was the son of an Anglican minister at St. Faiths Church at Narrabeen. Churches had a full attendance during the 50s as shops were closed and towns were quiet, but the 60s became busier and lax about attitude towards religion. The Reverend had a booming voice, a bristly moustache and, when he uttered the word God through his new dentures, it shuddered like a dramatic echo. He said God-d-d-d was all-powerful and knew what was in our hearts.

When it came to putting coins or buff coloured envelopes into the offering plate, we were racked by feelings of disquiet. *Could we have given more?*

"The good Reverend relies on our donations," said Mum. "He's got a church to run and a family of five to feed and, besides, I could pop off any time and you need someone like him to give you a decent burial."

"Don't die on us, Mum," I fretted. "I'll do all the housework."

The Reverend had a busy schedule spreading the word at schools, writing sermons, doing pastoral work and enlightening his flock of parishioners. The hardest job was keeping his kids in line. Some mornings his son was up at dawn, throwing pebbles at Jasper's window. They'd sneak away to surf, sometimes skipping school.

Once they took off for four days, saying they were going sailing, but hitchhiked as far as the South Australian border and slept on school verandahs, a padded police cell and a pig farm run by a wild-eyed Danish guy who kept them up all night demonstrating magic tricks. At a bar the publican suspected they were under-age.

Jasper said, "Gee mate, what d'ya take us for! Have a beer on us and keep the change."

The fifteen-year olds were treated to a couple of free rounds after that. Jasper could talk his way out of a paper bag.

When I told Mum I was getting confirmed, she wondered what that meant. I thought it was like having insurance against accidents and disappointments and if your parents upset you, the Big Man in the sky would sort it out.

Billy Graham, the American evangelist, caused an outpouring of religious fervour when he flew to Sydney, gathering up new recruits including the eager, the vulnerable and the impressionable.

The Reverend told us to pray for a parishioner who was in the throes of a nervous breakdown. The young woman had slipped, lost her memory and turned common, he said in strict confidence. She'd plucked her eyebrows and looked frightful and he feared she'd lost her way. I stifled yawns when he talked to a group of us about upcoming house parties and the *decision* and the *purpose*.

When a black Labrador slunk into Sunday School, he shot up from his chair and thundered, "Get out, thy Catholic dog!" The dog's owner assured him his Labrador was a Protestant.

Puffing on his pipe, the Reverend said it was a toss-up between Catholics and the commos (communists) on his loathing list. He thought the Anglicans had it pretty well sewn up and said we were God's labourers and should bring the lost souls of Collaroy Beach to church.

Some of the teens at church were quite devout for, at Fellowship, between scripture readings and rousing *Praise My Soul,* we were encouraged to share thoughts and pray aloud. I found it excruciating. I couldn't think of anything vital to pray about except asking God to rid me of a cold sore, or comforting a girl because she'd been dumped for going *all the way* with a boy.

"What sort of people are you meeting at church?" Mum asked when I told her about a girl engaged to a bus conductor. "I hope you don't get funny ideas and run off with people like that."

She and Dad attended more regularly after that, to show family unity even if it killed them. On Sunday evenings my sister was dragged out of the house screaming she hadn't finished her homework.

"It's boring, and Jonquil only goes to gawk at boys."

If Mum mentioned horses, Joanna pinned up her pyjamas with safety pins or brooches, flung a coat over the top and toddled off to the car in my sling-backs (shoes.)

"Jasper needs the Holy Spirit more than us," said Mum, frantically beckoning Jasper and the Reverend's son off their boards at Long Reef, her stilettos sinking in the golden sands. Once in the car the boys yapped about rip curls, wipeouts, hanging ten and pipelines.

"I hope you girls are behaving yourselves," she said, swivelling her neck if Joanna and I were forced to perch on the knees of Jasper's surfing mates who needed a ride home, or thought they'd come to church for something to do.

Although a short ride to St. Faith's church, Dad was annoyed by traffic, whether too fast or too slow.

"That sewer nearly got his water cut off," growled Dad, making us in the back seat snigger with fright.

"Shoosh, dear," soothed Mum reapplying lipstick in the rear vision mirror. "We're going to God's house to worship."

The congregation was usually in full voice as we stumbled in. Mum had an eye for fat women with large hats and always placed herself in a pew directly behind such a person.

"Move along, Dot," Dad urged as we filed into a pew.

"I'm quite comfortable, thank you," Mum said, and the rest of us had to climb or struggle around her while she smiled innocently and mouthed hymns. Dad's voice wasn't much either, a genetic defect passed onto us, although Joanna later sang in a band.

But Mum was a cunning old girl. She said she liked going to church for a good sit-down. Sometimes we wondered if she'd ever arise as the Reverend's sermon had a soporific effect. When he hammered on about the devil and sinners, his booming voice jolted Mum into temporary wakefulness. She'd give a little snort, hiss, "I was listening," reposition herself behind the be-hatted woman and nod off, her head slumping until we prodded her.

Dad said to let Mum sleep because she'd had a busy day vacuuming the lounge and de-heading the hydrangeas. Some of Jasper's mates did wheelies outside the church in their beat-up cars to get his attention. It prompted Dad to add a Commandment of his own: Blessed are the weak for they shall inherit the surf!

Even though Mum thought she'd end up in a mental home with the traffic of youths knocking on the door and Jasper sneaking up the driveway clutching his surfboard, our house was open to Joanna's giggling friends who also shared an interest in horses. At fourteen, she was having mood swings. When she refused to go swimming saying it would give her fat legs and bosoms, she was covering up an excuse common to all women. How do you wear togs when you've got your monthlies because sanitary pads were bulky and swelled when immersed in salt water? We hated having our periods or *girlfriend* or other monikers like *George, the curse, that-time-of-the-month* and *got-you-know-what.*

On me rags was a 50s expression. It made us spotty, grouchy and depressed because we couldn't perch on beaches in our bikinis, and had to fib about why we preferred basking on the sand in hipster pants instead of wallowing in the rolling waves.

Although the pill and tampons had been invented they were not widely available, and young teens would have been too embarrassed to front up to a chemist. Mum never made me go to the pharmacy to buy pads but she suggested I take a peek in the window at their display. It was a new range of *Jonquille* perfume that became a popular gift from boyfriends and workmates.

The blushing young chemist, on seeing me with Prinky Poo, sprang from behind a collection of *Jonquille* and invited me in to admire his display.

While he engaged me in conversation my brain cried, "Jonquil! You are a ripe young lady now and he knows you get it. Talk your way out of that!"

Whenever he asked Mum about me, doing rapid eye blinking, Mum replied I was not ready to go out into the big wide world yet.

Mum got on with Canon Newth, the headmaster. She helped in the canteen at Jasper's school, an hour away by bus, over the Sydney Harbour Bridge. He gave her two tickets to see Giaconda de Vito, the touring Italian violinist, although Jasper had all but given up on the violin. The cultural night was a temporary awakening, but soon Jasper was inventing plausible excuses why he couldn't attend school. He broke a thermometer putting it by the heater.

"You haven't got a temperature," said Mum. "Get into your school clothes now!"

Canon Newth rang to say he'd caned Jasper for playing hooky and dumb insolence.

Mum was distraught. "I'll chop up your ruddy surfboard! Your father's paying good money for you to get a decent education. When you get a job and leave home you can do what you like."

Canon Newth said teachers are afraid of the headmaster, who is afraid of the department, who's afraid of the officials, who are afraid of the government, and they are afraid of the parents who are afraid of their children, and children are afraid of nothing!

Jasper's teacher came to the house for a visit. Mum thought Jasper needed a psychiatrist to expunge his surfing obsession. Jasper spoke in short jerky sentences, he wanted freedom and to not be treated like a schoolboy. When asked about the purpose of life, he said it was to enjoy oneself.

Mum was irked. She flung slabs of cheese between eight butter-less chunks of bread into a bag for his school lunch, with a note: "This required little effort on my part and left me more time to enjoy myself."

Mum told the exasperated form teacher about *an element that comes to the house and gives him funny ideas*. But she didn't know what to do about it.

The *element* was a twenty-year old male nurse who was a guru to young teenage boys. He'd been scarred by an alcoholic father and having to help his mother raise the family since he was sixteen. His views on life were warped and anti-social. He preached to his adoring following that parents' views are bullshit and surfing is the way of life.

When Jasper whined, "Ma, whaddaya got against him? He's orright. He plays chess," Mum capitulated.

She let the interloper into the house and served coffee to talk with him about the importance of an education. His brooding presence caused moral panic with like-minded mums on Collaroy Plateau whose sons went to private schools. If he didn't bring that *antidisestablishmentarianism* bum into the house, Jasper could have his mates at weekends.

Since our house was strategically placed between popular surfing beaches, Mum complained it was like Pitt Street. There were youths under the willow tree fixing up dings on their surfboards, or poking around in decrepit Chevvies, bread vans and ambos (ambulances) Jasper had towed home.

The latest hits blasted from a transistor radio interspersed with racy DJs with adopted Americanisms. Instead of saying hello it was *hi*. Gee whiz became *crikey dick, shit, strewth* and *Hector Crawford*.

"Put a hat on, you'll ruin your complexion. I hope you're not getting boy-mad," Mum shouted through the kitchen window when she saw my legs dangling from the top of the septic tank.

She'd caught me gazing at Jasper's surfing mates. When Cliff Richard's syrupy tune *Lucky Lips* aired, I wondered when my own lips would get to be lucky.

Mothers had a wealth of expressions they spat out at intervals: *Bide your time for no decent man wants you if you are fast* (available) and *marry in haste—repent at leisure.* They told us they had eyes in the back of their head and could tell when we were lying.

If we were too sick to go to school then we were too sick to play outside or watch TV. We were told to be thankful for small mercies, eat our vegetables because they were good for us, and if we were too full to eat dinner then we were too full to eat pudding. Regarding body piercing, if God wanted us to have a hole in our ears He would have put it there.

Mothers also said, *Pick it up, I'm not your maid* or *Pick it up before someone trips over it and breaks their neck,* and *If you have the energy to stay up all night then you can get up in the morning. The oldest should know better,* and *If a job's worth doing, then it's worth doing well.* The biggest threats were *If you don't learn how to cook no one will marry you* and *Always wear clean underwear in case you're in an accident and get taken to hospital.*

When the lovesick young chemist said to Mum, "I'm worried about Jonquil, about the cultural aspects," Mum told him I wasn't interested in surfies because I was still in love with Liberace, which wasn't strictly true.

He sighed.

Mum didn't get it. In a gentlemanly way he was warning her to protect me from someone with loose morals a few doors from us. Chemists are like doctors and priests—they can't blab.

He was referring to a teenage nymphomaniac.

Chapter 16
Brenda the Bender and the Stomp

While the 50s had been a time of growth and development with post war immigration, an influence of European culture, a mass programme of free polio vaccinations and the beginnings of rock 'n' roll, there was disquiet that baby boomers, the new generation, were challenging the rules. The early 60s gave rise to those fears because jobs were plentiful and teenagers had money to buy records and dictate fashions. We told our parents to get hip, and that they just didn't dig our generation.

Our soldier daddies had been advised to put the past behind them and resume normal family life when World War II ended. We never reflected on how hard it was for them suffering haunting flashbacks, or perhaps their sweethearts marrying someone else.

Warehouses and giant supermarkets didn't exist. Instead, tiny shops in arcades specialising in chocolates, gateaux, Pierre Cardin shoes, Norma Tullo suits, fur coats, yoghurt bars (the new rage) and coffee shops tempted us. *Continental* had an exotic twang and people thought overseas goods must be better than our own home brand, although our mothers made a fuss if we went out with their sons.

The uncouth called Greeks and Italians *wogs* and *dagoes*. In fact, they were New Australians who worked long hours, employed their kids in their fish and chip businesses after school, and began living the Australian dream. They embraced the Australian vernacular and their dogged effort created a work ethic that lacked in some sons of established families of British stock. Those spoilt boys rode on the merits of their surgeon or lawyer dads. Their affluent parents, who appeared in the social pages of *The Sydney Morning Herald,* had sprawling homes with a swimming pool and sea view, and gave them sports cars for their eighteenth birthdays. They didn't want their son marrying that tramp or trollop, but someone with equal social and money status. If he got a girl in the family way they could afford to pay for a hush abortion and the frightened lass had little choice but to acquiesce. It worried wealthy parents that an opportunistic upstart might steal their son's heart; they could be dragged down by in-laws from the wrong side of the tracks.

Australians detested the snobbishness of the British class system but those living in upmarket Sydney suburbs enjoyed their social status. Life at home was unpleasant if a daughter became romantically entangled with a boy of mixed blood, especially a smattering of Aboriginal. She could be disinherited or sent overseas on a P & O liner to a relative in England, to become sensible. Nowadays people romanticise about their colourful bloodline, but in the 60s it was about pedigree. You relied on your family for support for there were no pick-up agencies, which are prolific now. Adoption was also an answer for unwed mothers. If a girl was sent to the country no one sympathised about her sluttish behaviour and it was her fault for not controlling herself. The fear of being alienated from our parents and besmirching the family name was a mental contraceptive.

There were no credit cards so people paid by cheque or cash and weren't impulse-driven. Immigrants brought old skills. Since footwear was expensive, shoes were re-soled and re-stitched until our toes curled. City gutter gratings were a hazard to stilettos. Stooped men with bushy eyebrows and guttural accents fixed watches and mended broken dolls.

Male hairdressers in white coats gave our menfolk short back and sides, and sold pipes, tinned tobacco, cigarettes and shaving cream. Women got perms and wrapped a nylon scarf around their hair-do before boarding a bus home, clutching parcels wrapped in brown paper and string. They made sure dinner was ready before their spouse, the breadwinner, came home. And *Never talk to a man on an empty stomach* was the housewives' motto.

It was worth the long bus trip over the Spit Bridge and vomiting into a paper bag, to view the Christmas display on the children's floor at department stores. Fairy grottoes, Pedigree bride dolls, pedal cars, tricycles and decorations thrilled us. Santa, on a throne of velvet, had bewildered kids hoisted against his belly while mothers beamed behind a cordon. Santa might nip back to a storage room, to check on his reindeer if a terrified child wet his knees. A few had hip flasks, and whiffy breath, to lessen the pain of impossible promises. Others needed retraining for inappropriate responses: *Bugga off, kid. I'm on me smoko break.* And *Reckon a couple of tinnies wouldn't go astray.* A child asked Santa what he'd like for Christmas.

On Christmas Eve we joined neighbourhood kids from the Boy Scouts, Girl Guides, Legacy or church, and went carolling. We got the odd *Front off, you've woken the baby,* or *Piss off and annoy the neighbours instead.* A few widows in fluffy slippers offered fudge or men lurched to their reindeer and mistletoe-emblazoned door and threw handfuls of Liquorice All-Sorts into the dark. Cosy pyjama-clad families were glued to TV screens watching *Scrooge* from *A Christmas Carol* or *the Vienna Boys Choir.* On Christmas day, if Mum felt up to it, she'd suggest we go to church. "It'll make us feel better. Afterwards we'll have a lovely roast duck and pull crackers. Can you oblige for one day out of your life, son?"

"Aw, Ma, waddya take me for!" and Dad replied, "A surfing bum."

So Jasper took off, and Mum turned on Dad. "Why did you have to ruin Christmas Day saying that? The boy's sensitive. He was nice to you. Did he or did he not give you a nice pair of socks?"

Mum hid presents in her wardrobe behind a collection of town hats, or in the stocking drawer covered with nylons and corsets, or beneath a pile of high-heeled shoes. She always placed Dad's clothes on the bed so he never noticed his own gifts hidden in his underpants.

The dog gave us things Mum couldn't bring herself to give, like wax for Jasper's surfboard, and she'd laugh while my sister squatted on the floor and curled the dog's fur with her new hair tongs. "You better not get us an over-shoulder-boulder-holder," we warned her. "Or a whopper-dopper-flopper-stopper." Mum said she wouldn't dream of giving us a bra. How embarrassing for Dad if we unwrapped such items in front of him!

Christmas Down Under is heralded by crickets and cicadas at dawn, and the promise of a blistering heat wave, so we rose early. Dad and I sprinted down to The Basin for a daily swim, hoping it wouldn't be littered with bluebottles and jellyfish. Dad said the run cleared your head and got your bowels working nicely. If a child was surly then they hadn't evacuated and mothers served stewed prunes on cornflakes for breakfast and more prunes and custard for pudding. Christmas Day was for treat food from dawn till dusk. If Jasper's surfing mates hung around, Dad muttered, "Haven't those louts got families? They should be home doing the lawns. Shove them in the army, that'd sort them out."

Mum was more charitable. She had an affinity for lost souls, those who'd lucked on hard times. She cared for several children from a large family when a friend's Chinese husband drove to the Blue Mountains and blew his brains out because his shoe business collapsed. A Mormon family sporadically dropped off their daughter when travelling to Hawaii to build temples.

Mum was confused between them and the Jews so she didn't cook pork but refused to deprive herself of a cup of coffee or a nocturnal pick-me-up when slaving over meals.

"Don't mention the word bacon if you can help it," she warned.

Another had a daughter who quit eating at fourteen when a dancer at her ballet class said, "Crikey, youse got fat legs." The desperate parents offered her to us at regular intervals because our family had a reputation for being fast and noisy eaters.

"Just shove it down your gonga like this," we urged, making slurping noises and flicking spaghetti strands in and out of our mouths and belching loudly. The anorexic kid blinked with astonishment at our vulgar display but Mum let it pass just this once. She said not to mention the word food either which was a big ask because that's what we thought about several times a day. She refused to pander to the kid by making special meals. Instead, the little bag of bones improved our social life because Mum initiated our help.

Jasper's surfboard was strapped onto the roof of our Wolseley and Mum drove long distances to Sydney beaches. We ate sandy barbequed chops and waited hours while she frantically beckoned Jasper in from the horizon. Mum thought horse riding fuelled hunger pangs so we visited several ranches around Sydney. The kid was bored but my sister wasn't.

"Let me go to dancing lessons at the surf club," I begged. "It's real good exercise and it will give you-know-who an appetite."

Mum was bothered. "Speak properly. Don't say real. Say really. And I don't want you getting an appetite for boys who work in butcher shops or hardware stores."

"Ma! The way you're treating me, I'll end up being the oldest virgin in Collaroy."

Mother was speechless. And, like the blushing chemist who inquired after my health, she had good reason.

Three doors from us on Pittwater Road lived a promiscuous angelic-looking teen with long blonde hair. Known as Brenda the Bender, she gave herself freely to adolescent schoolboys, lifeguards and the surfing fraternity. She also gave boys a nasty disease. Several mothers met in the pharmacies getting identical prescriptions. My brother smirked sheepishly when Mum explained dinner was late because she'd taken him to the doctor.

"Let this be a lesson to you," she said, banging pots and pans in the kitchen. "Never wear anyone's swimmers. They give you a rash." When trying out new togs in a department store, Mum shouted through the drapes, "Leave your undies on." It was scary to think brand new togs were disease-riddled.

Brenda was a menace to us chaste beach bunnies. We were saving ourselves for the future while she was giving free loving away. Youths parked their cars outside our house and loped in the dark to her awaiting limbs. Joanna and I peeked through the curtains of our attic bedroom to figure out which boys were dirty little rooters. Society turned a blind eye to male sexual activity for it was commonly said a son should sow his wild oats before settling down.

Karen the Grunter became competitive. She was short, plump and available. Girlfriends of surfies felt threatened and, in moments of desperation, several succumbed to passion in the back seat of panel vans. "Me boyfriend dumped me, the ratfink," they said regrettably as we lay on the sand getting red and blistered.

Listening to lurid details and sympathising with a tearful teen beat the boredom of peering at our boyfriends showing off hanging ten, which meant ten toes over the nose of the surfboard. Hang eleven described a nude male surfer.

When the boys emerged shivering from the water, snorting and spitting, they sat in male packs sharing their wave experiences, an Australian trait unknown to Greeks, Italians and Lebanese; they preferred to lie side by side with a girl on the sand and seduce her with sweet nothings. It took a few chug-a-lugs of Tooheys Ale to embolden the average Aussie to tear away from his caveman group and seek out a girl he fancied. Besotted surfboard riders chasing waves up and down the coast were surfers as opposed to surfies who were seen as parasites hanging around beaches. Midge Farrelly was a huge inspiration to the surfing cult as was his rival, Nat Young, who visited our home several times. Jasper became a skilled surfboard rider and competed in major competitions around northern beaches. Licking a Gaytime ice cream in a crowd of zinc-nosed supporters, on sand that burnt your feet and sun that reddened your backs, we peered at figures in the watery distance for hours.

Surfies and Rockers were enemies.

Rockers had distinctive Elvis Presley black greasy hair and surly bad-boy looks, wore leather jackets and alighted from their motorbikes with a menacing gait. Their girlfriends were silent and supportive accomplices with pastel-coloured lipstick, eyeliner and teased hair encased in a scarf after a wild ride to the beach suburbs. Lippy surfies, fuelled by beer, shouted, "Rack off, cockroaches," and "Get back to your own turf." Police zoomed up when scuffles erupted outside the Collaroy Surf Club as thudding stomping dance music and electric guitars screamed into the night. Sand rumbles between the opposing gangs at various beaches caused headlines.

Squares were the goody-goodies who behaved conservatively, a parent's dream. "I may be a square, but at least I'm a Collaroy gentleman," snapped a ten-year old to his foul-mouthed sister. Mum didn't think any gentlemen lived in Australia, let alone our beach town.

Soshees, a derogatory term for society teens, wore duffle coats and lived on the North Shore. *Citymobbers* came over on the ferry from inland suburbia. *Ho-dads* were junior surfies and *gremmies* were young inexperienced surfers.

When a woman whispered she and her son had been praying for Jasper to see the light and mend his ways, Mum was embarrassed. "To think we've sunk this low," she muttered.

Melbourne Cup is an annual horseracing event, which causes national hysteria in Australia and New Zealand. Teachers placed bets, as did pupils. There were emergency staffroom meetings around race time and class monitors sat at the teacher's desk and kept order. When Jasper was asked to take over for a few minutes, the boys flipped up their desk lids and crouched around a smuggled-in transistor. As the race commentator's voice pitched to a frenzied crescendo so did the pupils.' Jasper's voice of authority boomed down the corridor, "Shuddup, you pack of bastards!"

Canon Newth knew Mum was desperate to get Jasper into the Royal Navy and was giving him a chance of being in command, so to speak. Across Australia there were fierce debates whether the Melbourne Cup should become a public holiday since some teachers had told kids to stay home, and were sacked for doing so.

Aged seventeen, I wanted Mum to be less strict.

"It's not fair," I complained. "I'm the only one in the family who helps you."

"Darling, I don't know what I'd do without you." I didn't mind chores, just inequality.

While Mum was focussed on getting my brother into the navy, it created drama keeping him in school so he'd get good references. Although my sister and I felt loved, his behaviour and career was all-consuming, and Joanna often over-nighted with school friends. When Mum poured us a small sherry before dinner, I felt very close to her and much older than my siblings. Mum said the local boys were not right for me. "One day we'll go back to England and you will meet a nice man."

Whenever I accompanied her to the shops in Collaroy, cars tooted their horns and grinning boys waved bronzed arms out the window. "It's because of your hair," she said.

"I'd prefer they liked me for my brains," I said, and Mum gave a small doubting smile.

Sick of seeing the anorexic kid picking at her meal, Mum relented about dancing lessons if Jasper chaperoned us. Word spread and girls who had a crush on my fifteen-year old brother knocked on the door saying their mothers would let them learn, too.

Wearing stomp outfits, which were skirts with straps, frilly blouses, nylons and sling-backs, small bows in our hair and painted faces, we minced down to the surf club after Jasper. He usually deposited us at the entrance and nipped off to the cinema to watch Board (surfing) Movies or check the talent at the coffee shop. Or he sat on the wall outside the surf club with mates smoking a cigar while the waves roared and crashed metres away. They could talk endlessly about surfboards with pointy noses, rounded ones, twin fins, square fins and the changes from fibreglass-coated 9foot 3inch boards to the latest model.

Collaroy Surf Club was the pivotal suburbia focus for entertainment, weddings, funerals and club meetings. We paid four shillings a lesson to Olga Shaw, a professional dancer and suntanned mum. Her dress code was respect. Jeans were out; ties were in.

"No," she said, as I eyed a hunk from Narrabeen Boys High. "He's too tall for you," and she partnered me with a swarthy Catholic lad from St. Augustine's. It felt quite brazen dancing with a boy from another religion.

In the early 60s you mingled with your own kind. Since most schools in Sydney were same-sex, dancing was an icebreaker. We girls absorbed whiffs of Ipana toothpaste, hair lotion, garlic and the toxicity of a quickly bolted-down meat pie after tennis or swimming lessons. Some boys had clammy hands, rumbling tums or more base odours, and galloped like donkeys in Latin dances, sniffing back runny noses and bruising our shins with winkle-picker shoes. Others were bosom watchers. One stuffed a torch into his long red cardigan pocket. We could never be sure if it was that gadget or something more sinister prodding us. Those who took liberties were called fresh. Our partners breathed in our hairspray and Charlie—a new perfume we dabbed on cotton wool and plunged into our bra. Some cheated and grabbed their mum's hankies to make their tits look bigger.

Olga stopped the record player to shout, "Dance closer!" She grabbed her son and spun him around the room in a waltz.

"Like this. Be brave." We tried. "No, no," she said, and brought out a collection of 78s and jammed them against our stomachs. We broke out in telltale sweat as the records slipped and rolled onto the floor. She taught us the latest dance crazes, too—the monkey, mashed potato, elephant, slosh, the shimmy, the bunny hop, tamoure, Martian hop and variations to the stomp.

The stomp was a sensational beach dance where bands played to packed clubs up and down the coast. The Collaroy Surf Club pulsated to the deafening sounds of guitars, drums and a writhing mass of teenagers pounding their feet every Saturday. Burly bouncers manned the door, checking passes. When musicians twanged blockbuster hits like *Bombora*, *Wipeout* and *Pipeline,* the crowd danced frenetically and the floor was in danger of caving in. Dad called the stomp brainless jungle music, and Mum said, "You only meet low types there."

"If Jasper gets his hair cut, he can take you," said Mum. When he returned with hair short on top but long at the back, Mum said, "Since it's half a haircut you can go for half the time."

It was addictive, crazy, wild. Barefoot surfies gave you a nod meaning Wanna dance? In a hypnotic trance you faced each other and stomped, no body contact and not much eye contact either. Above the din you might be the recipient of brief niceties—"Jeez, yer a gas-lookin' chick. Got a boyfrin?" I got the odd drongo. One had crusty lips and rivers of perspiration down his beetroot face. After a few minutes, he said, "Jeez, me guts are crook. Moynd if oy siddown?"

After a Saturday night stomp I arrived home to find Mum looking faintly excited.

"I've been thinking. Daddy needs a holiday," she said. "Let's go to New Zealand for Christmas and leave him at home. That poor man deserves some peace."

Everyone thought it a good idea, especially Dad!

Chapter 17
Meeting the Rellies in New Zealand

As the days drew closer, Dad became more excited about our departure. He'd miss Mum, of course, but some weekends he'd sit stupefied by the traffic of youths in and out the house, Johnny O'Keefe singing *Shout* on TV, transistors blaring the latest releases from Roy Orbison, Elvis, Dion, and new surfing tunes—*Surf City, Monsoon, Shindig, Murphie the Surfie, Heat Wave, Stomp Fever,* Jan and Dean, and the Beach Boys' hit singles.

"Can't hear myself think," he'd roar. "Hurry up and go now!"

Since he wasn't domesticated, Mum baked oodles of steak and kidney pies and apple tarts, which she stowed in the freezing compartment of our Kelvinator. She bought drip-dry shirts for the office, wrote notes reminding him to squirt Jeyes Fluid down the lav and feed the dog.

We were disappointed with the *Patris*; the Greek ship was smaller and less luxurious than the P & O liners we were used to. Excitable noisy passengers with foreign accents lugged colourful boxes tied in string, unlike our smart suitcases. Mum didn't expect a fanfare of neighbours but they turned up with boxes of chocolates, streamers and champagne. Then got stuck into the grog as she played hostess with her gracious manners and crimson lips.

"What's happened to your face? It's gone blotchy."

"I might have hives, Mum," I said.

"Let Doctor Loomis have a look. He's a vet. He knows about funny diseases."

"No, she hasn't!" blurted my irritating sister with her giddy classmates in tow. "She's been pashing her boyfriend and they won't let us in the cabin."

"Rack off, hairy legs," I snarled.

"Don't use coarse beach language, darling. Say your goodbyes up on deck, it's much healthier for you."

Mum distractedly peered out the porthole. Then her face contorted into a horrified silent 'O' similar to the famous painting *Scream* by Edvard Munch.

Trotting up the gangplank to the chanting of *Surfer Joe*, my brother clutched a surfboard. He had a cortege of surfing mates. Mum was going to faint but rallied; it was poor manners to display feelings in public. She was not going to air dirty washing by revealing internal strife and disappointments. She'd frequently dish out epithets like *Remember, FHB!* (Family Holds Back) meaning let guests tuck into the food first, and to politely decline extra food with, "No thank you. I've had an elegant sufficiency." She winced hearing, "Ta, no. Oym as full as a goog," or "Oym stuffed," or "Crikey, it's that hot, oym sweating."

"Horses sweat, men perspire, women glow," she corrected. "And that is not an adjective."

Three days later we sailed into Wellington harbour. We were treated to a Mediterranean diet, and Greek and Cypriot migrants singing a mixture of *Waltzing Matilda* and homeland songs on the evening dance floors. Mum was coming home. In quiet moments at Collaroy I'd flick through the family album while Mum knitted and she'd name our relatives.

"You take after Enga," she'd say. "She's artistic, but you do have a streak of Ollie in you."

Dad's oldest sister, while funny and perky, had a stubborn madness. I flinched at the sting of my recessive impure gene. Jasper, she said, looked like her side of the family but he was over-confident and charmed the wrong people. Joanna didn't look like anyone but she had a quick mind and was good at scrabble.

We staggered to Aunt June's Combi van lugging duty-free liquor, transistors and cameras. Mum's brother, Rear Admiral Washbourn, now Chief of Naval Staff, had shifted his family from England to a home overlooking Wellington harbour. Since they'd arranged a cocktail party in her honour, Mum told Jasper to wear a tie and look naval. I was to act with decorum.

"You'll meet the *crème de la crème* and they might have nice sons." When I said I had a boyfriend, Mum added, "Yes, he's Australian. Do you want to live in Australia forever?"

Living in a beach suburb one may have stolen a boy's heart but it ranked low in preference. Surfing came first, a beach keg party second, cruising in noisy Holdens and Dodges checking out the talent or looking for birds to take to parties came third, while we chaste teens scored the crumbs, if we were lucky.

Lying on the beach with a bunch of girls, we dissected boys from hot to loser and confided how far we'd gone sexually, known as going upstairs or downstairs. In our circle the worst any upstairs girls did was to emerge from the flicks (movies) looking rumpled, her bra swung round to her back. Love bites and passion were blamed on movies like *Sound of Music*, *Gigi*, *Paint your Wagon* and *Breakfast at Tiffany's*. Sydney beaches were a hotbed of bikinis, boards, rolling waves and sun-splashed freedom.

Opportunities arose for playful interaction on the beaches, even for girls who had a face like the south end of a north bound camel. Another saying was *You don't have to look at the mantelpiece while stoking the fire*, avuncular advice given to horny lads over a beer.

Cousin Liza, at nineteen, gave us a Tiki tour of the capital where folk music poured out of coffee shops. "Heard of the stomp?" I asked. But she liked Eartha Kitt and the Kingston Trio.

"What are the waves like?" asked Jasper, as we peered at tramlines and hatted pedestrians scurrying past solid buildings and pokey dairies. Wellington had an austere orderly charm.

"I'm off," he said the next morning. Then he picked up his surfboard, and hitched up the North Island to Piha Beach, renowned for its waves.

Aunt Enga lived on a sheep station in the small settlement of St. Arnaud, south of Nelson. She met us at the Picton ferry, which runs a service between the North and South Island of New Zealand, with a lunch hamper. She and Mum were close so they acted like schoolgirls, preparing a roast mutton meal with butterscotch pudding, or lunches and tea for the shearers.

We followed Uncle Gerry over steep terrain, rounding up sheep, his face purple and language coarse when his dog ducked off to chase a rabbit. Enga was working on her book about the pioneering history of our family, the Washbourns. Most nights we watched slides of our trip to Europe two years before, or Enga told ghost stories. If we heard strange noises, she'd bellow, "Are you there, Mr Cummings?" He once lived on their farm, brewed beer in the shed and died an alcoholic.

One afternoon, while walking back towards the house down a long drive, Mum said, "Looks like Enga's got visitors for afternoon tea."

The roomy house had gracious old furniture and beds with fluffy eiderdowns. Before we reached the homestead, two figures went inside. My aunt insisted no one had visited all day.

Since Enga arose early, she'd bring us a tray of tea and chops for breakfast, saying ting-a-ling at the door. That quaint wake-up call came about when her married friends were invited by another couple to a tennis party in Blenheim. After a sweaty game the hostess went to make tea and the host offered his male guest the use of a shower. When the kettle boiled, the hostess popped her hand around the bathroom curtain and playfully yanked on her man's crown jewels. Ting-a-ling, darling. Tea's ready. But she'd got the wrong husband.

"It's Australia," said Enga, handing the phone to Mum. Had something happened at home? Trans-Atlantic calls were expensive.

"Jasper's got in the navy," shouted Dad down the line. Mum began weeping with relief, and my aunt brought out her South African Dry Fly sherry.

"It's not quite six o'clock," said Mum. And everyone sat on the sofa glaring at the clock. On the dot of six, we toasted Jasper and his future.

"How dry is your Fly?" tinkled my aunt to her husband, after our third sherry.

If Dad had been here, he would have placed an empty glass on his bald head until someone noticed, which Mum thought endearingly quaint. She was just glad a mighty force like the Australian Navy felt Jasper had potential, even if he looked like a prize fighter on the interview day. He'd arisen at dawn to surf but was beaten up by drunken louts at Long Reef who ordered him off the beach. He arrived home bloodied and bruised with a black eye and swollen lip. Happily, the Australian Naval panel were impressed by Jasper's pedigree and chest expansion, twice the normal average, which he acquired through surfing.

From a sheep farm we motored to an orchard in Mapua in the Nelson region. We stayed with another of Mum's sisters and her large brood who were busy with the apple season.

162

Mum suspected that side of the family voted Labour because they worked on the land. She was pretty sure Enga was a National voter. Politics, religion, your age and how much money you had in the bank, was never discussed.

Mum was relieved when Jasper eventually turned up. She regretted telling him about his acceptance into the Australian Navy; he nagged to go home early for last minute surfs and farewell parties. Mum said, "I don't want to kill your father. He's a good provider and I'm quite fond of him. He doesn't deserve to have loutish youths with low IQs and passion for surfing invading his home."

"Aw, Ma, don't talk about my mates like that. What have they done to you?"

Mum continued to think the surfing cult was time wasting and made youths unbalanced.

Onekaka, in Golden Bay, North West of Nelson, was where our New Zealand relatives gathered annually on family land. As a child, Mum and her five siblings were shipped to Uncle Arty's, their bachelor great uncle, who'd bought fifty acres bordering the beach between the Onekaka river and the Kaituna stream. They'd laboriously grubbed gorse and manuka by hand.

The children were treated to bowls of clotted cream from his three pampered cows, lavish helpings of strawberry jam and breakfast of fresh snapper or blue cod. They gathered shellfish, ate bread baked in a kerosene stove and spent halcyon days fishing, swimming and playing cards by lamplight.

Mum's two brothers, whether home in Nelson or holidaying at Onekaka, spent their waking hours building or sailing boats so it was not surprising they joined the navy. Decades later, we fifth generation Washbourns experienced a similar holiday.

The three original dwellings on the land were called The Beacon, Uncle Arty's and Pooh Corner. Our family was allocated the latter, a slightly derelict beach cottage, used as an occasional library for locals, a footstep onto the sand where water lapped lazily.

Enga's family owned Te Mara, a cottage overlooking the inlet. The incoming tide brought fish plopping out of the water, pukekos and oystercatchers. The receding tide exposed mussels, pipis and cockles.

A cottage, known as The Admiral's, was being built on a cliff top as a retirement home for my seafaring uncle. Uncle Richard dug a long-drop toilet that commanded a spectacular view, and erected a pole beside it bearing the British flag. Hoisted, it was a signal that someone was sitting on the throne and half-mast meant business had finished. If you were out at sea with a good pair of binoculars, sailors knew when the Admiral was in residence.

At Pooh Corner rats, penguins and wekas had crawled through the floorboards while the cottage had been locked up. Mum sniffed in disapproval, then promptly got someone to take us into Takaka to buy disinfectant, buckets and detergent. We dined by candlelight, cooked over a primus, played cards and fell asleep to the scuffling of native animals in the bushes and the sound of the sea crashing just metres away.

When all the relatives gathered for Christmas, our days were filled with expeditions to spots our forebears ventured in the mid 1850s, peering at old gold mines and family graves. We eighteen Washbourn cousins, mostly teens, followed our stout-legged aunts on gruelling tramps, carrying food hampers and flagons of giggle juice. Mum and her sisters reminisced between snippets of geology and native flora and fauna from Aunt Enga.

"Time for a flagoon," (flagon) suggested my brother whenever the older members stopped for a break. "You lovely ladies needing liquid refreshments?" The aunts wiped perspiration from their foreheads and proffered plastic mugs for a beer. Perhaps Jasper did have the makings of a naval officer. He got on famously with his cousins and was viewed as high-spirited and charming by older people.

On Christmas day we sprawled on the beach outside Uncle Arty's. We'd decorated fir trees with balloons and tinsel. The sun-hatted oldies warned us to move out of the sun for it'd ruin our complexion. Despite primitive cooking facilities, our aunts baked delicious fare, enjoyed with home brew, teasing, laughter and lots of presents.

Jasper had an egregious sense of humour. When the older cousins decorated the walls of Pooh Corner with posters of

Italy for a New Year's Eve party, he proffered his own ghoulish Dada work of art—a bloodied tissue from a nosebleed, which he popped behind a glass frame on the mantelpiece.

Candles flickered in empty Blue Nun, Mateus Rose and Chianti bottles in straw baskets—popular alcoholic beverages of the 60s—when teenage friends of our Kiwi cousins arrived in open jalopies (no seatbelts then), wearing Bermuda shorts and sloppy Joes. Guys wore jeans made fashionably old and faded by dragging them behind cars.

New jeans were for gays, although in the 60s they were called *bent, queer* or *one of those*.

I demonstrated the latest Sydney surf craze, *the stomp*, to Jasper's precious 45rpm instrumentals. "It's king, get amongst it," I said, and the Kiwi teens wildly embraced it.

Other superlatives for 'great' were *stoked, way out, too much, bewdy* (beauty) *bottler, a blast* and *gasser*. Kiwi teens used *super, montyfab, neato, neatax, choice, helluva neatie, deadly, ripper*, even *tickety-boo*.

Mum was supposed to be at The Beacon seeing in the New Year but she turned up at regular intervals flashing a torch.

"Don't be so embarrassing, Ma," I hissed. "Hector Crawford! No one's playing *bottoms!*"

"What's up with your old lady?" asked a Nelson Boys College guest.

"She thinks we're having an orgy."

To appease her, we built a bonfire on the beach, limboed on the sand and formed a long chain to dance the conga up the gravel track to The Beacon. The grown-ups were warbling Christmas carols and rum-fuelled hymns, hideously off-key.

Parents worried about their daughter's virginity and reputation, and were vigilant. Boys had to look presentable, state what time they'd bring you home, and the porch lights glowed. Arrive late then all hell broke loose. An irate pyjama-clad father lunging to the door would start off neighbourhood dogs, causing a domino effect of lights switching on up the road.

I appreciated their rules, especially if rich boys took me out and expected something. Are you a *good* girl or a *nice* girl they'd murmur, their mitts fiddling with buttons. I never knew the correct response but they weren't getting my goods, like Brenda the Bender.

At Uncle Arty's, we were fascinated by a trunk filled with old letters and photos. Mum became skittish about past relationships for she changed the subject. Were they from her old lovers? I wondered. I was keen to know who resembled Great Great Aunt Susannah who played the harp and burnt the tips of her fingers with a poker to harden them for plucking. And why did Mum marry Dad when she was engaged to a New Zealand naval officer?

A 1940s letter from an elderly relative warned Mum about settling in Australia '...*it is a thoroughly bad country to raise a family in (owing partly to the strong strain of criminal and coloured blood, perhaps.) Then again, it's a mere prejudice that makes us believe that New Zealand is perhaps the finest country to live in for those who love the mountains and the rivers and lakes and so forth. Also, I believe, the people are a better lot than the Aussies and that counts later on in raising a family...*'

Excitement mounted when the launch *Manga* anchored off Onekaka wharf to collect Uncle Richard for naval duties in Wellington. People lined the shore, waving. Since Uncle was feeling indisposed for the night, his teenage daughter took command. All Washbourn relatives were invited aboard the 72ft. vessel for a beer, which prompted cousin Liza to assert rules when the officers asked who'd like a drink.

"Only those fifteen and over may have one. I'm sorry, Gerald, but I have to draw the line somewhere," she said to a disappointed cousin while his older brother just scraped through.

My fourteen-year old sister said she preferred smoking. When given a duty-free cigarette she demonstrated the drawback and blew smoke rings into the air.

At night the captain and his crew rowed ashore with four crates of beer. As the large orange moon hovered in the sky, Uncle Arty's relatives gathered around a beach bonfire where we Aussies felt a warm connection to family, history and men of the sea.

Most nights the aunts tucked into mussel and pipi stew while we teens barbecued on the beach.

"I hope you're not leading your cousins astray, Jasper," said Mum, shining her torch into the campfire. She'd heard bawdy laughter, a belching contest and clinking of bottles.

"And make sure you go to bed at a decent hour. And no smutty jokes."

"Buzz off, little titties," growled older cousins if Joanna crept out to join us. "You're too young to hear grown-up stuff."

The holiday nearly ended tragically when Jasper and two cousins borrowed Uncle Richard's runabout *Minxmaid*. A gale force 8 or 9 wind whipped up. The boat snapped its moorings, leaving the boys stranded on the broken wharf. Jasper dived off as the *Minxmaid* drifted out to sea.

The current was too strong so he swam back to raise the alarm. Despite warnings to stay on the wharf until the tide receded, the brothers, Julian and Gerald, leapt into the sea and swam for their lives. Mum put them to bed with a hot water bottle and coffee laced with whisky to stop their uncontrollable shivering.

Aunt June was furious, but relieved the boys survived, and locked up the canoes for the rest of the holidays. Police were involved and the *Nelson Mail* reported the ordeal of an Admiral's nephews and his boat being swept out to sea. We spent fruitless days searching along the coastline for *Minxmaid*. Mum said she would go to work to pay for a replacement boat but not to tell Dad.

"Once your brother is in the navy our worries will be over," she said.

Chapter 18
Beatlemania

A fortnight after Jasper entered the Royal Australian Navy, tragedy struck.

On 10 February, 1964, *Voyager*, a Daring Class destroyer, and *Melbourne*, an aircraft carrier, collided while taking part in training exercises at night near Jervis Bay on the S.E. coast of New South Wales. The *Voyager* was sliced in two when it crossed the bow of the *Melbourne*. Though 232 officers and sailors survived, 82 lives were lost. It was Australia's greatest peacetime disaster.

Jasper was one of forty privileged cadets chosen across the nation that year. While safe at the naval base he was horrified by the tragic collision. His earlier letters moaned about his feet blistering from marching; the old boy bullying style, popular in English boarding schools where juniors kowtow to seniors, paled into insignificance. At his initiation ceremony, new recruits were ordered to carry huge poles and slither down its greasy surface while having peroxide and other muck thrown at them, before being squirted with hoses.

Jasper wrote that while his backside was covered in bruises two cadets were knocked unconscious. One broke his arm and the other was a chronic asthmatic and nearly died. Mum smiled when he ended his letter saying he was on the brink of enjoying himself. She posted off a parcel of fruitcake, marshmallows, biscuits, condensed milk, coffee and a mug. Next time could she send some surfing magazines?

Dad thought the introductory rough and tumble would be the making of him; life in the forces is no place for sissies. He hoped his son would come home on leave, call him Sir, and have candid man-to-man chats about the wonderful opportunity he was given, perhaps expressing gratitude. Dad was disappointed.

Jasper's passion was crouching under a monstrous curling wave, and the comradeship of his surfing mates. They paid for surfboards by hawking newspapers to food outlets, selling recyclable glass bottles and lost balls at Long Reef golf course, or part time jobs at the local garage. It was unusual for parents to buy surfboards for their kids for, like pop music, it was considered a time-wasting teenage fad. Pursuing a career was all-important.

"You don't understand, Ma," explained Jasper. "Life's short. I could end up under a bus and never have enjoyed myself."

Mum told him to stop listening to stupid philosophy twaddle from his halfwit friend who worked in a mental home and had hair past his shoulders. He works with lunatics so his brain is addled. "Your father hasn't spent a fortune slaving in the office for you to listen to rubbish from a drifter. There must be something wrong with him to fall out with his parents."

While baby boomers were infatuated with music and fashion streaming out from America, Australian housewives slavishly followed a weekly routine with set days for washing, ironing, mending, scrubbing and baking. Youngsters descended from mulberry trees with stained faces and tummy aches while mothers made marmalade and jam. Loquat trees were cut and burnt when fruit fly became a problem. Dazzling white nappies fluttered from Hills hoists. Infants were wheeled in bouncy prams to catch sunshine and gaze cross-eyed at plastic beads strung above their faces. New mothers ran themselves ragged, spot-checking the angle of the sun and hoping the family cat hadn't sat on little Pammy's face.

A wooden playpen kept toddlers safe inside and outside the home. Some weary mothers admitted to climbing into the playpen to read an American magazine uninterrupted, while toddlers plucked snails and ate dirt.

Mothers made chocolate crackles, fudge and toffee apples for school fetes. They quipped, "An apple a day keeps the doctor away, but two apples a day keeps the dentist away." Going to the dentist or murder house filled us with dread. Parents of teens wrung their hands over their daughter's pimples, posture and puppy fat. It was unusual to see an overweight child and obese people were so rare we thought they must work in circuses.

Mothers worried about daughters reading in poor light cautioning, Men never make passes at girls who wear glasses. Four-eyed sons were exempt; they looked academic, university material. Parents who could afford it indulged their shortsighted daughters with contact lenses, hoping their investment would help her find a suitable husband. Australians clung to remnants of Britain by hanging up prints of haystacks and hunting dogs, and reserved a corner for oak cabinets crammed with Royal Doulton, Crown Derby and Wedgwood bone china tea sets. It made them feel connected because Australia was a new country, finding its identity.

As school kids we were encouraged to feel proud about penal settlements, hydro dams, the Sydney Harbour Bridge, the emerging opera house, Albert Namatjira, the Aboriginal painter, Sidney Nolan, William Dobell, Russell Drysdale, Daisy Bates, Henry Lawson, Ned Kelly, Banjo Paterson, boomerangs, didgeridoos and Rolf Harris.

We gave pennies to the Flying Doctor Service, lepers and outback missions. We heard tales of Aboriginal families going walkabout after dismantling dwellings provided by the government, and using it for outdoor cooking. It was illegal to sell booze to Australia's indigenous inhabitants. And crew cuts weren't very popular in Australia despite American marines sporting the porcupine look. Mum said it had to do with nits.

American child models advertising Lux and Pears soap were stunningly pretty, as were their youthful mothers with their unblemished faces, in stark contrast to tanned Australian women. Betty Crocker Instant Cake Mix was for lazybones, but jelly crystals were common party treats. The rest of the world was called overseas and we thought everyone in China worked in rice plantations, or factories making transistor parts. We called them chinks and could barely tell them apart. Mum said she was sure Chinese parents could identify their kids.

American articles unsettled Australian women, like the Masters & Johnson and Kinsey surveys on sexuality. Some psychologist suggested women felt deprived not having that extra bit of flesh below their navel; hosing a garden was considered a substitute. Mum said that was utter claptrap, but she and her neighbours crept out at night to water their roses to avoid being labelled frustrated sex maniacs.

Dad liked to climb onto the roof with a hammer and nails, sometimes bellowing out to Donny's mother over the fence about the price of meat. Mum thought he was safer up there than in the garden mowing over her new plants. Larger homes had a rumpus room, a hangout pad for teens and supervised parties.

We had the slummy back verandah, where a dozen or more boys sprawled, munching freshly baked biscuits, chuckling over Mandrake, Phantom, Superman, Dennis the Menace and Donald Duck comics, playing monopoly and cards, waiting for favourable surf conditions.

When Mahalia Jackson belted out her gospel tunes, Mum asked Jasper to turn down the sound on the record player. "Your father is trying to think beautiful thoughts."

"Gee, Ma. She's singing about God. And you force us to go to church. No wonder our generation's confused!"

The early 60s produced whimsical chirpy sing-along hits, which made us dance and feel glad to be young. Roy Orbison and Gene Pitney lyrics tore at our heartstrings, an invitation to wallow in misery if we'd broken up with the opposite sex.

"Sorry, Libby, darling," I said, removing Liberace's newspaper clippings from my attic wall. "I've got a real boyfriend now and have my needs. But I'll always love you."

When an article screaming scurrilous headlines *Mad about a Boy* appeared about the ageing pianist, I didn't despair over my idol's sexual preference. Adoring middle-aged housewives around the world posed more of a threat.

Information about pop idols was limited but became increasingly available when markets saw the buying power of teenagers. Initially, black singers like Sam Cooke, Chubby Checker, Fats Domino, the Ronettes and Crystals girl bands, made famous by Phil Spector and Motown, didn't appear on Australian TV.

Our parents laid aside colour prejudice and admired the likes of Martin Luther King, Louis Armstrong, Sidney Poitier, Winifred Atwell and Sammy Davis Jnr. The White Australia Policy excluding all non-Europeans prevailed until its abolition under Prime Minister Gough Whitlam in 1972. After that, there was an influx of Indo-Chinese refugees thus coining the word *multiculturalism*.

Collaroy, and other northern suburbs, hosted weekend surf carnivals and stomps. It became a hotbed of lanky sunburnt teens on Saturday nights when ear-splitting rock bands performed at surf clubs.

"You'll never meet anyone decent there," warned Mum. "Stay home and read a good book. It'll improve your mind." But she relented when bubbly teenage friends knocked at the door, their hair teased and backcombed, wearing pastel lipstick and a splash of *Somewhere*, a new Avon perfume.

Dad said he couldn't understand why anyone was interested in twanging guitars. "Gutter snipes," he snarled. "No beauty in that."

"It's just a stage the youth of today are going through," soothed Mother. "I'll make you a nice cup of tea."

"You're a good woman, Dot. You know how to look after a man."

Col Joye and the Joy Boys, the Atlantics, the Delltones, the Denvermen, the Echomen, the Telstars, Billy Thorpe and the Aztecs, and diminutive fifteen-year old Little Pattie singing *He's my Blonde Headed, Stompie Wompie, Real Gone, Surfer Boy,* entertained a frenzied sweaty mass at monster beach dances.

Some surfies loped off to their woodies (surfboard carrying cars), a Toohey in one hand, the other around some chick. Tears of rejection made our mascara run when a boyfriend grabbed some tart's digits in the melee. We thought about killing ourselves, despite the eager horny youths draped on the beach wall discussing the surf. We felt misunderstood by parents who wanted us to conform and do the right thing, for what would the neighbours say?

When pop stars crooned songs of angst and heartache, dads wanted us to turn that rubbish off the radio and go mow lawns. We wondered how girls avoided getting 'knocked up', and thought used condoms discarded along Long Reef beach were skins off sea creatures left by the turning tide. Mothers didn't enlighten us if we brought one home snagged to an oyster shell after rock hunting.

Boys were seen as brave Lotharios if they plucked up courage to ask for French letters at the chemist, blushingly mumbling their condom wants to a pharmacist, who'd give them a lecture on morality. Today, youths would be lauded for taking precautions and offered a selection of slinky or rippled flavoured connies.

In Britain, condoms were called Durex, but in Australia it was a brand name for sticky tape. Aussies, like friend Janet, on their O.E. in England, were surprised to be directed to a chemist in London for a bit of sticky tape.

"You want a roll?" asked the pharmacist in disbelief. Janet was shocked when handed a giant packet of condoms. "I didn't mean those filthy things!" She fled the pharmacy in shame.

When Billy Jay of The Sundowners made eye contact at dance class, girlfriends who visited to play records, gossip about boys, and inquire after Jasper, were mildly jealous. I thought he was cute. But I knew Mum wouldn't approve of his tight jeans, pointed shoes, cardigan and greasy slicked-back hair. Parents' jaundiced view was that anyone who played in a band was deliberately avoiding getting a real job, but girls idolised guys whacking drums or crooning over electric guitars.

One of Australia's finest cricketers, Sid Barnes (1916-1973) and his family lived in the house behind ours. He impressed Dad with his prowess as opening batsman in thirteen test matches, scoring three centuries, but the man was strange. He was a bi-polar sufferer. To avoid mowing lawns, he built a large concrete shed to indulge his musical children who'd formed a band called Strings and Things. Mum thought Drums and Bums more appropriate.

Sid Jnr. was Jasper's surfing mate, a funny, tough, freckled youth who played drums, his older sister played bass, Dave Lee guitar, and Doug Parkinson vocals/guitar. They had gigs at The Antler Hotel in Narrabeen and enjoyed a minor hit under their new name The A Sound.

Some neighbours moaned about the racket but my sister and I crept down to the back fence to listen to them practice. While cigarette companies sponsored some sporting events and bands, we thought menthol tipped fags wouldn't poison our lungs and improved the quality of our breath at kissing time.

Surfing music took a back seat when Beatlemania gripped Australia. Whenever the Fab Four's latest hit was played on commercial radio by popular DJs—Bob Rogers, Mike Walsh, John Laws, Ward 'Pally' Austin and Mad Mel—queues formed outside record shops hours before opening. Parents were dismayed when sons grew their hair long in front and told them to slick their fringe back before going out. We girls ruffled our boyfriend's hair when they came to the door. It was embarrassing being seen with a nerdy boy with short back and sides.

When it was announced the Beatles would be touring in June, 1964, hundreds of teens camped outside the Sydney ticket office overnight with blankets and cushions, clapping their hands and chanting *Love Me Do*. At David Jones, fans rushed through the department doors, knocking over clothing racks. For £9 five shillings, I secured five tickets. And told my sister that if she wanted to borrow my sling backs, step-ins (corset), white lipstick and pink rose-patterned tight nylon pants, she'd better keep her distance from my boyfriend. Or I'd tell Mum about her and Bugsy in the Chevvy.

In Amsterdam when news media reported excited Dutch fans leaping poles and jumping in canals in an effort to reach their idols, police warned they'd use hoses if such riots occurred here. The big stories were sightings of two crocodiles in Manly reservoir, and a dirty-faced prowler who'd slipped a rope around a pensioner's neck. The gutsy great-granny fought off her attacker with a bowl of custard. She went on TV to offers tips from her ordeal.

It was expected we'd scream at the Beatles concert after reading papers. Surf City in King's Cross, an ex-picture theatre converted to a stomp venue, hosted bands like The Arrows who played Beatle music interspersed with sugary hits. Giant footprints and surfing pictures decorated the walls while the band played under flashing lights. Joanna learnt to do piercing whistles when rounding up dogs in New Zealand and these egged the band on to play louder.

The excitement of the music made us all slightly mad. Wacky Mad Mel on 2SM radio had fans knit a ten-metre long scarf to present to the Beatles. A Keymania radio promotion had youngsters scrabbling round Sydney suburbs searching for the correct key to a Volkswagen with consolation prizes of Beatle watches, transistors and Top 100 records.

Dad liked the Beatles; they were British and sang melodic ballads. Once, he got excitedly silly, jigging around, whacking our backsides with a rolled up newspaper, the volume turned up to drown out the neighbours' hymn singing. The Beatles put Dad in a good mood.

The Beatles concert could be described as temporary insanity with girls screaming and fainting. Supporting acts under the flashing blue lights were the Phantoms, Sounds Incorporated, Johnny Chester in elongated red shoes and Johnny Devlin in a leather suit, writhing and twisting on the floor. Impatient fans booed and flung eggs.

When the Beatles emerged to sing eight songs beginning with *Long Tall Sally,* the crowd went wild with kids stamping on seats and yelling hysterically. Suddenly it was over. We were pretty well deaf when police rushed the Fab Four off stage. It was whispered John Lennon had a penchant for Asian women, though he was married. The others had English girlfriends. That didn't deter youngsters climbing walls, using ploys to touch their heartthrobs.

During the year Jasper was in the navy, Mum hoped he'd mature and follow in his uncle's footsteps. When he came home for long weekends, the house was once again infested with his mates. Dad coped by incarcerating himself in the bedroom, office work and endless cups of tea fortified by homemade wine. She agreed to parties involving Jasper's naval friends, so long as he didn't invite surfie bums.

"Aw, Mum, I'm cut when you say that. They're my friends."

"They're not the sort of people with our values."

"But, Ma, some of their parents own yachts."

"They probably won money on the pokies and are undeserving. We don't know their backgrounds. Please, darling, we just want the best for you. Make us proud."

Then Joanna complained that her school friends had much nicer homes than ours.

Mum said, "That may be so, but we know where we come from." Dad said our lineage traced back centuries to nobility and our surname, Strathern, meant Valley of the Eagle.

Our first party began benignly, for Mum slaved all day in the kitchen making party food while Jasper went surfing. Joanna and our high-spirited friends helped concoct punch with apple and pineapple bits in Mum's home-brew with claret, cherry brandy and soda water.

Sid Jnr. began thumping his drums in our lounge. He said, "Jas said youse were havin' a turn here." Mum gave Dad a stiff

175

drink and cotton wool for his ears. She reminded him nice people were coming so would he try not to call rock 'n' roll teenage muck and be pleasant, even if it killed him.

When Jervis Bay cadets arrived in taxis with bottles and cans of beer, Dad greeted them wearing a tie. Mum said, "How lovely to meet you," before ducking into the kitchen to check the sausage rolls. She wasn't expecting imported booze or Jasper's mates sneaking in bleach-blonde girlfriends with pouting white lips. Once lights were turned off, Mum said, "Is this absolutely necessary? I hope you're behaving yourself, Jonquil." She was not happy when a guy with a squint draped his arm around me. He didn't look naval, because those afflicted with poor sight were not signed on.

I was going through a phase of fancying guys with deformities—doubled-jointed, a dash of impetigo or large nostrils. Polio sufferers were especially attractive for they looked like fallen soldiers. I never met a thalidomide victim. I thought they lived in the western suburbs.

When Mum spied Jasper and his surfing mate jigging around the room with chair covers and cardboard boxes on their heads, she served strong coffee. The noisy evening ended with Jasper's outburst on discovering his mates urinating on his beloved surfboard. The slummy back verandah had become a carnage of stomped-in food. One cadet, who later had a distinguished naval career, upchucked on Mum's bedspread. Surprisingly, Mum admitted it was quite a good party despite a broken meat dish, a flowerpot and half a dozen glasses.

To encourage Jasper to stay in the navy, Mum tried everything to make him happy. His naval friends came to stay and she hid her disapproval when a car tooted outside during our dinner. "Coming for a chug-a-lug at the rubbity-dub?" Jasper invited. The cadets looked confused but followed his lead, returning later in a wobbly state.

"That boy won't bow to authority," said Dad shaking his head.

At the end of the year Jasper rang. He'd failed all his exams.

"But," he added brightly, "I got my licence now."

When a letter from the Navy confirmed his expulsion, Mum did what any other depressed and disappointed mother might have done. She cried bitterly into the sun-kissed basket of washing on the back verandah, then got an axe and chopped up his surfboard.

Chapter 19
First Job, First Love

Jobs were plentiful in the 60s. We hadn't heard of the dole. The only noticeable unemployed were workers stirred up by unions marching down the main street of Sydney waving banners about their rights. Dad thought they were a pack of communists. It annoyed him when he and a colleague from Blue Star Shipping, who eschewed over local and world events at a gentleman's club at lunchtime, became blocked by ranting maniacs.

He clung to his Britishness while Jasper clung to his Australian upbringing, both unable to find neutral ground. Mum hoped the navy would have united them.

"It's stupid wearing a tie and slaving in a city box," scoffed Jasper. "Live for the day. Enjoy nature, the waves are beautiful."

And he twanged his guitar on the back verandah.

Mum said if he wanted to live under our roof he had to get a job or go back to school. He quickly found work at a polling booth, cleaning a butcher's freezer, coffin-making where a stiff sat bolt upright in a fiery furnace, grease monkey at Young's Garage, digging sewers, baby-sitting, and even agreed to further education if Mum could be a bit more open-minded about his mates. Dad was aghast. Sons don't make demands. They behave and don't question.

Donny's mum was no comfort. She voiced her opinions in that strident Australian way.

"Heather, we all have problems. The wretched railways demanded Bully be muzzled for a train trip to Woy Woy. How do you muzzle a bulldog's flat face? The damn thing kept slipping off, so I had to give him a tranquilliser. Now that's a worry!"

A Kiwi friend reminded Mum about real pain, for all three daughters had broken her heart.

"My Barbie fell in love with an Arab from Jordan who was on the Board of Education at Melbourne. She insisted on going back to Palestine, and being his Number Two wife even though his first wife had three kids. Poor Barbie had to live in a tent, wear rags and was miserable because her husband was away most of the time. No one spoke English. She got ill with worms and couldn't leave the tent. After six months we had to cough up £250 for her airfare home. My second went to America after marrying a Czechoslovakian and discovered he was already married. And Sue is plain lazy. She's got a nice flat in Surfers and doesn't want me to visit."

"I wouldn't do that to you, Ma," I said.

"I know, darling."

And she let me curl up on the couch and listen to adult conversation.

"You can say anything in front of Jonquil," Mum said when couples visited after dinner for a drink in our lounge.

The men smoked and talked about cricket. Women knitted and talked about their problem kids. Mum proffered shrimp and oyster nibbles and emptied ashtrays. I absorbed the intricacies of an adult world with its small joys and colourful disappointments. Evenings ended with Dad yawning and Mum politely asking, "How about one for the road?" meaning a final tipple before departing. Little thought was given to drink/driving.

Saturday nights for girls with their latest heartthrob was the ultimate, but not to have a date felt like cruel rejection. Friday night you'd be panting with anticipation, wearing uncomfortable curlers in your hair and playing syrupy records to solidify the sweet ache of expectancy. Saturdays were spent thinking about *him* while he converted a car, told dirty jokes, went surfing, or helped his dad so he could have nocturnal freedom.

When I found myself without a date one Saturday, I was hysterical. I'd been a two-timing cheating little cow and deserved it, but parents see positive attributes in their kids. "You're above them, darling," said Mum, calling a crisis conference in the kitchen while pouring a sherry. Dad had a back injury and was resting on his bed rattling his English newspapers.

"Christ, Dot. My back! Do I have to get up?"

"This is not about you. It's about your daughter."

He staggered into the lounge and made us wait while he lit his pipe and collected his thoughts. "Trouble with women is they've never learnt to keep their mouths shut and look mysterious. Man is the hunter. Let him make the chase."

Mum added to the sting. "You've had too many late nights, Jonquil. I never understood why anyone saw anything attractive in you at 2am."

When I revealed my worst fear was marrying a thick-necked Aussie bloke with sun-blistered ears who'd spend his evenings at a pub while I raised snotty-nosed brats in a flat, Mum poured another sherry. I said, "I think God's come into my life and…"

Mum interrupted. "I don't want you going to that church party. It'll be full of grey-haired old women trying to convert you."

"It's not like that. It's teenagers who've seen the light. I think my calling is to marry a missionary and go to darkest Africa and help the natives."

"Doing what?"

"Dunno. But I'm a bit worried a missionary will make me read the Bible all the time."

Mum said my broken heart had undermined my confidence; she knew just the answer. June Dally-Watkins. This iconic woman ran a successful charm school in the city where etiquette and manners, for a weekly course over three months costing £23, would help young women gain poise. I should ring Ingrad to see if she'd go. Since we were best friends and spent hours on the phone, her parents said it sounded a nice thing for teenage girls to do.

Our first lesson taught us how to sit and stand, turn gracefully with shoulders back, and rub lanolin into our knees and elbows.

"Don't reveal the inside of your arms," warned the guru. "They are white and ugly."

The second lesson was about exercise, a subtle reminder you were more employable and attractive if you kept yourself trim, though Italians liked fuller figures.

Ingrad and I were pooped after breathing exercises and, when we ran to catch the double-decker night bus, we were confronted with a sickly reminder. We were investing over two week's wages to attract a man. The lessons were informative and enjoyable but men who rode upstairs on the bus looked boring, smoked, and rattled evening newspapers, while downstairs the intoxicated lurched on and fell asleep on our shoulder. The crabby one-armed conductor didn't care, but he'd be in your face if you didn't produce your ticket on spot inspections.

Deportment included sitting in front of a mirror, skirt slightly above the knee having chosen a flattering sitting position where the lighting was kind. By make-up lessons, Jasper had agreed to go back to high school and Mum was fretting over Joanna who was lying listlessly on her bed worrying about fat legs.

"For God's sake, you're not adopted. You've inherited the Washbourn legs."

"Like upturned beer bottles," grizzled my sister. "Why'd you breed us, Mum?"

Mum thought Joanna needed a psychiatrist, or worm treatment.

Other lessons included manicure, hairstyling, wardrobe planning, adjusting our handbag while walking erectly, and speaking into a Dictaphone. Upset my *faux pas* was lazy speech I vented my rage in my diary which was hidden under a loose floorboard in my attic bedroom.

At the graduation ceremony, thirty-three proud mothers wore their best and clapped enthusiastically as we modelled sports and evening wear they'd made for us. June Dally-Watkins, gracious and immaculate, presented diplomas and said something nice about everyone. She said I was small, pretty and cute with a lovely name.

I would have traded in one of those superlatives for bright or smart.

"Sorry to hurt your feelings, Ma, but I don't want to end up like you with awful kids and a husband who gets ratty filling out his income tax." Mum didn't want me to ruin my life either. "I've changed my mind about marrying a missionary, Ma. I fancy a good-tempered Englishman who smokes a pipe, pats a big dog by the hearth and recites poetry, or a cuddly Italian with a nice singing voice. But I'm worried his back might be smothered in black curls and he'll wear gold medallions around his neck."

Mum said my profound thoughts called for a Cinzano Bianco. Daddy could wait a few more minutes for his dinner as she was thinking Italian, too.

Cocktail hours with Mum were fun. When she wasn't weeping into the sink worrying whether her daughters would end up marrying a foreign lavatory man or a Catholic, and a son destined to be a perpetual beach bum, her brain was a cornucopia of ideas. She'd have been a woman's libber if it was invented then but, like women of her generation, she was keen to be seen as doing the right thing.

Jasper blew it with his wilful attitude and my parents never recovered from their disappointment. And Mum said I would be more attractive to boys if I was unavailable.

"I don't want you looking vacant and empty-headed like a shop girl. You need to have an air of mystery about you. We'll learn art and Italian. I'm sick of your father's mood when he's trying to quit smoking, and Jasper's friends treating this house like a social club. We should go to Italy on a nice Italian ship and study art in Perugia."

The art class was lively and Mum excelled at portraits. The teacher was so impressed he asked if he could buy the portrait she'd done of me. "I think he likes you, darling," said Mum.

When Jasper played up Mum went through her Picasso period and churned out blue nudes. I was embarrassed going to class with her, but Mum said she hadn't painted in specific bits. We did abstracts using acrylics, sand and toilet paper and commended each other's work.

"I see Jonquil's painted a naked male playing a violin," gushed some spinster. I was appalled when the art teacher put on his glasses to have a closer inspection.

"It's meant to be a sinking ship," I said to Mum. "I'd never paint a naked chap with a ding-dong. I've never seen one and I never want to."

Mum said she hoped I wouldn't either as they were ugly little things. That verbose spinster was silly, she added. Marrying a bad-tempered man would soon cut her down to size.

In the 60s, people used quaint terminology for hidden body parts. When a new wave revolution in the 70s said we should say the actual word or we'd mess up our kids, we were shocked. Uttering toilet to a boyfriend sounded crass and unromantic. Popping off to the ladies, need to powder my face or slipping out to the twinkle, la-de-da or the toot was sufficient.

Men said they were going to see a man about a dog, point Percy to the porcelain or shake hands with a man's best friend. They proudly referred to their manhood as monsters, which sounded frightening as it was only a zipper, the back of a Buick at the drive-in and brief unbridled passion that could ruin our reputations. Australians misunderstood American guests asking to go the bathroom when they simply wanted a urinal, not a bath or shower.

The Italian teacher loved us for Mum was keen and I was blonde. Mum had all day to whip down to the greengrocers and practice but I was tired after work and yawned a lot. The Italian professor produced photos of his eligible son while I peered at other pupils, including two good-looking priests. I thought it a terrible waste they were sacrificing themselves to God when they could have virginal me. Maybe Mother was right about the attractiveness of non-availability.

I took up German and yoga, briefly. The German lessons were structured and lacked warmth and levity like the merry Italian classes. Images of Hitler and marching boots poisoned our generation until later in the 60s when youngsters travelled and hippy flower-power spread its love tentacles. Yoga didn't have the calming effect I imagined. The air was punctuated with pregnant women, in leotards, hoisting their limbs and expelling wind.

Learning Japanese was frustrating with its squiggles on the blackboard. When asked what a word meant, the tutor smiled and shrugged. "Velly solly, no meaning Japanese," and I wondered why Asians couldn't pronounce their Rs. At the end of the year, it was a relief to pack up. We celebrated at an ethnic restaurant. The Japanese farewell was polite, formal, atmospheric. Guests with knee transplants struggled to tuck their legs under a low table laden with exotic dishes, while a trickling fountain made the weak in bladder head for a bamboo cubicle.

The Italian meal was raucously cheerful with priests singing songs of Italy made popular by Dean Martin. The waiters joined in and the Chianti flowed. Mum was right. The call of Italy was coursing through my veins, too, and I didn't want the evening to end.

Saturday's *Sydney Morning Herald* listed pages of job vacancies with firms seeking typists and stenographers. Mum suggested finding a shorthand/typist job with a travel agency because of travel concessions. As I was scared, Mum said she'd come to the interview. She donned her hat and gloves and we took a bus to Centrecom, the central Sydney employment agency where a young woman gave me a minute speed-typing test. And World Travel Headquarters was seeking a stenographer; the manager was interviewing now. So Mum and I click-clacked in our chisel-toed shoes to find the right building.

"Of course they'll want you," she said confidently. "I bet you've travelled to more countries than they have," and she spat gently into a tissue and wiped grime off my face, and dusted my shoulders for imaginary dandruff.

The boss emerged from a glass cage surround at the end of an elongated office room where women clacked noisily on their typewriters. He was a rambling interviewer. I worried about Mum pacing outside in the corridor clutching a string bag and hopeful heart.

"Why on earth did he keep you so long?" she said. "My feet are killing me."

"Mum, I'm going to hate the job. I want to stay home with you. I'll never find my way around the city. I hate growing up."

"What you need is a nice cup of tea and a cream bun and I need a lavatory. We'll go to David Jones and shop for smart outfits for you, and put them on Daddy's account. You can pay him back later if you get the job."

Another lengthy interview followed inquiries about family, religion and schooling. Attending a private school weeded out other hopefuls. Wages were £11 a week gross, hours 9am to 5.30pm and one Saturday morning a month.

My new job initially robbed me of the womb-warmth of home, the comforting crashing of waves pounding against Long Reef cliffs, and the suburban familiarity of neighbours pegging nappies out while husbands warmed up the engines of their Fords, Holdens or Chryslers. The first week was a nightmare; the boss was bad-tempered but Dad said, "Don't be a quitter," and Mum said, "Perhaps he's having a bad day."

As the bus rolled through beach suburbs to the city, hatted pedestrians climbed aboard and the bus conductor growled directions. "First seddown (set down) Cremorne," meaning that was the stop you could alight at, not before. Busty office women in twin sets gossiped and crocheted, moustached men flicked through their briefcase and young office workers stood for older people. Pancake make-up hid pimples and freckles and girls chewed gum while discussing boyfriends and their trousseaux. On leaving school it was assumed they'd meet a guy of the same religion and values, and he'd propose. In anticipation they bought a carved wooden casket with brass clips called a glory box and each payday bought linen, glassware and crockery at sales to add to their treasure trove.

My workplace was divided into three sections: Australian, European and North American travel with a woman at the helm of each. I worked for the Greyhound Bus Company whose slogan was *99 dollars for 99 days. See the USA. Go Greyhound.* My Indian boss taught me how to compose itineraries, decipher bus schedules and convert American dollars on the adding machine to Australian pounds, compile monthly reports, use the Gestetner (copy printer) and franking (postage) machine. Also tips on making frothy instant coffee.

Everyone smoked at their desk, muttered expletives while using Tippex to correct typing errors on multiple carbon copies, and discussed anyone taking too long in the Ladies. Sometimes the air was thick with bitchiness between the three women bosses; it was disloyal for junior typists to talk to the warring side. The boss shrugged, helpless and impotent. He had his own problems; Snookie, his foul-mouthed wife, was suspicious of him holed up in an office with a dozen women.

"Tell her I'm out of the office," he'd bark, amidst a mess of papers, a phone at each ear.

I got a dissertation on her lungs. "Me throat's like the bottom of a birdcage, love. Strewth, it feels like a bird's left its calling card in me mouth and buggered off. What's that galoot up to? Is he or is he not in the office?"

We told fibs to protect him and junior stenographers bore the brunt of mood swings from bosses under pressure at home

185

and at work. The boss chewed, mumbled, received phone calls and flicked through files during dictation. He'd parade up and down the office and lower his voice at crucial names. When asked to repeat, he'd shout. He'd indicate you were an imbecile if you asked him to decipher his alterations, his incorrect spelling, balloons and arrows. Since his work was more urgent than your social life he'd breathe down your neck or glare at the wastepaper basket filled with screwed up letterheads while you retyped corrections, painted Twink over errors, and missed the bus.

Mum chuckled when I told her it was easier to catch the bus than accept a lift with the Beatle-fringed boyfriend. In my city finery he'd ask me to push his Vauxhall backwards to get it started. He didn't trust me to steer; I'd put it up a telegraph pole under his driving tutelage. If it conked out he'd roll up to the garage and ask for two shillings worth of juice (petrol.) The muffler fell off charging over potholes, and my head hit the roof. He got his kid brother to hold in the gearbox while skidding around corners to keep the engine charged. Once, car keys flew out of his hand and into a gutter.

Jasper later bought his bomb for £5 and converted it into a beach buggy until it became skeletal metal and fizzled.

Chapter 20
The Teen Social Scene

"Speak up, enunciate clearly," Dad barked, home from work to find us huddled on the sofa weeping.

"Prinky Poo's dead. She got hit by a car."

After a stunned pause he said, "For heaven's sake, it's only a dog. Life's not a bed of roses. Where's my dinner?"

Mum called Dad a heartless beast and Joanna bawled hysterically. Our beautiful little Lassie-type dog had turned into a limp fur coat.

I sprinted up to my attic room where I wept onto my Liberace photo. His permanent plastic smile offered some normality, as did the rumbling of night traffic on Pittwater Road.

Dad's reaction was generally attributed to war trauma.

Mum ran sobbing to her bedroom saying she wanted to go back to England. Some husbands would have struck their wives for such defiance. But Dad—never! He sat in his city suit in the dark, smoking a pipe, confused, reflecting. He loved Princess, too, and would nurse her on his lap, blow smoke rings into the air, read Shakespeare and listen to decent music.

Joanna's face was so swollen she refused to go to school. Mum was too upset to go to art class. Jasper left a note on his bed saying he'd gone to think about life after he flunked his exams. He stowed away on a ship to New Zealand.

Despite Jasper's disappearance, our house on Pittwater Road remained busy. His mates dropped by keen to fix radios, lamps, the lawnmower, or help Dad tinker under the bonnet of the car. When Mum was in her Italian tiling mood, our home buzzed with surfie boys prostrate on the bathroom floor. I made cups of coffee and whipped up cakes.

Cadets from the naval college asked after Jasper and Mum invited them to stay long weekends. They were the kind of sons she wanted. She didn't mind Joanna and me puffing on Alpines into the night over cards and cups of tea. They took us to the Long Reef Surf Club stomp just up the road. And they wrote thank you notes.

In one was a message of love to Joanna, but I distracted my fifteen-year old sister. I knew she preferred teenage drummers in bands, not nautical guys with potential to become admirals.

We played ping-pong on our verandah, but when Dad said the exercise would stop me getting fat, I became a better player than him. He delivered backhanders and tricky ball spins. I won by default. It taught me taking huge risks was less rewarding than a steady approach.

Mum grimaced when I beat competitors.

"Darling, can't you let him win sometimes?"

"But that'd be cheating, Ma."

It was empowering outsmarting the opposite sex since inequality was pervasive. Men doing the same job as women got paid more and it annoyed a new underground movement called feminism.

The office relaxed when the manager went overseas. The spinster bosses didn't bitch, and when one discovered the manager's cabinet stocked with spirits, we enjoyed the spoils at our tea break. Everyone smoked and the manager's legacy was to strengthen us in feminine unity, despite living in Sydney suburbs revealing your socio-economic status.

When attending travel league luncheons, or after hours drinks with overseas directors at the Chevron Hotel, we preened under glaring neon lights in the Ladies. We checked our stockings for snags, squirted *Madam Roche* on the inside of our wrists, behind ears and down our cleavage, pinched our cheeks for colour and lavishly sprayed our back-combed hair before clutching minute handbags and striding in uncomfortable stilettos to the venue.

Women moaned about sore feet. They couldn't wait to get home, kick off their shoes and girdle, have a cuppa, a Bex and a good lie down.

The girdle, corset or step-in was the grown-up version of girl's suspender belts. Its clips snapped onto sheer or patterned stockings and ruthlessly moulded fleshy hips and stomachs into a slender shape. Since no girl dared be seen in it, it was an aid to chastity. The all-in-one panty hose became a welcome replacement. Gorgeous gussies or frilly lacy panties worn over the girdle was a lovely gift from other women, but too intimate a gift from men.

Pointed patent leather shoes with thin soles gave us bunions and foot deformities. Mum maintained one must suffer to be beautiful.

Complimentary cigarettes, salty peanuts and pickled onion, cheese and pineapple bits on toothpicks were typical snack fare, as were some airline BOAC lads with a roving eye. Rascally travel agents addressed our busts. Some tough walnut-faced women in the travel industry, after too many vodka stingers or Harvey Wallbangers, got frisky with anyone with an American accent for it smelt of money and connections.

When boozy baggy-trousered managers returned late from lunch and swayed over our desks for dictation with their flies undone, what could you say? In the 60s you used euphemisms. It was too blunt to tell them the truth. If they failed to interpret frantic typists' eyeballs swivelling southward they needed help, such as, 'Something is flying low today,' or 'You've left the trapdoor open.' My boss preferred, 'I think I see a little dickie-bird.'

The biggest threat to a typist's reputation was the office Christmas party, because some pranksters thought it funny to mix drinks. One year I ended up in a broom cupboard flirting with a shy Lebanese office boy after spiked Advocaat and cherry brandies, but emerged intact except for smudged lipstick around my earlobes. I called it my Lebbo period. But then I committed the ultimate sin, which Aussies call the technicolour yawn. My sweet boyfriend with missing side teeth and hands riddled with eczema from using a printing machine was so caring, Mum invited him for Christmas dinner.

Ashamed, I thought of purging myself by going into exile somewhere, perhaps a convent. Mum said not to be silly, even nuns could go astray and get a bit thirsty at communion.

The next day, she whipped up a rich brandy sauce and thrust boiled threepenny and sixpenny silver coins into the Christmas pudding. My boyfriend was smiling broadly—he'd never been peppered with so many kisses in all his life.

"Jeez, you're a bonzer chick," he said. "Mum is dying to meet you. She loves your name."

In the 60s, parents clung to traditional values when it came to affairs of their children's hearts. Dads insisted on shaking hands with a daughter's new beau while mothers sniffed for grooming, speech defects and job prospects. Fathers of sons were attracted to good-looking young females while mothers had a nose for immigrants, cheap beach tarts and strident twanging vowels.

Twenty-first birthdays were momentous events. You were officially an adult and given a large silver-coated key to the door. It meant you could vote, drink and wed without parental consent. The age was eventually lowered to eighteen due to social changes and the Vietnam War; if you fought for your country you deserved equal rights in drinking and marrying.

Twenty-firsts were an occasion to indulge in a new frock and elaborate hair-do. Parents hosted buffet banquets of curry and rice, chicken and pineapple, Neapolitan ice cream and fruit salad. Orlando white wine was followed by coffee and champagne. Some girls wore chiffon dresses with a Tom Jones sleeve, or the unflattering empire-line frock, which had people guessing, especially if an engagement was announced. Pastel-coloured frocks with long puffed sleeves and teased hair with little bows was the in thing.

Boutiques selling nightwear for maidens had lowly paid typists and stenographers longing for fussy nightgowns usually reserved for the next big event—the scary wedding night! They were so beautiful they could have been ball gowns.

Bachelors wore ties and gawked at girls. Some parents hired bands if their repertoire extended to demure foxtrots and barn dances. After a few Bloody Marys and Screwdrivers, the evening morphed into a kaleidoscope of teens twisting, jiving, stomping, and necking in bushes or sports cars.

When the birthday person opened presents during the fruitcake offering, guests gathered to witness facial inflections of delight over a casserole dish. Usual gifts were fancy cigarette lighters, wine glasses, towels, bone-handled cutlery, pottery, cup and saucer sets, egg timers, musical German beer steins, and ashtrays.

Some parties ended belligerently. One son was caught with a bleary-eyed bimbo.

"It's moy life now, Dad. Youse can't tell me what to do."

His dad responded, "Yer twenty-one now, son, so yer can bugga orf."

Three months later Jasper turned up sporting a beard after his stowaway adventure. Sprawled on his bed, strumming a guitar, the prodigal suggested renting a room at home so he could be free to come and go.

Dad was flabbergasted and slunk off to his shed.

"That boy looks like a beatnik."

Mum wanted to know why her son wore shorts with a broken zip and acted so base. After a family conference he reluctantly, yet again, agreed to go back to school, but was annoyed when Mum pasted a sign on the front door: Jasper is studying. Keep out.

"Ma, you can't do that to my mates. They're good blokes."

Mum said true friends wouldn't jeopardise his chances of getting a proper education.

My brother caused catfights between girls and furious boyfriends who'd been dumped. He was funny, ebullient, opportunistic and likeable. If his shady deals turned sour he shrugged. That drove our parents mad because he wouldn't take life seriously.

Joanna went to Queenwood Private School because zoology was a subject and she liked matters medical. Maybe she'd end up helping brain-injured wallabies and wombats. When she wasn't scowling through a long fringe, demanding zookeepers cease slaughtering wild brumbies for lion tucker and offering to buy one for five dollars from her pocket money, she was showing off with school friends pretending to be go-go dancers.

They chortled, burped and whistled in the dark on the long narrow backyard where the fervent religious lived on one side of the fence, Donny and his parents in the brick house on the other side, and Sid Jnr. banged on his drums in the house behind. He was practising latest hits like *It's Good News Week* (Hedgehoppers Anonymous) with its dark lyrics about dropping bombs and pollution.

The mid 60s saw a shift in music from crooning syrupy heartache and rebel rousing twanging to lyrics voicing global concern. Sam Cooke's *Another Saturday Night* reminded girls that guys, too, looked forward to that day of the week after Friday's payday.

Tragically the singer (1931-1964) was fatally shot, robbing rock 'n' roll of a black musician with immense talent who made people realise we all felt the same about life, love and chances.

The 60s Australians were paternalistic towards Abos who were seen as feral, not bright, and living in the outback. American TV depicted Afro-Americans as maids or chauffeurs.

Australia was mostly a white society then and dark-skinned people were not visible.

Our diet of TV was mainly American imports like *The Donna Reed Show*, *77 Sunset Strip*, and *Twilight Zone*. Or English—*The Rag Trade*, *Benny Hill* and *The Two Ronnies*. Dad said you couldn't beat British drama or humour. Australians were flexing their talent and producing shows for children like *Skippy, the Bush Kangaroo*, and *The Mavis Brampton Show* with its satirical sketches. TV ran from midday to midnight but hours were extended with more TV stations opening.

The Australian home help wasn't seen as subservient. The employee was referred to as my little cleaning woman, what would I do without her? Shop assistants irritated customers by chatting above serving. Australians considered everyone equal, whatever the job, especially when the trade unions became powerful and dictatorial, supporting blue-collar workers.

Female reporters frequented restaurants with a pencil and notebook, and approached well-dressed groups. If you were connected to a wealthy family you were photographed. Despite wearing a Norma Tullo linen ensemble with boater hat at The Brass Rail, a reporter sashayed off to another table. I'd failed the society pages for she'd asked, "What is your father's profession? Is he a doctor?"

The Beatles and Rolling Stones overshadowed surfing music. Some parents disliked their children attending the stadium to scream and faint over singing groups like Peter, Paul and Mary, Gerry and the Pacemakers, Ray Columbus and the Invaders and other overseas bands who'd sold smash hits. They feared their darlings might be contaminated by riff-raff— the bikies, rockers, hoods and seamen from the *Chusan*.

Folk music soon became associated with drugs. Going to The Attic at Kings Cross was an excuse to cosy up on the floor with your date in the dark. Or stare at a longhaired hippie straddled on a stool strumming his guitar in a hypnotic trance. Back-up girl singers with long printed frocks and long hair added melancholy spice. You left the venue gulping air and wondering if the world was really so stuffed up.

Boyfriends wanted to shield me from the seamier side of life, such as prostitutes with large sores on their legs, lurching tattooed sailors and drunks collapsed in doorways. My dates were perfect gentlemen walking on the outside of the pavement and opening car doors. When we got home my Lady Muck image vanished. The porch light would be on, a reminder to be in bed by midnight or else!

"Bedtime now, your father can't sleep," Mum would call.

Or she'd fling open the lounge door, crying, "Kindly have the manners to spring apart when I enter the room."

It was humiliating seeing a face lathered in Ponds Vanishing Cream, hair in curlers, a tatty dressing gown.

"I'm acting with decorum, Ma. We're only playing records."

There wasn't time for hanky-panky with singles lasting around two and half minutes. Just when you were about to brush lips to *Be My Baby* (Ronettes), *And Then He Kissed Me* (Crystals), or *Will You Still Love Me Tomorrow?* (Shirelles), the record had finished or was stuck on a scratched groove.

"I'd never be immoral with you, sweetness," boys murmured. "You're the perfect girl for me. Will you wait for me?"

A turn (party) down the road or the olds (parents) are away was an invitation to crash a respectable home. There, teenage boys in white jeans swayed to new releases clutching a stubbie, while bleach-headed girls in cut-away shifts and the Mary Quant look (severe short hair and fringe, black eye-liner and pouting white lips) gyrated under backyard lights.

Jasper knew of every party. Sometimes he'd find someone to escort me. He owed me since smashing up a Hillman Minx he pressured me to buy and had no intention of repaying. Brothers could prowl the neighbourhood but sisters were under the thumb of protective parents.

When a local doctor returned home from the pictures one night, he was astonished to find his beautiful beach home infested with beat-up cars laden with surfboards in the driveway, beer bottles encircling the picket fence and boys drunkenly singing Bra-bra-ber-Anne, to the Beach Boys' hit *Barbara Anne.*

"Where's my little girl?" cried his fur-coated wife.

When told the teen was upstairs in their bed with a local lad, her response was astonishing. "Oh, thank goodness for that. I didn't want her catching a nasty cold outside."

Other daughters would have been grounded indefinitely!

Gold Finger, Rock Around the Clock, Help (Beatles), *Lawrence of Arabia, Gigi, Mary Poppins, Summer Holiday* (Cliff Richard) and *Windjammer* were some of the popular movies playing at the Collaroy Odeon in the mid 60s. A low-lit coffee shop with candles flickering from raffia-wrapped wine bottles ended the evening. It gave you time to decide whether you'd hold your date's hand walking home or feign a nasty cold and put them in your pockets.

An unoccupied table in a dark recess with a single candle glowing was in memory of the poor guy who couldn't pay his bill, or so warned the owner.

While church delivered *Power and Glory* magazines and preached a code of morals for teens—attraction, proposal, acceptance—bushfires across New South Wales broke out regularly, girls wore baby doll pyjamas, and parents wrote lists of house rules.

Youths sprawled around the back verandah with engine parts and surfing magazines. Their cars blocking the driveway were the final straws for my parents. Mum wiped her teary eyes over Jasper refusing to get a decent job, and we sat down to a nice roast chicken dinner.

But when Joanna's date turned up and she got up to leave, Dad said no. Mum just wanted a peaceful family meal. In the fracas Joanna's dinner plate ended up on her head. Mum wailed her dinner was spoilt and Sis ran out the door sobbing with chicken and gravy running down her face. Her boyfriend screeched down Pittwater Road doing burnouts like a police escapee.

A couple of hours later, when Joanna crept indoors cuddling a fluffy toy koala, Dad was laughing and Mum knitting.

They were selling our Collaroy home and buying a house in a suburb where surfies felt intimidated and unwelcome.

"Jasper's made his choice about his lifestyle. We just want the best for our girls."

Chapter 21
Sex in the City

When our house in Mosman was burgled Mum was mildly peeved.

"No one would've bothered at Collaroy," she said. "Far too slummy with Jasper's decrepit vehicles."

Lights from passing traffic on Pittwater Road, night dog walkers, and Jasper arising at dawn to surf, limited temptation. Our new home in Park Avenue was at the end of a cul-de-sac, built against a rocky cliff where shrubbery and dark footpaths provided cover for robbers.

"Ma, they've taken my Liberace records!"

Mum said it wasn't the work of gay extremists. She was more worried about family heirlooms hidden underneath the house, between dirt and concrete piles. She clambered out, her hair matted with cobwebs, waving Great Aunt May's silver salver and candlesticks.

I looked for clues while Mum sighed over cigarette butts found in Joanna's room.

"Probably the work of gangsters from the Balkans," she said. "God, I hope they haven't gone through my drawers. Hate to think they've parcelled up my undies to send back home to their wives. They were getting a bit baggy round the waist."

I had visions of swarthy men with droopy moustaches, battered fedoras and trench coats with deep pockets filled with stolen treasures.

She said, "These people are desperate. They'll take anything."

Our home was footsteps away from a leafy park leading to the Mosman jetty where people commuted to work in the city.

"You might meet someone nice on the ferry," Mum said. "Take a book with an interesting cover and try not to look too vacant, darling."

Regulars met at the wharf, perched in the same seat, and quietly read their morning papers. Dad was a tease. If we were about to cast off, he'd remove his hat and, in an affected English voice, turn to me and say, "Excuse me, madam. Is this boat sailing today?"

"Shhh, Daddy!" I'd blush into my book. "Don't be a twerp."

"There's a young man with a nice big head staring at you. Would you like to marry him?"

"God, you're embarrassing. I'm not travelling with you again."

I hoped no one thought we were related or that he was my sugar daddy.

Despite living in a wealthier suburb just off Pittwater Road, Dad shuddered on hearing the neighbour's strident voice. She was calling to her hen-pecked husband; he'd holed up in the bowels of his house, which he'd converted into a movie theatre.

"Lal! Me washing machine's gone crook. Get your skinny arse up here or there'll be bobsy-die!"

"A woman's voice let's her down," Dad muttered, his teeth clenched onto his pipe. "Prefer your Kiwi twang, Dot," and he plunged a playful kiss on Mum's powdered face.

"Stop it, Fairley. You're annoying when you're in a good mood."

Jasper's cars were still a sore point; his old ambulance with surfboards on top lowered the tone of the neighbourhood. When Jasper traded it for a souped-up Bentley, Dad was interested but both parents remained disappointed he lacked direction. "The navy didn't want him and the army doesn't either," Mum said. "He's going to be a brickie's labourer all his life."

Our feral brother with his film star Troy Donahue good looks and misdirected energy fascinated Joanna's Queenwood school friends, daughters of well-to-do parents. He'd cock his leg over a rolled-arm sofa in the lounge, strum on a guitar singing his twisted version of *West Side Story*—"Maria, I've just met a girl called Diarrhoea"—and entertain them yarning about drunken parties, dodging police, meeting American pop stars like Bobby Rydell, his near-miss shark attacks out surfing, and how he lost a bet raising money for Spastics (polio victims) at a social. He was the funny bad boy who refused to bow to the niceties of society, a refreshing enigma for teens who felt constrained by parents' expectations about their future.

If Mum wasn't bundling up clothes for the Aborigines, making parsnip wine or stamping on grapes in the bath the Italian way, scolding Joanna for sniggering over the rudest words she could find in the dictionary, shopping at the Bargain Centre for imported clothes, dipping into Colin Simpson's *Wake Up in Europe* for future travel, she'd be planning a do.

"There's an eligible bachelor at your father's work," she said. "Give him a chance. He can't help his silly surname." I said I'd never marry a man with an embarrassing name.

At work, when compiling itineraries for travel agents, we'd chuckle over names like a Pio Bott, someone Greenslit, Smellie, and Higginbothams. Anyone with a cock-name would never get past first base with me. And Smith and Jones were too common. When I married I wanted a name with a continental touch.

Be-aproned mothers had their heads full of handed down anecdotes and epithets and annoyingly spouted them. Our worries became our mums. Mine was; to wed or not to wed?

Not yet twenty-one, I'd had several marriage offers but one chap was particularly persistent. I sought Mum's advice for I'd need her approval. Many girls were engaged in their teens. Once they left school it was expected they'd find a job, get married and start a family, and the husband would be the single breadwinner. Society called ambitious girls selfish for having a career and taking jobs from men, though there were plenty. Nurses were exempt.

Girls were on the prowl for a suitable mate of means after dating losers. Losers included guys who wore Speedos to the beach (lifeguards exempt), those without a car, those tied to their mother's apron strings, and those who expected to be favoured sexually for wasting their money on you in the first place.

Don't come the raw prawn with me, a groper might say in the back of a Holden after a night out at the local. His mates drank in a bar but he'd paid extra so he and the sheila could drink a Pimm's, shandy or gin sling in the Lizard Lounge watching Howard Morrison or the tuneful Quin Tikis from New Zealand. Girls wanted to be liked for their personality and looks, but after a few schooners guys weren't fussy. Surfies had the same drive, which we beach bunnies discussed as we lay on the golden sands hoping the beach inspector wouldn't evict us for wearing tiny bikinis. Some girls cut out a boyfriend's name from paper and lay it on their backs waiting for the sun to burn them. When at a dance that night wearing a Trent cut-away frock, it revealed *Gary* or *Brian* in white on a blistered red back.

The thrill of riding a wild wave made some surfies randy; they'd prance up the sand clutching their boards and blowing jets of surf out their nostrils–What a ripper. Fan-bloody-tastic. How's about a rouse-about? Any of youse chicks up for a shag?

After telling them how disgusting they were, we might offer a girl's name if she had nicked one of our boyfriends. We hoped it would tarnish her reputation, get back to her parents and she'd be grounded for a year.

In the 60s guys asked the girl's dad for permission to marry his daughter. A father wanted to know if his little girl would be well provided for and, over a few beers, quiz the lad about his job prospects. Mothers eavesdropped, pretending to be arranging gladdies (gladioli.)

Sons were advised to have a dekko (look) at their girlfriend's mother. She'll turn out like that. And they were encouraged to marry someone from the same socio-economic group.

Leaping from a close family to a mother-in-law whipping up baby gowns on the Singer sewing machine, knitting booties and shawls in anticipation, saved you from being labelled an old maid or lesbian.

Since 60s mothers were queens of their kitchen, their daughters lacked cooking experience. A bride who could only bake one pudding might, eventually, be asked, "What's for sweets?"

"Pineapple Surprise."

"Well, it's no ruddy surprise anymore!" Since he'd married he was entitled to lots of nookie. If she'd submitted before marriage she was labelled loose, so it weighed heavily on Catholic girls for the Pope declared the pill a sin. She was expected to control carnal desires (his) until the wedding night, then breed like crazy and raise lots of little Catholics.

There wasn't much literature for girls planning to be brides. It was hearsay and innuendo, American TV and the shenanigans of film stars. While church preached morality, American and British pop idols were divorcing, free-loving and living like we never imagined. Our lives seemed staid in comparison with *Sex and the Single Girl* and *Boys and Other Beasts*—a popular read. Girls spent hours preening and practising a pout for a date at a drive-in in a two-toned Zephyr. There was more action in the car than on the big screen.

It was flattering to think someone wanted you badly enough they'd suggest marriage before testing the goods. Good girls were like vintage wine; ready to be uncorked once the gold band was planted on the fourth finger. Nice girls were like an opened bottle of Cold Duck wine; savoured but still marriageable. Or was it the other way round? Others were called soiled or damaged goods, but they still got hitched.

Some friends pranced up to the altar like bumptious Barbie dolls. "Bet she had to," we said jealously when spying them in the social pages of *The Sydney Morning Herald*. "How did she land him?"

We prayed there'd be enough men left on the planet for us. Mothers told daughters, 'Bide your time and your turn will come.'

When Mum said I'm not living in Australia when your father retires, not over my dead body, I felt unsettled. Should I feel allegiance towards Australia, the country of my childhood where we sang *Advance Australia Fair* and people could tell what school you went to if you said advarnce instead of advaaance, or England, country of my birth, where Dad remained patriotic. Or New Zealand, Mum's homeland, where she had oodles of relatives and some social standing?

"So where do you want to croak, Ma?"

"London, perhaps. It'd be quite pleasant having a quick coronary at the Tate Art Gallery looking at a Turner, don't you think?"

No, I thought, I don't want you to die. I want to live in the same country as you.

She might be flighty and say mad things, but she was our rock. She rescued us. If we were stranded after a party, crying over a boyfriend, dropped stitches when knitting a jumper or broke something, she fixed it. Mum took us to the pictures (movies), concerts, and the music hall and, at the drop of a hat, conjured up food for unexpected guests, even welcoming Jasper's naval friends long after he'd been kicked out.

She let Joanna and me to go to Surfers Paradise with Margie and Rozzie, two wacky sisters, whose parents had homes in Mosman and Palm Beach, because a bunch of medical students they knew were holidaying up there. It sounded safe. We didn't tell her we whistled, hooted, chortled and waved our bikini tops out of the window as we cruised up the east coast of New South Wales. But we refused to sleep with these hunks and they broke our hearts. We'd found their large box of condoms in the fridge, so in a moment of drunken despair we scattered them across the floor of their apartment while they were out getting laid.

But not Boomer; he looked after us and married Rozzie the following year. The others called their beach pick-ups grubs, and, after the holiday, went back to their own girlfriends. Surfers Paradise was a sizzling hotbed of bikinied typists, nurses and hairdressers, and roaming horny youths seeking sun, surf and sex.

So, should I say yes, no, or maybe? Mum included Dad in my marriage quandary at tincture time (cocktail hour.) He chomped on his pipe, looked thoughtful, then said, "I don't think you'll do much better than him."

"But he's Australian," I said.

Dad said he couldn't help it, poor chap. He was nice and steady and could talk about cricket, what more could I want?

Well, frankly, I wanted Liberace. He'd been my pin-up boy since I was eleven and whenever he appeared on TV my heart fluttered wildly and I'd scream at anyone who dared breathe while he sang. If I closed my eyes hard enough I'd imagine sitting next to him at the piano, watching his bejewelled fingers dance across the ivories, and he'd wink at me. That luscious wink on TV ripped into my soul and made me deliriously giddy. "Oh, Mum, don't you think he's divine!" Mum would smile absently and say Mmm if she had pins in her mouth when sewing, or Yes, darling, I think you two suit each other very nicely.

I'd even make a current boyfriend watch TV if Liberace appeared on a special. "Isn't he gorgeous?" I'd swoon. The beau worried he wouldn't get a quick fondle of my tit when saying goodnight if he disagreed. I knew Libby wasn't perfect because he went to the toot, and there was a slight suspicion he wore make-up and a wig at home. I tried to block that bit.

"What do you say, Ma, about you-know-who? Do you think he's a bit too decent for me?"

"You don't want anyone indecent, do you? Let's all go to Mackerel Beach for a wee chat."

My parents had bought a one-bedroom holiday cottage called The Doll's House on Pittwater for nearly £3000, complete with fishing tackle, snorkels, old food, deck chairs and a first aid kit.

Mackerel Beach was an isolated haven, accessible by ferry from Palm Beach or by foot through Ku-ring-gai National Park. There were no cars or phones, and the clear waters lapped against yellow sand. Kookaburras sang in the gum trees by a stream that wound through the back of the section. Since the cottage had no electricity we awoke at dawn and went to bed at dusk after fishing, rock climbing, floating on lilos around the jetty and sizzling sausages. We went there regularly, passing our old home at Collaroy on Pittwater Road, honking the horn and wondering how the new tenants had settled in.

Mum said Dad didn't know much about women but he might give sound advice. Dusk turned to charcoal. She lit candles and brought out the sherry.

"We're talking about your daughter's future, so put on your thinking cap and don't hurt her feelings. She's sensitive."

Outside, frogs croaked and wildlife rustled in the bushes. Next door an old codger played *You Made Me Love You* on his honky-tonk piano.

It was hard to know where to begin. Mum never uttered the word sex. And she wriggled out of taking us to a mother/daughter film at Narrabeen High School since a friend's mother had sighed her relief, saying to her sixteen-year old, "Thank God that's over with. Now you know everything."

Boys were always hot topics. Some girls came to work sporting hickeys on their neck, a sign someone wanted them.

To make a mercurial boyfriend jealous, we'd pinch our own neck so he'd think he had competition.

When I described my earnest devoted chap, a ditzy blonde in Accounts thought he was the type to do his business under the blankets. She made him sound dull. I was shocked when she said she nibbled on her boyfriend Froggie's ding-a-ling. She said Froggie was now in the slammer for armed robbery. "Bet moon-doggie's missing his greens," she said. And she wasn't referring to vegetables.

One colleague said if you truly loved someone you'd do anything for them. When she got home to her high-rise flat she'd whip off her clothes, put on a *Speak German* LP and cooked in the nude. It made her husband happy. Once a window-cleaner got an eyeful.

My sister's school-friends were a mine of misinformation. While the Rolling Stones bleated *Can't Get No Satisfaction,* we lay entwined on Joanna's bed puffing Alpines. Margie's sister married Boomer, a doctor, so had old medical books about diseases. There were pictures of grotesque tongues and one of a chap whose manhood was so large he had to cart it around in a wheelbarrow. I'd never seen a naked man, except the statue of David, and shuddered at the thought of being landed with a husband and an over-large surprise.

One teen said she had a fling with a guy who was AC/DC. He lathered her with raspberry ripple ice cream and sensuously licked it. Would my new groom do the same, perhaps splatter me with blancmange or junket? What would Mum say if she saw my clothesline clogged with stained sheets? Could I keep his fetish a family secret? I was getting cold feet.

"Mum, we have to talk about my connubials. Do you think I have good taste in men? Do you like him?"

"Very nice. A bit brash, but Dad said he's solid and faithful, so don't expect perfection."

The Penfolds sherry was making me a bit cross-eyed, but it emboldened me to ask anyway.

"I know babies aren't your favourite subject, Ma, but he's the type to want them. Don't worry, we haven't done anything disgusting yet. But what if I fall once I'm married?"

"Put up with it, just like your poor father and me."

"We might have albinos. Same colour hair. You know, defects. I learned that in biology."

Dad said I had more brains than he'd given me credit for, but he was irritated he couldn't get reception on the transistor to hear the latest cricket score.

Mum said it was unlikely I'd breed cretins. The Scandinavians were nice looking types but they spent half their life in bed since it was so cold over there, and what about the Japs and Chinese? They all had black hair and weren't worried about breeding blackheads. And pity your poor father who's got no hair to speak of—so what else did I want to know?

I couldn't cook but Mum said if you burn something, just whisk off the black bits and smother it with cream. And I couldn't sew because Mum made me hate sewing.

"His Nibs is well-heeled," she said. "You'll never have to slave over a sewing machine on a slummy porch trying to make ends meet like me."

We gazed at the last drop twinkling in our plastic sherry goblets. My head was a kaleidoscope of glittering harbour lights, golden sunsets, Ave Maria, cherubs, Mr Darcy from *Pride and Prejudice*, boy sopranos and Liberace flicking back the coat-tails of his tuxedo as he sat down to play Tchaikovsky's *Piano Concerto No1 in B Flat Minor*.

"And he's very masculine and sporty, Ma, and you know I hate sport—except sun baking and riding in a sports car."

Mum said she understood. It was difficult living with a cricket fanatic who yelped with excitement when England scored an innings while neighbours were batting for the Australian side. Then Dad would be downing cups of tea while they clanked bottles of Tooheys.

"When in doubt do nowt," said Dad, and Mum offered more advice, "Don't marry a man you could live with. Marry a man you can't live without. He's a good catch but deserves a girl who adores and lives for him. Perhaps someone with a horsy face and fat legs."

"So why do you think he wants me?"

"Your hair," she said. "It's your best asset."

After we blew out the candles I hopped into the little camp bed in the kitchenette and my parents climbed into a double bed left by the owners.

"Thanks for the chat," I called into the dark. "Hope I'm not cramping your style!"

"You don't think we indulge in any of that nonsense, do you?" Mum said. "It's been a perfect day. I caught an octopus and a small white fish, probably poisonous, and haven't worried about Jasper's long hair and insalubrious friends."

Dad beat his chest, and roared, "Roll on death."

Chapter 22
London in the Swinging 60s

If girls didn't have a sparkler on their finger by the time they were twenty, there were other options—such as travel, or doing the big O.E (overseas experience.)

The lure of shipboard life and holiday package tours to the Continent encouraged youngsters to save their pennies, although on 14 February, 1966, decimal currency kicked in. Dollars and cents faded out pounds, shillings and pence. Parents looked forward to mail with foreign stamps from their gallivanting offspring and shared their news with anyone who'd listen. Neighbours muttered sourly that Australians should see their own country first. It was unpatriotic not to have explored every inch of Godzone.

I got discount fares working for World Travel Headquarters and booked a coach trip around Australia. The guy on the front desk said I'd need a gun and Mum suggested I go on a nice cruise to New Caledonia. But a love-boat full of randy females competing for uniformed crew, or being targeted by hairy-legged lads in jandals, intent on duty-free and opportunistic lays, felt emotionally exhausting.

But I hankered to see the harshness of the Outback, climb Ayers Rock, camp under the stars and boil a billy by a billabong. Australia's landscape of mulga scrub, shanty towns, glowing red sunsets, inebriated white guys roughing up their lubras (aboriginal women), corroborees, jackaroos, opal mining in Coober Pedy, and the mix of coach passengers made a memorable holiday. Two jillaroos said they arose at dawn, tucked into a plate of steak and eggs, then rode miles to their fencing jobs, in the nuddy, before the sun became unbearable.

As the bus rumbled through the desert, passengers burst into song to keep the driver awake. Australia was still a man's country for women were not allowed to drink at the bar, even in remote towns.

Dad said he had good and bad news. He'd told The Firm he had young daughters so when he renewed his five-year contract to return to England he couldn't leave us to flounder alone.

"Since your father has been a faithful worker, The Firm has broken all rules and given you girls a free passage to England. But not Jasper," said Mum. He was a male, over sixteen, and had obligations, such as the call up in Vietnam.

The American president LBJ—Lyndon Bain Johnson— arrived in Sydney on October 22, 1966, where half a million people lined the streets, many fluttering anti-war placards. Mothers marched along Pitt Street bearing banners. *Save our sons.* Others waved pro-American slogans. *Go all the way with LBJ.*

Jasper protested, "I'm not going to fight in a country I've never heard of and slaughter beautiful women and kids," and he surfed from dawn till dusk until his knees became so swollen he was declared medically unfit.

When we boarded the *Orsova* the following year, our cabins were crammed with neighbours, workmates, school friends and old boyfriends clutching flowers, chocolates and streamers to farewell us. Jasper stumbled up the gangplank in party mood with surfing mates and bottles of champagne. Joanna and I were bubbling with excitement. Mum said not to get too friendly with the stewards because they weren't our type.

As we rounded the Great Australian Bight she warmed to a Japanese passenger and tried to extract the secrets of her youthful skin over deck quoits. Dad warmed to those connected to The Firm who took us on port sightseeing trips, while Joanna ditched her school studies to ride lifts with bellboys and chat with boys in the band. I had a few Mardi Gras with Norm the refrigeration engineer in the Tavern, and ogled the Welsh bass player in a band before realising his sweet poetic outbursts were drug fuelled. Many passengers warmed to our family. Perhaps we looked ordinary for first class passengers?

Mum played scrabble with a dowager who lived permanently on-board. She had two cabins: one for sleeping and the other for her wardrobe. Another had racehorses in Europe, and there was elegant Mrs Weston of biscuit fame with five children and a sixth on the way.

A wealthy wrinkled mother and middle-aged daughter duo with dyed platinum blonde hair and broad New York accents thought Mum was a darling. They invited us to their lavish cocktail parties sprinkled with titled passengers. Mum smiled through a swish of diamonds, sequinned stoles, tuxedos and flounced frocks to glimpse me surrounded by handsome uniformed brutes. I lapped up their charm, knowing sailors had a girl in every port.

"Ma, it's not fair, those white stewards earn £50 a month and Goanese stewards only get £12."

Mum said that was probably good money for them and what was I doing talking to stewards?

Liftboys earned 15/3d a day and would lose a day's pay if they were too familiar with passengers. They became subservient if an officer entered the lift. Joanna was cheeky and outgoing, for she loved the English cockney accent. It reminded her of the Beatles. As the *Orsova* steamed out of Australian waters, Mum was slightly more relaxed about us going out at night when the ship berthed at exotic ports.

"Don't you girls spoil our trip by getting murdered." On 26 January, 1966, three Beaumont children had disappeared from an Adelaide beach. It still remains one of Australia's most famous cold cases. Peering anxiously from the boat deck, Mum couldn't tell if we were mingling with stewards dressed up to the nines in their paisley shirts, cravat, leather jacket and flared trousers, or officers out of uniform.

Travelling from Australia to England by ship took five weeks and every day was devoted to sheer indulgence, starting with a cabin steward serving a tray of tea and biscuits before the first or second breakfast sitting, and a newsletter of the day's events. Depending on the lurch of the sea and how jaded you felt, you rolled over until the poor cabin steward said there was a captain inspection and he had to make the beds.

Every night there was an event to look forward to such as a frog race, bingo, quiz nights, a casino or French Night where waiters dressed in a theme. On Ladies Night we lit cigarettes for men folk and had them fill out a dance card, giving us a chance to waltz in the arms of a hunk we admired but were too hesitant to speak to.

At Hawaiian Nights we teens were roped in to decorate the ballroom, waiters served roast pig and those wearing grass skirts twisted to a lively band until their outfits fell off. Mum wasn't pleased when Joanna nicked her salmon-pink corset and danced around with it on her head at the Mad Hatter's parade until she won a prize for *Corset's a hat*. Another donned a chamber pot and went as *Night Trots*.

Crossing the equator meant aquatic high jinks where a tubby seaman, dressed as King Neptune, threw people coated in ice cream and strawberry juice into the swimming pool. Waiters set up a smorgasbord on deck. Ships housed around 2000 passengers and crew, giving opportunity for smouldering romance and secret yearnings. If Mum didn't appear for dinner we knew she was seasick so we'd duck down to tourist class to join a livelier crowd.

When the ship berthed in Singapore and Colombo, a taxi driver and company car was at our disposal. Mum had Joanna hailed over a loudspeaker. She told her she was coming with us and not spending the day swimming with the bellboy.

"You girls are lowering the standard by smiling at stewards," she snapped. But she didn't mind me nipping down to the officer's quarters for cocktails and never asked what I did after that. I wasn't going to share my erogenous zones with those smug lads with upmarket accents.

After seeing snake charmers, dodging honking cars and scooters, tropical downpours, botanical gardens, mosques and palaces, we trod up the gangplank with duty-free hairdryers, transistors, binoculars, tape recorders, cameras and reels of film, typewriters and jewellery.

Trouble in the Middle East was worsening, and in Aden passengers were advised not to go ashore. While the ship steamed through the Suez Canal, Thos. Cook offered an overland excursion to view pyramids and sphinx, three-thousand-year old tombs, the perfume palace and a chance to ride camels, all of them named Moses. We arrived in Port Said late as Nasser had his troops out which delayed the ship. Soon after, the Suez Canal was blocked off and ships travelled through the Panama or around the horn of Africa.

Before departing, passengers leant over the ship's railings pointing to souvenirs and noisily haggling, with baskets on rope being hauled up and down. When Joanna fancied a toy camel the Egyptian seller bellowed he'd give it to her in return for her top. She whipped off her blue skinny-rib jumper and threw it down. "Dis not good, lady. What else you have?" and

Joanna rushed down to her cabin and grabbed a piece of used soap, laddered stockings and half a packet of cigarettes. When she hauled up an ashtray, she screamed, "Give me my camel, you..." The rest of her tirade was drowned out by the ship's blast. Off to Piraeus.

"I had a better time than you," she jeered as Mum, Dad and I staggered back with blistered feet from exploring the richness of Athens. The wharf was noisy with inebriated crew singing *Rule Britannia*. "So where did you go? Little fart-face (a deckhand) was looking for you. Gee, you have terrible taste in men, Jonquil. Did you buy me anything?"

In Cannes, Mum made Joanna tag along with us saying she'd see French horses at the changing of the guard at the Monte Carlo palace. In Marseille, Dad went off his head about late nights since we weren't appearing at breakfast and Joanna was becoming dreamily cross-eyed at the mention of a steward's name.

In Lisbon, Joanna took off with some passengers to see the riding school at Estoril. Mum and I marched behind Dad, clutching a guidebook, charmed by overhead washing fluttering from poles and twisted alleyways offering a taste of Portugal. We lost Dad somewhere between Lisbon and the train ride to the picturesque seaport of Cascais.

"Excuse me, but will you kill me if I speak with your daughter?" Mum swung around to see a swarthy young man trailing us.

"Mum, I did not give him the come on," I said. "I'm not a sex fiend."

The fleshy young Liberace-look-alike indicated his suit to imply he was respectable. We were upset over losing Dad, so we explained we'd lost a bald Englishman wearing spectacles and holding a map of Lisbon. Amazingly, Antonio found him and, since Dad spoke Spanish and our rescuer understood several languages, we drank Portuguese port and beer to celebrate.

We took the train back to the *Orsova*, with bags of gorgeous Portuguese shoes, and the oily youth with luscious eyelashes who had an affinity for blondes.

"I knew your hair would come in useful," Mum said.

Antonio begged me to write and we shyly shook hands goodbye. Dad actually shoved me into his arms. "Say goodbye properly," he ordered as a commuter train puffed towards us. I had seconds to indulge in fervent Mediterranean lips that smelt of intrigue, garlic, and a sensuousness lacking in surfie boys back home.

On arrival in the Mother Country, most anxious parents worried over how their youngster would cope. They wrote letters to distant relatives in England, asking them to keep an eye on young Carol, Barry or Johnny.

That was the last thing Aussies wanted.

It was the Swinging Sixties and, apart from gawking at the Tower of London and cheekily coaxing a smile from Beefeaters outside the palace, youths were keen to pub crawl, see Carnaby Street and soak up the psychedelic atmosphere. After a couple of nights at a hotel or youth hostel, many Aussies gravitated to Earl's Court, known as Kangaroo Valley, for cheap accommodation and to hear a comforting Australian accent.

Jobs were plentiful and resourceful Australians were in demand since they had a good work ethic. Cheerful nurses were paid well working night shifts for the titled gentry. One randy nonagenarian lord made a miraculous recovery, arising from his bed like Lazarus, chasing a Kiwi nurse around the bed with his walking stick. There was temp typing for girls with secretarial skills, au-pairing, cleaning hotels, even waitressing at the trendy Tiddy Dolls restaurant.

In London, for a whole month we were guests of an extremely wealthy man who was grateful to Mum for housing his teenage son when he was doing his Australian O.E. Charles was respectful, polite and obviously well educated, but we had no inkling of his dad's fortune. Once he let slip his father had a large room devoted to his ties but we said Yeah, yeah. Pull the other one. Dad enjoyed chatting about England and Mum said she'd like Charles for a son, and what a pity Jasper was a poor influence taking him to keg parties with a bunch of louts. Later Charles said living with our family was one of his fondest memories and wished he had normal parents like ours.

"So, your father owns some apartments in Kensington?" I asked, nibbling snails for dinner at a posh hotel while Mum and Dad quaffed champagne and a Fortnum and Mason meal with Charles' dad and his bank manager.

Charles shook his head. "No, he owns the whole block, and a few other properties as well."

London was wildly exciting once Mum's blood pressure settled after blowing us up for taking a train to Southampton to wave our favourite crew off. If we weren't being generously feted by Charles' family, there were shows like *Hello Dolly, Danny la Rue, Desert Song,* the soap box speeches at Hyde Park, endless shopping, and young passengers from the ship to meet for connection and drinks.

Girls in mod clothes screamed excitedly over the Monkees in a nearby hotel, the movie *Ulysses* was gender segregated and cost a pound, barristers in top hats inhaled snuff at fashionable pubs along the Thames, and it was considered racist not to embrace lonely Malaysian or black students for a one night stand.

Vegetarian hippies in long frocks handed out flowers in Piccadilly. Fashion shops were converting to midi-jean skirts and long boots. The model, Twiggy, sent mixed messages; the thin were in reprieve, some chubby folk became anorexic, and the rest of us relied on boyfriends to remind us we were hot chicks.

While our parents toured, Joanna au-paired for a Jewish family. I worked for a travel company and found an Australian girl to share flatting costs. It was a confusing thrilling lonely city, pulsating with chance. In the bustling crowd along Bond or Regent Street a voice whispered in my head You're never more alone than when alone in a crowd. Overseas was okay but nothing beats returning to your mum's fatty roast, freckled siblings clamouring for a souvenir of the Queen stamped on a mug. And a sunburnt fiancé hoping you had got travel out of your system.

Some girls said loneliness was the reason they accidentally got knocked up. Then they had the terror of abandonment in a foreign country and trauma about their parent's reaction when they returned home cradling a real-life souvenir with a hint of Pakistani or African blood.

So while pubbing, late nights and dinner parties with guys was fun the noise caused a fuss with the housekeeper. I didn't want those inebriated lads, mostly Australian, camping overnight in our room. I was called frigid, Victorian, a prude, and told I looked like a woman but didn't act like one.

Since London was so liberal and impersonal, some Australians became uninhibited to prove there was no false sense of shame in toying with drugs and sexual activity. Asked if I was the sort of person who looks out of a window or up at a window, I didn't know what to say. I hated the emotional blackmail and became miserable.

When our parents boarded the *Adelaide Star* in a Jaguar they bought for £400 they were reluctant to leave us behind. Mum became anxious.

"There are plenty of nice men and horses in New Zealand, you know," she said.

Once their ship sailed life became more riotous, the flatmate bitchier, the housekeeper angrier, and Joanna gaunt. I felt anxious, pressured and hung-over at times, but not willing to cave in to Aussie lads craving canoodles and a familiar accent. While thinking some men were pitiful creeps for making me feel abnormal, I was more disappointed in Aussie girls who flung open their legs and ended up at our bed-sit weeping into cheap plonk about how used they felt.

I knew it would end in misery for the tarts who said I was brainless and inhibited. I hated confrontation.

Hitchhiking with cousin Pops to her parent's thatched roof cottage in Colchester on her weekends off from nursing saved me from utter depression. My stooped aunt was as kindly and welcoming as her older childless sister a bicycle-ride away.

"Hello, Popsy, darling," gushed aunt Ollie at the front door of her two-up two-down semi-detached, puffing on a Woodbine and adjusting wrinkled stockings on her skinny legs. "Is that your little Greek friend?"

On hearing my name, Ollie let out a rapturous shriek and embraced me so hard my bosoms swung around my back.

Since London was a city of excess and razzamatazz, Wimpy Bars and Lyons tea houses, regal taxi cabs and red double-decker buses, the aunts worried we'd fall victim to depravity—perhaps a homeless man lurking from the shadows of below-pavement bed-sits—or worse, we weren't eating properly.

They filled our arms with strawberries from the garden and pressed the odd pound note in our hands.

Andrew, in a nearby flat, whose mother was a concert pianist and father an art dealer, restored my faith in men. He was a gentle impecunious English student. It cost five shillings to stand at the Proms and nothing to admire his dad's collection of Fragonards. Pity he was recovering from some unworthy girl.

We hitched to the Isle of Wight, an island of boarding houses, fortune-tellers and weird people dancing with animals in a music hall, and joined an 8-day camping trip to the Munich Beer Festival for £16. We danced on tables, clutching beer steins. A German brass band in national costume played boisterously, and plump Fraulein in dirndls sprinkled sawdust on any projectile vomiting.

I was surprised when some German lads apologised for Hitler, their sorrow and shame raw and deep. Several coach companies around Earls Court offered cheap package tours and, plied with gallons of red wine and cheese, it was hard to resist them. Some tour leaders stumbled up to our bed-sit and one blubbered he missed Australia. When Dad said his firm would pay for our return fares, it was a happy reprieve. After selling crockery and eating off pot lids, my flatmate flew home. I had a final fling on a 28-day tour of Spain and Portugal with young Aussie and Kiwi girls.

I screamed the first night in a pensione; a girl with a wide Julia Roberts' smile, a curvaceous figure and a desire for the handsome coach driver had left her prosthetic arm on a bed. Most girls were pleasant and conservative, like the one with a glass eye, the alopecia girl, the one with a gammy leg from polio, the one born without kneecaps, the one who had noisy coughing fits and flung herself upside-down doing postural drainage, and the one with a sweet face but ankles as fat as her knees. The oldest guy on the trip was a postal worker who chased me down a hotel corridor clawing at my clothes. The tour driver said he'd fix the problem and took him to a brothel. The next day the creep sneered in my face. He'd met a real woman—she was like a rattlesnake.

At night, Spanish girls were safely locked up while their Antonios, Manuels and Pedros roamed the streets or gathered in bars. That trip was a magical blur of sangria, serenading matadors and students strumming guitars. I arrived back in London with a flamenco guitar I couldn't play and a book bursting with addresses. I was exhausted but happy.

It was time to catch a ship home.

Chapter 23
Domestic Bliss - *Not!*

Joanna and I travelled back to Australia tourist class on the *Oriana* and treated the voyage as our last gasp of unbridled freedom. It was nearing Christmas and the ship was full of youngsters returning home from their O.E. We were mismatched in a four-berth cabin with two elderly women.

"You naughty girls, going to bed so late," they chided when we climbed into the top bunks as dawn broke.

Nightly, we sang long after the bar closed to *Where Have all the Flowers Gone* and *King of the Road*. Joanna flirted with the band and I flirted with everyone else.

When the ship docked in Sydney and we heard Mum's voice demanding the steward unlock our cabin door, we frantically tried to clear up evidence of a party.

"I know my daughters are in there," she cried.

It was not the welcome she, Dad nor a trail of friends expected—empty beer bottles and a startled older Maori passenger clutching her pallid teenage musician lover, hiding in our wardrobe. If we were popular with everyone else, we weren't at home.

"We've had a big year," I justified. "We need time to adjust to reality. Gee, don't you want us to have fun?"

In the excitement of going feral—a tornado hitting our suburb and the tragedy of Prime Minister Harold Holt's drowning at Cheviot Beach—Mum agreed to us inviting a few people from the ship for a party. Expecting there'd be a sprinkling of officers, she made delicate ham sandwiches, sausage rolls and provided Coca-Cola.

Mum was appalled when half the cabin crew turned up with duty-free ciggies, cartons of beer and bottles in paper bags.

"They've got funny accents. This'll kill your father."

Dosed on gin, Dad went to bed while Mum knocked on the door every hour on the hour, calling, "Isn't it time your guests left?" and Dad bawled, "Tell those bastards to go home."

At dinner the next day, fuelled by a sleepless night and a bad day at the office, he decided to give us a talk about the birds and the bees. He thumped on the table over a bottle of hock shouting he didn't send his daughters to private schools to have them running around with riff-raff. A true gentleman, he said, speaks the Queen's English and mates quietly in the dark.

Joanna barely stifled her giggles.

"Gee, you're rude, Dad."

Mum cried, "What sort of talk is that to give to our vulnerable girls? Shut your trap and eat your dinner." Afterwards she said, "Never marry a short man. They say odd things."

Apparently other fathers were embarrassing, too. One said her boozed-up dad staggered home from the RSL, became confused and piddled in the budgie cage.

Dad became irritated translating letters from Spain. "Who are these sewers writing this filth to you?" He squinted at flowery handwriting ending with *Receive a firm embrace, Dear One. I like you very mush,* (sic) or *You are my life's girl, greetings to your family*.

I was vague who was who for I'd met so many Antonios.

When fragments of black fuzz tumbled out of an envelope bearing Spanish stamps, Mum nearly fainted. "How did this get past customs?" she screeched.

"It's not botty hair, Ma. Jeepers creepers, you're suspicious. Not my fault they like me. I did not go around Spain rooting people. In fact, you should be proud of us. I bet Joanna and I are the only virgins left on Pittwater Road."

"Let's polish the silver. We're having nice people for dinner tonight," Mum said.

For Christmas that year I gave Dad a book called *How to Stop Worrying and Start Living* and Mum gave me a Cliff Richard record in Spanish because she sympathised with my tearful attempts poring over a *Spanish Made Easy* manual. She refused to let me join a Spanish, Greek or Italian club because I'd meet a poorer type.

Only the desperate leave Italy she said; she'd put up with discomfort to be able to paint lakes, eat scampi and chat with charming Italians who had lovely manners, like kissing your hand on greeting. I had visions of fat garrulous mamas in black, boiling pasta and chiding chubby offspring, toothless revered grannies with chin hair, barking out orders, while paunchy husbands quaffed wine and played cards with male relatives.

I didn't think that sort of life suited me. Maybe Mum was right.

When Joanna and I chatted to a French guy, who reeked of garlic, and invited him home, Mum was upset. "We thought you liked Continental people," we muttered.

So he didn't remind her of Pierre Cardin or Yves St Laurent. He was suspiciously lower class French. And she promptly drove him home to his lodgings out in the wop-wops, a suburb we'd never visited. We marvelled at Mum's sniffer-dog intelligence. She wanted us to associate with boys who met her standards.

If a guy thought your mother didn't consider him a gentleman, it was the ultimate insult.

"Crikey dick! What's with your old lady? Is she up herself or what?"

"Are you a snob, Mum?"

"Just a little, darling. And proud to be so."

Although they loved their teenage daughters, some fathers were emotionally remote while mothers were supportive, protective and critical. Men expected to be head of the household, and challenging their authority made trouble for mothers who were caught in domestic conflict between their weary spouse returning home from his important day at the office and confrontational teenagers. Americanism and rock 'n' roll upset the status quo. Mothers had to be peacemakers to smooth friction.

Nancy Sinatra's *These Boots Are Made for Walking* was a funky liberating hit warning guys that modern-day girls were unwilling to kowtow. Lesbian thoughts were a secret shame. Similarly, it was tragic for gay men who feared having electric shock treatment to make them normal, or who had unhappy unfulfilled marriages to please their parents and society.

In 1958, Liberace was involved in mendacious litigation with the British newspaper *The Daily Mirror*. Veteran columnist, Cassandra wrote the visiting pianist was the deadly, winking, sniggering, snuggling, fruit-flavoured, sentimental vomit of all time.

Fruit implied he was gay. But admitting homosexuality would have ended his career. For a flamboyant musician, who'd dedicated his life to entertaining and inspiring millions, he had to lie under oath saying he was against the practice because it offended convention and society. Women adored him, hoping unrealistically he'd notice them in an audience and relieve them of a boring husband. Gay entertainers at Kings Cross were tolerated because it was glittery showbiz and saucy fun.

Life at home was lively.

If Mum heard a Cockney voice asking for us she suspected the *Oriana* had berthed in Sydney and promptly banged down the phone. She worried we were attracted to funny types of people.

When Jasper rang to say he'd been in a car crash, Dad said Jesus Wept, but Mum corrected him. No, Jasper had wept. He'd swerved to avoid a child and hit a post. The car skidded and, as he fell out of the door, the vehicle passed over Jasper's head and ribs. He was in hospital with a swollen face, stitches to his nose, fractured ribs and tyre marks over his abdomen.

Days earlier he'd become a dad to a baby boy. Mum thought he was too irresponsible and the girlfriend far too young to cope, but when she visited the fretting young mother and cradled her grandson who looked like a mini-Jasper, there was no more talk of adoption. She bought clothes and blankets for the baby and, when Jasper came for dinner, ebullient as usual, bearing a celebratory bottle of sparkling wine, Mum laid out the silver cutlery, cut roses, lit candles and cooked his favourite meal.

Women were receptive to husband's moods.

Dad wanted peace and quiet when he got home from the office and, if Mum had any big news, she'd wait until he'd changed out of his office clothes and sat in the special armchair with a snifter (sherry) and his pipe and tobacco at arm's reach. She handed him the mail but hid the bills until he began puffing rings into the air listening to his favourite music—*My Fair Lady* or *Scotland the Brave*. The sound of bagpipes made him crazily cheerful. He'd rip up the volume of the bagpipes, leaving open-mouthed guests clutching drinks and blinking uncertainly. Unless it was New Year's Eve, it was a cue he wanted to go to bed and he didn't care how rich or famous they were.

Mum was a great hostess and people were reluctant to leave. If they didn't take the hint, Dad rattled the Austrian cowbell and shouted, "You bastards, haven't you got a home to go to?" Mum smilingly gathered up armfuls of fur coats and handbags and received pecks on the cheek from jovial men and their wives smelling of Tweed hand lotion.

No one was offended by Dad's outburst.

They thought he was quaint and amusing for they sent notes or flowers thanking Mum for her delightful party. If they rang, she got an earful of who tumbled down the garden path and who ended up in the wrong car.

When the Scottish travel writer, Elaine Cunliffe, came for dinner, she was greeted at the door with a room full of laughing folk sipping out of Mum's red Venetian glass goblets. They were all connected to The Firm, part of the Lord Vestey empire.

In her book *The Wandering Moon* she described Dad as *eyes gleaming naughtily behind round spectacles, hair so scanty that he seemed bald, who airily waved his hand introducing her to expatriates, intelligent enough to adjust themselves to Australia!* She wrote furiously in her notebook describing our elegant lounge-room and the meal. *Fish, served with the usual additions, reclining on green, fish-shaped plates, followed by steak and delicious succulents served by the pretty daughters of the house and their friends. From the basement came the ghostly strains of organ music.* She was referring to a church organ we'd bought at auction and hauled under the house; the organ needed warming up using foot pedals.

Joanna and I entertained our friends playing *A Whiter Shade of Pale, Yellow Mellow, Love is Blue* and other current hits by candlelight until Dad rigged up an electrical cord. If Mum didn't hear the organ wheezing, she nipped down the steep path lined with blue agapanthus, striking matches or flicking a torch into that black earthy cavity to make sure our lips weren't cemented onto someone of the opposite sex.

Mum's parties were often more fun than our teenage ones for the food was better, everyone laughed heartily and we weren't trapped in dark rooms with boys groping us. Or pretending to be happy if someone nicked our boyfriend crying, "All's fair in love and war." Lesley Gore's *It's My Party and I'll Cry if I Want To* was often too close to home.

Like many women, Mum gleaned recipes from the *Australian Women's Weekly* bought with her housekeeping money because she wanted to win Crozzle, a crossword puzzle where competitors juggled words to reap the biggest scores for a huge cash prize. When Mum shared a main prize with several other winners, a schoolgirl from Tonga wrote to Mum requesting to be her penfriend. I imagined it was so hot in her part of the world students went to school near naked.

When the schoolgirl sent a photo of herself more clad than most Aussies, and a parcel of shells damaged by customs, Mum thought we didn't need to send her blankets or my cast-off clothes. She looked black, smiling and happy. She was an island girl and I was a city girl. Perhaps she was more content than me; she had so little and I had so much. Her letters were humble, Christian-flavoured, and she made me think about what I wanted in life.

I'd had several proposals and at the end of the night rewarded rich boys who dined and wined me with reluctant tongue-kissing in their MGs, Mustangs or Pontiacs, but worried about germs and getting strep throat. I acted like a precious princess but, like many guys of the 60s, they behaved gallantly having met parents like mine.

Dad shook hands and chatted about cricket. Mum proffered a nip of sherry and nibbles. We then slipped out into the velvety night, my hair a twirl of heavily lacquered ringlets from Marilyn's Hairdressing Salon and my Thai silk gown shimmering, newly made by Mum who'd pored over patterns at David Jones. I hoped an outrageous kindred soul might whisk me out of middle-class suburbia. Liberace didn't know I existed, apart from sending a couple of signed photos from Hollywood.

But still, when Mum and I watched late night wartime romantic movies on TV, we ended up wiping our eyes for different reasons. She was having flashbacks about old naval beaus who reminded her of handsome Hollywood stars like Charles Boyer, Gregory Peck and Cary Grant and the joy of life BC (before children.) I was churned up by familiar stirring music Liberace played on his TV shows. Once I confessed to

Mum I'd never find a guy as decent as Libby and she wasn't dismissive saying I was a dreamer or silly.

"What's wrong with me, Ma? I don't want to marry just anyone because they want me, but I don't want to be left on the shelf."

"Bide your time, darling. You were born in the wrong century," she added unhelpfully.

She said if I couldn't find anyone suitable in Australia, she had friends in New Zealand who had sons. I felt safe, loved and glad she was interested in my happiness. Dad on the other hand thought I was too fussy. When I said hotly, "You just want Mum all to yourself," he threw his hands up in the air.

"What have I done, Dot?"

And Mum sorted us both out. She always did.

Jasper was evasive about settling down and said he'd marry his girlfriend once she proved herself, and what was wrong with the baby's name? Clynton, Dad sneered, wasn't that a vulgar cowboy name? Mum suggested he choose something nicer, like James. My brother remained a continual source of angst and discussions. Dad said if only he stopped louting on his surfboard and got a proper job he could be a decent chap.

Mum said he was a law unto himself when she lost money on shares he 100% recommended. Jasper had a keen mind and worked at surfboard factories, trading cars and shouting his mates at pubs. He even enlisted on a yacht sailing the world with a wealthy American serial monogamist until trouble aboard curtailed the adventures.

Australia's unpopular commitment in Vietnam, becoming a dad before he was legally an adult, and being tamed by staid conventions was not what Jasper had planned. Australia provided all he wanted; golden sands, challenging curling surfs, mates who thought he was king, and the energy of being in the now. While his mates remained loyal and keen surfers, most married young and were constrained by a mortgage and the little woman restricting their freedom. Some felt Jasper epitomised how life should be lived.

Mum began a Thai silk business from home and revelled in parcels of gorgeous material from Thailand. Claudette, a French woman she hired because she was pushy with a fascinating accent, was her help when orders started rolling in.

Flamboyant men from trendy boutiques loved Mum and called her dahling. One even had a pet kangaroo called Nefertiti.

"I'm going to raid that thieving woman's wardrobe," Mum cried when Hildegarde reneged on paying for a large order; her company had gone bankrupt. Seething and upset, Mum drove to the woman's mansion at Point Piper only to be confronted by guard dogs and a foreign maid behind tall iron gates; her mistress had left the country.

Mum bought Dad an Afghan hound for his birthday thinking perhaps I'd meet a nice man by exercising the dog. She got that idea from a movie.

But Yasha was an embarrassment. In the park, she was a hindrance to any chance love encounter. She yapped at other dogs and frequently squatted. Mum said she was retarded and needed a psychiatrist. The dog, a cowering nervous wreck, randomly piddled in the vacuum cleaner cupboard and on our bedspreads. The vet said she didn't have a bladder problem. He suspected she'd been an abused puppy. Mum returned her, demanding a refund.

In 1968, the world was more chaotic because US troops massacred civilians in Vietnam, which encouraged more longhaired youths to become conscientious objectors. Martin Luther King and Robert Kennedy were assassinated, Jackie Kennedy married Onassis, John Gorton became prime minister to Australia's population of twelve million, St Vincent's Hospital performed the first heart transplant and Tony Hancock committed suicide.

We saw *2001: A Space Odyssey, Planet of the Apes, Chitty Chitty Bang Bang, The Odd Couple, The Graduate,* and sang along to *Hey Jude* (Beatles), the Bee Gees, *If I Only Had Time* (John Rowles), *Cinderella Rockerfella, Yummy Yummy Yummy* and *Tiptoe Through the Tulips.* Australia's first quintuplets were born a year earlier. TV shows included *Star Trek, The Saint, Dr Who, Hawaii Five-0, Four Corners* and *The Andy Griffith's Show.*

Bushfires broke out at the beginning of summer, and in November people lost homes in the Blue Mountains while Ku-ring-gai Chase, Penrith and St Ives burned, sending a pall of frightening yellow haze blanketing Sydney. Daughters complained about weight gain when some mothers put them on the pill while others resorted to Tenuate, an appetite suppressor.

Jasper took advantage of a petrol strike in July that year by driving to Lismore in Big Henry (his Ford) while Jimmy Hendrix and Otis Redding tapes thumped in the cab. He purchased 150 gallons, which he sold for twice the price, but gave a discount to the guy who lent him a trailer and drums.

I worked on the 28th floor (of 50 levels) of the newly constructed Australia Square tower. Initially, I was flummoxed by a very boring question posed by the Industrial Relations Manager at Alcan Aluminium. I'd been singled out from a large typing pool as someone who might have a few brains, which surprised everyone, including myself.

So how did I feel about trade unions and being a Girl Friday? That involved toting up figures with lots of clerical work. The thought made me go cross-eyed. I was still dealing with *Oriana* flashbacks—locking lips with a British racing driver in the cavernous ironing room while the ship's engine hummed, ploughing through choppy waters around Africa, and the night watchman flashing his torch along the corridors.

How could a man, so old at thirty, have lips so tender when he roared around a racetrack for a living?

"Sounds fascinating," I said, jolting out of my reverie and smoothing down my hot pants. Lying little toad, Jonquil, cried my brain. You're here for all the man-action around this busy office, and aren't trade unionists commie-bastards? And the only maths you enjoy are adding and subtracting guys you like or ditch!

The girls in the typing pool yapped about fiancés or studied childbirth books. The sketches were vague from the foetus somersaulting down a swollen belly to nipple squiggles, while men were portrayed as benign eunuchs, their winkies, diddle-pops or dickie-di-dies considered salacious belonging to doctor's text books. We didn't say the 'p' word. Too crude.

Men bought the *Australian Pix* for its busty cover girls, scandals and jokes. We got them from rubbish bins at the beach. It was more daring in the late 60s with Australia undergoing massive cultural and political changes. We chuckled over risqué cartoons like the one of a rough-looking couple sitting on a beach gazing out to sea with an oil tanker on the horizon. The guy has his arm draped around his girl, saying, "How about a little on-shore drilling?"

Joanna got a job at David Jones training as a buyer. She spent the whole year in the shoe department sniffing deformed feet, infatuated with the Display boy. Their eyes met but they never talked. She just became thinner.

"He touched me in the lift," she squealed excitedly.

"He touched you in the where?" boomed Mum's voice from the kitchen.

Similarly, I was going through a one-sided trauma.

As sisters we travelled to work in the city, on the same ferry, reading Dorothy Dix, an agony aunt who answered questions in a magazine. It was mostly teens wanting advice on attracting a man without looking too bold. A friend solved her dilemma by sidling up to a hunk at a party and blurting, "Jeez, aren't ya husky!"

One correspondent wrote, "My husband and I are both sterile. Will this affect our children?"

I fancied a young man on the ferry, but classy girls didn't make the first move. It was seen as desperate and cheapened you. Men lost interest if you were too available for they were the hunters and they decide whom they want for their life partner. Every morning I hoped Mr Gorgeous would sit next to me, strike up a conversation and tell me he wasn't married. Joanna thought he had a whiff of Italian about him for we agreed he was foreign-English. She could be my best friend or worst enemy.

When he sat next to me one balmy morning as the ferry nodded towards The Coathanger (Sydney Harbour Bridge), I began hyperventilating, until Joanna said, "Jonquil! Stop extending your nostrils! You're making them go sticky-outy!"

I was mortified.

"It's the ferry ride. It reminds me of gondolas. Don't you adore Italy?"

And I glanced sideways to see if there was any guy-reaction.

Joanna stared at me in lofty silence, yawned deeply.

"Have you got a mirror?"

I scrambled in my tiny handbag.

She said, "Have a geek at your teeth. You've got orange bits in them."

I nearly howled. Now he'd think I had nostril and teeth problems and would be a liability. And for the next few days I sat in another part of the ferry. I wanted to clobber my sister.

Mum said in her day young ladies dropped a lace-edged handkerchief, which gave the guy and the girl a chance to connect. Possibly by the late 60s guys were wary of touching delicate nose rags after Asian flu hit Australia and paper tissues gained popularity.

When I alighted from the ferry late one December afternoon after work in 1968, Mum said she'd been to the travel agency. She thrust a brochure in my hand.

"I'd love to do it, but your father wouldn't agree. The agent did this trip ten years ago and raves about it. Interested?"

Chapter 24
Doing the Hippie Trail

"Mum! This is the adventure I've dreamed about!"

The brochure read Grand Indiaman 1969–An expedition for the modern day Marco Polo following the age-old caravan routes through India, Afghanistan and the Middle East to Europe. It stressed expedition rather than tour, taking us across mountains, deserts and into the remotest parts of some primitive countries where hotels ranged from pretty good to putrid.

The 103-day trip included travelling on the *Oriana* from Sydney to Hong Kong, flying Cathay Pacific Convair 880 Jet to Bangkok then to Calcutta to link with the Indiaman coach.

Mum said, "I'd love to come with you and see all those temples and people dressed in funny clothes. But I can't leave your father. Go while you're free and haven't got any blasted children to tie you down."

I handed in my notice at work causing a mild uproar in the typing pool. A typist with bouffant hair said she knew someone who'd done a trip across Asia. It was terrible, really rugged, and everyone got sick. And what about that Aussie who sold his blood when he ran out of money in Turkey? Thugs drained him and flung his body in an alleyway.

But my mind was made up. I wanted to do the classic hippie trail, travelling by coach from India to London. It was affordable at $A738.00 despite earning only $40 a week. While typists spent their pay on their back hoping to attract a man, I was never going to be indebted to anyone. I squirreled my savings.

Sometimes I had bursts of generosity and hoped God smiled when I flung coins into hats of homeless old men clutching bottles of meths. Mum didn't smile when a migrant Swiss girl I met on a ship rang periodically for a loan. I felt sorry for her so far from home and pregnant.

"I can't help being hot," she said, making me wonder if foreigners had an extra steamy gene while we Aussies were sexually retarded. She promised to pay me back but never did.

"That low-quality girl speaks good English. She's lazy and using you. If you give her any more money, I'll kick you out of this house."

When the hot chick rang next time I told her I couldn't help any more. She wasn't upset. My relief was enormous. And Mum said, "You have to be cruel to be kind."

Europe on $5 a Day was a popular read for those intending to travel abroad. When the Beatles visited India in 1968 to a blaze of publicity, many youngsters felt the urge to explore the mystic East travelling by mini-buses, vans, clapped out cars and motorbikes. Some hitchhiked, sporting long flowing Jesus-locks, sandals and Indian garb, seeking enlightenment, adventure and/or dope.

Hippies were labelled pot-smoking smelly layabouts who wanted to save the world. The hippie parties I attended in Sydney were students who lined their flats with newspapers, lit candles, ate lettuce and lentils, and sat, yogi-styled, sharing a joint. Pictures of Indian gurus with beaky noses glared from their walls, and the latest Beatle LP thumped in the background.

I thought them boring for I was happy, optimistic and didn't care about the after-life. I cared about now. Jasper married once our parents flew off to New Zealand to buy land. Joanna followed them shortly after.

"Come for a lonely," begged a Chinese boy on the *Oriana* after we won the ping-pong tournament sailing towards Hong Kong. "We go to my cabin and drink beer."

I declined, but wondered if oriental boys had yellow peckers. Away from home, raucous beer-drinking Aussies partied hard. When a couple were caught doing the mattress-mumbo in a life raft among tinned food provisions, the girl justified it. She wanted to have a quick bonk before we hit the desert coz after that it's abstinence all the way.

The real adventure began in Calcutta where 120 passengers gathered in the lounge of the colonial Great Eastern Hotel to meet the drivers of four tough German Setras.

Someone said, "Try and get on Nick's coach. He's tops," so I scribbled down Coach No. 4.

Whirring fans kept thick steamy air circulating. Turbaned staff, dressed in off-white pantaloons, crouched among pot plants. After lively talk, ranging from the trots to being dragged out of sleeping bags, and itinerary change because of trouble in the Middle East, we split into groups to meet our individual drivers. They had several years' overland experience behind them. A couple of trainee lads would travel a few hours ahead to attend to passports, visas, change money and fix up hotel accommodation when not camping.

We eyed each other suspiciously. Could we stand the next three months together?

Suddenly there was a violent explosion followed by several sharp bangs, blood-curdling yells and scuffling. A waiter in a red cummerbund calmly reported a bomb had exploded in the courtyard; two people had been shot so he advised us to stay indoors.

The next evening a middle-aged Indian grabbed me in the flimsy lift, plying wet generous kisses on my neck. When I kicked him in the shins he gave chase down the long corridor. I frantically fumbled for the door lock aware of screams and sobbing emanating from a couple of rooms. The brochure was right. This was going to be an expedition.

Calcutta was a culture shock with its clawing heat, pot-bellied children with siblings strapped to their back, deformed beggars, betel-spitting men with gouged-out eyes, the limbless and the homeless. Women in saris bathed their toddlers under fire hydrants and emaciated cows ambled among rusted trucks, bicycles, rickshaws, ox-carts, peddlers, honking horns and meditating holy men. In spacious parks families flew kites as vultures soared overhead.

Our drivers told us to stock up for the Great Sand Desert and possible breakdowns. While we were haggling over corned beef, baked beans, nuts, lentils and dried fruit at markets, flies buzzed around blood-dripping carcasses. Rice was rationed and expensive.

When the first two coaches lumbered out of Calcutta, someone cried, "Hey! We've found a beaut hotel, the Fairlawn. It's cheaper, only 30 rupees including meals."

Run by a woman with extremely pointed shoes, a shiny frock, a shock of black beehive hair and Armenian connections, the colonial villa draped with bougainvillea, offered a serene refuge away from the vibrant crazy colourful city just metres outside the gates. It had a Somerset Maugham touch with its large shared rooms, army style cots and guests reclining in cane furniture reading outdated magazines and sipping beer at 6.50 rupees (about a dollar a bottle.)

Some Indiaman passengers stayed put at the Great Eastern while others dossed down in the Salvation Army fleapit. Half the passengers, including me, got food poisoning, were feverish and fell into deep sleep.

I heard a distinct New Zealand voice say, "Found the pills in my hen-beg," and blearily spied two pink balloons bobbing in mid-air. Still slightly delirious, I watched the balloons descend swathed in nylon froth. It was the rump of a cheerful Kiwi nurse in frothy baby doll pyjamas!

Trish, from Christchurch, was affectionately called Sister Trash for she hauled around a large dilly bag of notebooks, films, biros, face cream, bandages, toilet rolls, hair rollers, medicines and dysentery pills.

On this trip she probed prickles from passengers' feet after bush stops, and helped bloodied victims propped against wrecked overturned buses in godforsaken places. A good Catholic, she was keen to find a church, and risked the balmy sweet-scented black night where people camped on footpaths. And sounds of noisy brawls emitted from side streets.

"The Pope will understand if you don't go to Mass. It's dangerous," we warned, but she donned a scarf and later returned, intact.

"Let's be having youse," cried a Yorkshire accent. It was Nick, our driver, and thirty of us scrambled aboard. Goodbye Calcutta, hello world!

As the coach rattled over potholed roads, past tumbledown villages, in stupefying heat, Nick called over the microphone system. In remoter areas in India and Pakistan we camped at dak bungalows. These are government rest homes where you can sleep on the verandah and use the facilities inside. It's free but customary to tip, say a rupee, to the little man in charge. For a small sum he'd do his best to rustle up a breakfast or you could cook your own on the burners.

Our first night in Bahri we arrived in gathering darkness at a small outpost with a single hole-in-the-floor toilet and tap. Women first. Miserable with dysentery, one woman charged in on the boys' time, shouting, "Sorry, fellas, can't wait," and rushed for a squat.

We lost all sense of modesty.

Pushy passengers grabbed a gas ring while others fumbled with canvas stretchers and wrote up diaries. We slept under the stars, mainly Kiwis and Aussies, with a sprinkling of other nationalities from diverse backgrounds.

Nick said the Holi Day, Festival of Colours often got out of hand. All day long our coach was pelted with mud, stones and paint, with youths lying in wait behind bushes and bridges, hurtling rocks and chunks of clay or piling stones onto the dusty highway.

A stone smashed against the windowpane spraying me with shards of glass, but the ever-resourceful New Zealand nurse, Trish, ordered me to strip, rummaging in her dilly bag for tweezers and talcum powder.

There was even more excitement when Nick ran over a goat; angry villagers mobbed the coach, hammering and pounding on the sides, bawling baksheesh. As the crowd swelled, it became terrifying. Nick pointed to the shattered window, protesting it was caused by their hooliganism, and thought the goat had been purposely kicked into the middle of the road. After a payment of ten rupees the hysterical mob were appeased and waved us off to a chorus of Bye bye, come back again!

At Tilaiya Dam, we flung ourselves, and dirty washing, into the water. Across the field women patted cow dung cakes against the sides of their mud and straw dwellings. We were guests at a boys' boarding school so prosperous Sikh dads and mum swathed in embroidered saris and jewellery were evicted from front row seats as their youngsters put on a concert.

At midnight, we sat around our campfire chatting to Nick over steaming cups of tea.

"On every trip there's at least one silly girl who ends up getting raped," he said. "It's asking for trouble wearing miniskirts and accepting invites from locals."

He cast his eyes approvingly over my long flannelette nightie. Beneath a starry night we climbed into sleeping bags while sounds of a dogfight filled the night. Tenting would come later.

At the Nepalese border, villagers gathered to stroke or pinch us as our passports were scrutinised, upside down. At the hotel in Birganj we shared a squat toilet and a tap that kept petering out. The four drivers greeted each other and knocked back tots of rum while the agile climbed the fire escape and slept on the flat hotel roof.

To tackle zig-zagging ranges to Kathmandu, we used embellished buses called public carriers. They took us to where farmhouses, three-storeys high, clung giddily to scalloped hillsides and men in baggy pants, coats and jaunty printed caps tilled the soil. Six of us, wedged between the driver and his grinding gear stick, all terrified by the sheer precipice and narrow pass.

Our spirits soared when Kate, a gregarious Aussie physiotherapist, said, "Gather ye hymn books, sisters," dishing out rugby songbooks and sharing a bottle of ale.

The grinning driver whistled a Tibetan ditty through blackened teeth stumps as we sang bawdily into the pink sunset, waving to the mountain children smoking cigarette stubs.

I was so happy, so glad not to be hooked to the kitchen sink at a tender age. I was free!

We six crammed into a three-bedded room at the Snow View Hotel, and because Kate was bossy and funny we nicknamed her Mother Superior. Nightly she'd ask, "Have you sisters washed your three Fs (face, feet and fanny)? You'll get frightful diseases if you don't."

We'd rub Nivea into our cheeks and curl our hair while she read aloud from the guidebook.

When the avuncular Nick with a couple of passengers in tow arrived at the door with rations of Nepalese brew, we were in our nighties, hoarse and tired from the long mountain trek. The indomitable Kate turned up her portable record player, leapt from the bed and, in a fit of nostalgia for Sydney, waved her arms and cried:

Two arms, two hands, two steely bands
Beneath the Southern Cross I stand
A native of this foreign land.
Orrstraylia! You bloody beauty!
Up the old red rooster!

We whistled and cheered. Nick shook his head and said, "You sisters are a crazy bunch."

Dawn breaking over Mount Everest was stunning, as was hiring bicycles and exploring ancient cobblestone villages. Kate rode ahead to become sandwiched between a bus and tricycle-rickshaw but she emerged sheepishly, her orange flannel hat askew.

We briefly disowned Sister Jill when she wobbled into a fruit barrow sending the owner and contents tumbling down a hill. From the city of pagodas, temples, prayer wheels and gentle people, we headed back into India.

At night in the Bodh Gaya dak bungalow courtyard, irritated passengers cried out and flung shoes at dogs cavorting over our camp beds. At dawn we awoke to a massive shackled elephant with painted ears gazing down on us.

"Bodh Gaya is the Mecca of Buddhism," said Kate clutching a guidebook and sidestepping a worshipping mendicant. "Boozen-Suzen! Come get educated!" she thundered when Sister Susie wandered away from Buddha's tree of enlightenment to gaze at hippie beads at a souvenir stand.

In blistering heat we arrived in Benares, where it's the aim of every Hindu to make a pilgrimage to the sacred water of the Ganges. The road to the Burning Ghats thronged with elephants, camels, cows, itinerant musicians clanging drums and cymbals, monkey temples, curd sellers, contortionists and rickshaw drivers. Then we insisted on seeing the naughty temple carvings at Khajuraho.

Parched passengers descended on the sole shanty selling coke and beer and drank the place dry, groaning with disappointment when the famous temples were locked for the night. The suspense proved too much for Kate for she scaled the fence and caused a terrific rumpus when guards chased her with bayonets. Tom and Betty, a middle-aged couple, rewarded her with a bottle of beer, keen to know what she saw. But she was too busy running to take note.

Our favourite couple were the colourful Kiwis, Godfrey and Juliana, nicknamed Bumfrey and Banana. He was a chemist and she, years younger, a strapping girl with a passion for bananas. They slept with a sack of vegetables between them and when their reeking carton of cheese caused complaints, Banana had a cheese party, which most regretted the next day.

She became ill early in India but, like some other passengers, caught up with the coach later in the journey. Bumfrey said rum was the cure of all evil, and tenderly dosed his wife when she showed signs of flagging. When a spinster moaned about some hardship, Banana said in exasperation, "Oh, for goodness sakes. Lift up your legs and live!"

We'd had our fill of writhing amorous lovers and serpents immortalised on holy monuments. The guide's visitors' book was filled with travellers' names. Someone had written Oh, erotica! Debauched erotica! Curiosity got the better of us and we followed a man into a dark room separated by a curtain of dangling beads. His grimy fingers rolled the weed while his eyes darted nervously, making us feel like criminals.

"I'm not seeing rainbows or getting enlightened. Are you?" I asked after a couple of puffs. And, since Kate felt the same way, I said, "Come on, Blue, let's shoot through," and we sought normality in the brilliant sunshine.

The road to Sanchi was a mass of wild monkeys, wandering goats and cart-pulling bullock. Ramshackle stalls sold fruit at Sagar Village. Nick parked the coach, and said, "Let's be having youse in ten minutes. The natives are not used to tourists."

He was right. An excitable swarming mob surrounded the coach when we tried to re-enter. It was terrifying.

A British bride suffering from recurring dysentery stayed in the coach, but wailed in anguish at her groom bobbing in the swelling crowd, "Forget about them mandarins, darling."

Those amply endowed flung their purchases onto their bosoms and stretched out their arms to be hauled aboard to resounding cheers. Others waved frantically in a sea of dark faces and dirty dhotis pleading rescue. Nick counted us as locals hammered the coach, then he inched through the rippling crowd.

At Sanchi, a tourist Mecca for its stupas, thirst was again on our mind. After unloading the coach, Kate sang Beer is Best outside the shanty store. Locals poured out of huts and an impromptu concert was in progress. In the happy chaos children chanted, adolescents banged tin pots, Aussies chirped Waltzing Matilda, Kiwi passengers did the haka, and I showed toothless bandy-legged men in nappy attire how to stomp and jive. When the store ran dry, we linked arms and wended our way back to the dark bungalow to cook under the stars.

"Step on the gas, Nick," we urged when the other coach overtook us, its jeering passengers waving victoriously. Those sneaky blighters would take all the water!

At dak bungalows it was first in, first served. In our haste we discovered we'd left a young passenger behind. Nick was about to turn the coach around on the deserted road when a panting old Sikh, pedalling furiously on a bike, emerged on the horizon with the young Kiwi girl clinging to his waist.

A curious crowd gathered at the Indore compound, pointing, staring, spitting when we draped washed knickers and bras over a gleaming mounted canon, and cooked outside. When the sky blackened, we invited Nick to pull his stretcher alongside ours for he was a source of entertaining tales.

In the vibrant city of Bombay, we dabbled on the black market at a silk shop in one of the bazaars. When Trish's biro smudged on her $10 travellers' cheque, the dealer refused to accept it but relented when she howled noisily. Stopping in a city meant getting the coach serviced and much-needed love-ups for couples and willing drivers.

Collecting passengers from various hotels, we spied the two librarians in yellow shifts running down the road with suitcases, laughing hysterically. They'd broken the hotel loo! They yanked the chain and the china cistern crashed onto the floor. Nick made a quick getaway, and the girls giggled all the way to Ellora and Ajanta where we stopped to explore temples and caves dating back to 200BC.

"Hope there're no more bloody caves today," we moaned when Nick cried, "Wakey, wakey, blossoms."

We'd camped overnight in a peaceful garden. Exhausted from the long valley trek, I'd slept in my stretcher, oblivious to noisy dogs and mosquitoes.

In Rajasthan, known for its colourful costumes and silver jewellery, we set up camp in Bundi under trees in the courtyard of the circuit house. Dozens of monkeys vaulted overhead, enraging a spinster when one snatched her loaf of bread and defecated into her soup. Banana bellowed too; they'd swiped her bunch of bananas. Then a monkey piddled on my bed! During the night as monkeys whooshed from tree to tree, cries accompanied foul language.

From Jaipur, the Pink City, where tailors whipped up Punjabi outfits for those heeding Nick's advice about covering up in Muslim countries, a villager wandered into the dak bungalow at Fatehpur Sikri and offered a walking tour to the fort and palaces for a rupee each. When the tour dragged on, everyone lost interest and headed back to camp for a beer except Kate and me. Seeing me jotting his musings on toilet paper after my notebook filled up, the guide hugged me.

"I show you something velly interesting," he said. But I was bored and hot as we climbed a myriad of steps in a crumbling ruin. "My house over there," and, in the vast yellow landscape, Kate squinted through binoculars searching for a yellow speck.

The tour ended when she joked, "Ah yes. You have velly nice house. I see your wife. But goodness me, who's that creeping down your stairs? The butcher!"

At the Gate of Victory, a local claimed that for five rupees each he could dive from the top of a tall building into a tiny well. Everyone waited with bated breath while he grimaced, prayed and flexed his body before a spectacular plunge. By the time he emerged, some tourists had scuttled off leaving a livid wild-eyed diver screaming breathlessly.

At the Delhi YMCA an English girl on the coach, with a collection of horsehair wigs, scored several breakfasts by changing outfits, but when she lent them out, the waiters wised up. The owner of a music shop in Old Delhi said the Beatles purchased sitars from him, producing photographs and news clippings as proof. We left the store banging bongo drums and monkey rattles.

The juicy gossip was when a van driver, employed to travel ahead, turned up. He'd disappeared in Kathmandu and speculation was rife as to his whereabouts. Kate and I charmed him into taking us to a druggy discotheque, but he remained abstemious.

At the stunning Golden Temple at Amritsar we witnessed blind temple singers and the ceaseless readings of the Granth Sahib, the sacred book of the Sikhs.

Family planning notices pinned to trees read Small family, happy family. Some clinics offered a transistor to men who agreed to be sterilised.

After a month in India, gorging on lassis (yoghurt drinks) at fly-blown stalls, we were ready for the desert!

Chapter 25
The Turk Lurk and Persian Coercion

At the Pakistani border, uniformed officials sipped cups of green tea while checking passports. In the searing heat, money-changers paraded up and down the dusty featureless road insisting they gave the best rate—56 Pakistani rupees to $US10.

When passengers grizzled about the delay, Nick found a besotted border official staring at a passport photo. He wanted to meet this dimpled physiotherapist. When she strolled over, rivulets of sweat flowed from his brow. Five hours later we were on our way to Lahore, grateful that Jill had sped up the passport process despite being handicapped, writing with one hand and fobbing off roving pinches with the other.

Arriving in Lahore under a purple sunset, some of us splashed out at the Park Luxury Hotel while others trundled down the road after cheap accommodation. A hot shower and clean clothes later, we viewed each other differently. Even Nick wolf-whistled; he was used to frumpy chicks in saris and flannel hats and guys in muslin tunics, boots and with beards.

As a lively band serenaded us to dinner, Banana strode through the dining room like a champion racehorse, her long hair elaborately swept up, clutching her shorter husband's hand. Bumfrey was dapperly dressed in a pink shirt and multi-coloured cravat, his wild curls oiled and flattened. As the thoroughbreds slid into their seats, the band hit a few discordant notes. It took several minutes to get back into rhythm again.

No one was a wallflower that evening. The spinsters in their metallic satin frocks, plastic beads and chunky brogues foxtrotted with shiny-suited delegates. Nick pointed to a square ashtray stand with Use Me painted on it.

"You may as well hang that sign around your necks if you accept invitations from these lads," he warned. "It's just asking for trouble."

Lahore was a surprise—a sprawling chromium-plated city, vigorous and modern—where men were visible and women hidden or veiled. After donning robes, entering mosques, and viewing dozens of worshippers facing Mecca three of us flagged a passing horse and cart.

"Where you want to go? I take you museum or etceteras," said the owner. The latter sounded dodgy so we said Kim's Gun, having been brought up on Rudyard Kipling.

When the horse refused to budge the driver whispered soothing words, corrected its blinkers, examined its hoofs, and we were off. Then it halted after a passing cyclist rang a bell. The beast rocked his head wildly and dilated his pupils.

"He no good horse," said the driver as he delivered an almighty whack to its rump. We were thrown into a tangled heap in the cart and my jandal sailed onto the Pakistani highway. Cars swerved, honked, screeched, and roared by, while the horse galloped uncontrollably.

In Peshawar, a city of mud huts and minarets, Nick negotiated a run-down hotel for five rupees each per night. Three of us shared a bleak dank room where men in pyjama-type outfits and caps lurked. Kate was frightened and made such a fuss the manager lowered the price and included breakfast. We piled chairs against the door and were only woken by the wailing of muezzins calling the faithful to prayer at dawn.

Along the imposing Khyber Pass dotted with forts, we encountered swarthy mountain men brandishing ancient rifles, panniered mules and ox-wagons. We shopped at an underground bazaar at stalls selling hot curries, sizzling kebabs, mutton fat and fried camel and goat meat. Afridis, the mountain-race, were armed with rifles and daggers. Vendors offered contraband goods—cameras, transistors, watches and guns—smuggled from Russia and Japan.

At the border, Pakistani soldiers shared sweet tea, chapatti, and even their cushions and table. Proffering cigarettes, they insisted on being photographed, standing erect, proudly brandishing a silver badge and wearing a quaint hat with a gathered red scarf around it.

Crossing into Afghanistan was a photographer's feast where nomadic families, with babies strapped to mules or camels, peered coyly. Round-hatted locals stared from their boats of goatskins as we washed in an icy stream and set up camp at Jalalabad.

The base hotel in Kabul was *The Metropole* costing 120 Afghanis or $1.50 a night—a popular dive with English, Canadian and American hippies sharing joints around a jukebox.

The vibrant city was a tourist Mecca teeming with long-haired travellers, turbaned locals in baggy cloth pants and embroidered smocks, belching camels straying into the path of American limousines, Russian jeeps and decrepit bicycles. Black marketeers dealt smuggled goods ranging from televisions to opium.

A money vendor, well known to the drivers, was doing a roaring trade in a backstreet alley. After cigarettes, cups of chai, enthusiastic handshaking and slaps on the back, we waddled into daylight with bulging money belts strapped to our waists. Afghani goods were tempting, especially the embroidered suede coats, silver trinkets and carpets.

From the mountain village of Istalif, we boarded a rattletrap bus back to Kabul, perched on the roof rack amid spinning bicycle wheels and smelly youths. But on a narrow pass with treacherous ravines below, the bus ground to a standstill and the driver demanded we give him twenty Afghanis before continuing. We shouted for fifteen minutes, shaking our fists and hurling insults at the laughing rogue before agreeing to pay once back at the hotel. After trying that a second time, everyone pushed the man back into his driver's seat.

We took pity on one young passenger who appeared vulnerable, and we smuggled her into our room. She seemed to exist on vitamin pills and dried fruit samples from roadside barrels. The manager was suspicious, locating her under a bed gripping a Nepalese rug. But then he took her out for a lavish meal. When lights fused in the hotel lobby, the manager was caught clutching our waif-like Kiwi like a hot water bottle.

At Ghazni, a high-walled fortified city, tribesmen brandished rifles. A prowling guard reared his head over the wall pointing his gun while I was having a squat among camel dung.

Now we were entering the real desert, for wind raged across rippling sand dunes dotted with isolated mud villages and biblical figures. At a deserted crumbling fort near

Kandahar we camped, using torches and candles to cook by. Some guys had a final dope session before the border. Spying sinister figures lurking in the shadows with guns, we dived into trenches. The gunmen loomed, peered at our cowering bodies, grinned, shook hands and wandered off.

After too many dates and raisins, Jill got the trots.

"Help!" she squealed in the dark. An army of dung beetles were chasing her, gulping her produce, making her bunny-hop since she was in a squatting position with her pants locked about her ankles. She made frightful backfiring noises that we called dinner gongs. I couldn't help her; I was laughing too hard.

Back in Pakistan, Nick chose the *Lourdes Hotel* in Quetta. He'd covered this route several times and base hotels gave a party rate.

After exploring this bustling city rebuilt after a devastating earthquake in 1935, costing 35,000 lives, we found Kate doing a brisk trade. She was selling a bottle of brandy to a Pakistani willing to pay an exorbitant price, even though she'd had a few swigs. More locals trickled into the hotel grounds, sending us scuttling to our rooms to see what we could part with for profit. Tenders were called for stubs of lipsticks, holey socks, nylon briefs, frayed shirts, and stamps off letters from home. Banana had sold her large bras in India.

"Youse 'ave all been up since six and fiddled and dilly-dallied over them burners," growled Nick in Nushki. "It's not good enough. We've got a schedule to keep."

The wind and sand stung our faces. We had to push the coach when it bogged on a highway littered with submerged stricken vehicles. At the Iranian border we waited hours in the sandstorm while certificates were checked for cholera and malaria. Two girls needed smallpox injections, and a doctor performed a quick operation on Trish's finger with a thick rusty needle after she gashed it on a tin of Indian sardines.

Whenever the coach stopped in Iran, curious crowds gathered—mostly children with glittering skullcaps and men on donkeys. Guards at disused police barracks, or army compounds, watched over us at night if we weren't using base hotels.

In Bam we camped at a vacant dust-coated schoolhouse. When water petered out we leapt into an army truck to find the town water pump. Each time we hit a pothole we were thrown against the jovial Persians, spilling half the contents from the plastic containers, laughing like hyenas. During the night I awoke to a guard hovering over my stretcher, his hands creeping up my neck. He scuttled away but then he paced the floor, smoking in the still black night.

Heading out of Bam, it poured. The highway became a river. Trapped by floods, Nick told us to go explore a two-thousand-year old city ruin. That night we slept in nearby caves where I cooked a disastrous dinner for one of the drivers after a vodka party in Bumfrey and Banana's mud quarters. The next day he looked wan.

"Don't invite me again," he said. "I've got crapulence and had more bush stops than I care to remember."

The road to Kerman looked like a battle scene littered with bulldozers and tractors, and rivers of muddy water. It was hard to tell where the road was and, in the confusion, the other coach headed up to the Great Salt Desert.

In Kerman, Araj shook hands profusely with Nick, insisting we stay for the night at his new hotel or camp on his lawns. He happily let Banana take over his kitchen and boss his boys, even turning a blind eye when ten of us sneaked into her room for a shower.

We limped into Surjan with a punctured tyre before negotiating flooded mountain tracks and finding a perfect camping spot in a green valley.

"I'm happy, I'm so happy," I whooped, racing up and down the hills.

"Where've you been, little flower?" asked Nick. "We were going to send search parties."

"Just being happy," I said.

At night, three armed guards stuck their head inside the coach warning this was dangerous country for thieves and bandits lurked in the wilds. They urged us to move on. Nick pointed to slumbering campers on stretchers under the stars and, when he gave the men hot coffee and rum, they insisted on keeping vigil throughout the freezing night.

At dawn our sleeping bags were saturated in dew and the guards miserably cold. Disaster struck an hour later when the coach came to a standstill. Nick and some of the lads set off for help after discovering a broken axle and bolts that had ripped loose from a wheel.

A Persian offered to take us to see an ancient mosque built in a mountain up a stony track. Nine of us climbed into a Jeep and the bottom fell out of it. We sprawled on the ground amid curling springs and collapsed wheels, laughing. Undeterred, the driver led the way on foot. We trudged for miles over rocky terrain. Worried the trek was taking too long, we scrambled down a hill and hailed a truck crammed with peasants, runny-nosed kids and caged hens.

From Shiraz, the city of wine, roses and poets, where swarthy males surrounded the coach with roses clenched between their stained teeth, we camped near the ruins of Persepolis. Numb with cold, we pulled our stretchers into the smelly hole-in-the-floor latrines during the night.

Keen to see the cliff tombs of Darius and evade the ticket vendor, we darted up the hill at dawn. Soon enough we were bowling back down the hillside chased by an angry man.

Nick said, "Youse are a mean bunch."

But he had greater concerns. He'd lost contact with Coach No. 3, our coach was playing up and the English bride, miserable with Delhi belly, kept requesting bush stops.

By his feet Nick jealously guarded a sacred bucket used for passports and his booze. He was surprised when the bride asked to use his bucket.

"Petal," he said, "If you want to be sick, lean out the window."

"But, Nick," she sobbed. "It's not that end—it's the other!"

The dramas continued; she discovered her groom using her contraceptives for water-purifying tablets, we'd been towed through more floods, a bridge had collapsed and a wrecked Iranian bus was nose down in muddy waters tragically killing all its passengers.

Finally we limped into Isfahan, city of Shah Abbas with its blue domed mosques, bazaars, silversmiths and carpets. There were intricate carpets laid out in streets and trampled on, to be sold by dealers as genuine antiques, gleaming brass-ware, blindfolded camels crushing seeds for linseed oil and exquisite paintings on ivory with scenes from Omar Khayyam's poems.

It was annoying being constantly trailed by men. One said, "You think I am like wolf, a big playboy? I am lonely man. My women are all locked away."

Nick was alarmed at the number of carpets being stowed into the coach. But when he spied the Kiwi waif with randy Persians in tow, carrying her three carpets down the street, he roared, "Don't anyone buy another thing! I've a good mind to take these ruddy carpets to England meself and leave youse lot behind!"

Stopping for lunch on the road to Tehran, a jocose young businessman drove up in his white Mercedes. That night Karim showed us the sights of the sprawling city where people drove like maniacs. At the expensive Casbah restaurant, he airily said, "Don't worry. It's all on the expense account. I'll put it under forming good relationships between our countries. My father is very European in his outlook and does not like the Persians much. But my mother. Akh! She wears the veil, but underneath she wears the latest fashions from Paris."

He was shocked we were staying at the *Sherafat* in Tehran Avenue.

"Oh, my God, even Mother wouldn't walk around there on her own."

Outside his parents' mansion, a smoky perfume wafted by.

"Oh, that," said Karim, "is my father having a pot party with his friends."

Getting the coaches serviced put us three days behind schedule. Tetchy passengers ganged up on the drivers. We were virtual prisoners as the hotel was surrounded by mobs of men and crazy American hippies in Afghan coats fighting outside. But Trish and I braved the streets where sly men pinched our nipples as we walked past. Trish whacked one with a tennis racquet and I slapped another with a hot water bottle. Pursued by a lecherous lad, we darted into a showroom and hid in a carpet. The storekeeper was annoyed at having to unravel us from his Persian rug.

On our last night in Iran, we camped by the Turkish frontier with a view of Mount Ararat. Russia lay beyond. We pitched tents around a campfire, lustily sang hymns fuelled by fermented hops, and had to be rescued from an ablution block. Peeping Toms had battered on the door causing it to warp. With heavy hammering outside and us trying to free the door from the inside with toothbrushes, nail files and combs, it caved in.

Although disappointed at missing Iraq, Jordan, Lebanon and Syria because of political strife, southern Turkey was a wealth of archaeological history. Cheap hotels with lice-infested bedding were rife with intruders, forcing us to jam our beds against a door. In Agri, some guy hammered on the door, twisting the latch. We yelled for the bridegroom since he was a burly English bloke, but he'd rushed to his wife's aid; she was being molested elsewhere. Privately, we marvelled that a guy who wore socks and sandals had it in him.

When Trish complained of toothache, we found a shabby clinic where patients sat with bloodied cloths tied around their head. After drawing diagrams, since no one spoke English, the dentist grabbed pliers, clamped his hand on her forehead and extracted the rotten fang.

Nick was a happy man. He'd fallen for a redhead on the other coach and swapped her for two of our passengers. So he whistled contentedly, while we waited hours in the driving rain, watching the army build a temporary bridge. Every few hours, the workers downed tools and prayed on mats. Too wet to camp, Nick found a community hall. Frogs croaked all night as we slept. And the next morning when he opened the main door, banked up water cascaded in, forcing us to wade knee-high to the coach.

Trish and I stopped at a yoghurt café in Erzerum. The men inside grabbed us. One splayed his body across the closed door, looking out for customers. The other forced my head into a bucket of yoghurt. A third prodded my ribs and rump. Trish and I made so much noise kicking and screaming that we were hurled back out onto the road.

By the time we limped into Pulumur, through swollen rivers on a punctured tyre, I was gasping for breath, and suffering stomach cramps. Rain belted down in blinding cascades, while Nick dropped us at a chai shop and went looking for accommodation. I desperately needed a bush stop, so squatted in a nearby forest.

A Turk popped up from behind long grass, crying, "Tuvalet?" (toilet) and grabbed me. When I yelled with pain and revulsion, the molester ran off. Miraculously a little girl appeared. Grasping my hand she took me to her home with the usual squatters-hole. Her worried mother patted my forehead, embracing me.

That night, as thunder crackled, we laid our stretchers out in a crude schoolroom. I was feeling desperately unwell and my sisters became Florence Nightingale. The concerned Turkish family provided a hot water bottle when Nick declined for me stay the night in their home.

Indiaman passengers were unrecognised talent until that evening. Then something extraordinary happened. We gelled—even the staid ones.

Lying back on stretchers, we were entertained by Kiwi Tom, who'd once been in musicals and who rendered songs from *Student Prince* and other oldies. He was enthusiastically applauded, despite singing wrong lines and wrong notes to well-known tunes.

"Aw, Tom, c'mon down," pleaded his old wife, Betty, who camp-cooked in her apron and took photos with the cap on the lens. "Please, lovey, you've haddanuf to drink."

Tom was wonderful. Some strummed guitar, but Tom was memorable.

The rest of Turkey was a feast of sampling Turkish delight. Then, to the whine of Aw, not more ruins, everyone perked up in Ephesus. Nick said they sold beer along the track. And Susie led a charge at breakneck speed. She was keen to find the ancient brothel, which she located between old boiler rooms and fragments of columns and rubble.

Nick was accused of being a bully when he wouldn't stop in Izmir.

"Sorry, blossoms," he said. "We're going to Pergamon to see more ruins!"

"Youse a stingy bunch," he said later, watching us being chased by a choleric toll-keeper at night after sneaking through Hadrian's Temple. "It's a pity youse can't be that quick getting away in the morning."

Disappointed by Troy, we boarded the ferry at Canakkale where the captain let me steer his ship to Cape Hellas. Kate was so excited we were visiting Gallipoli that she climbed onto the top deck and entertained passengers with a Scottish reel, rattling monkey drums and blowing whistles. At night I crept up to the memorial to think about the heroes of WW1 and a ship, *H.M.S. Jonquil,* which was lost at sea.

In Istanbul, at a covered bazaar, we bought leather coats and monkey-puzzle rings.

"You are a very fine darling," shopkeepers murmured. "You are a nice honey. For you everything free."

Yenner's Lokantra was a bustling hippie dive. The extrovert owner tucked flowers in our hair, kissed cheeks and gave free food. This was true international flower-power brotherhood. We were invited below to inspect a typical Turkish kitchen. But I opened a cupboard and dozens of hens flew out, squawking, crapping into pots and fluttering upstairs to where diners shrieked. The hens were caught and thrown back into the cupboard to get on with their laying.

In Greece we sold our blood. There was a sign outside a monastery warning no one would be admitted wearing slacks or short skirts. We rummaged in our luggage for nighties, quilted dressing gowns, even men's jumpers and raincoats to hide our offensive flesh.

In Athens, American marines called out, "Say, honey. Just plant yourself on that slab against the Aw-crop-pollis so we can capture a real perfick shot."

I gave them a film-star stance. When two of our sisters appeared breathlessly through the columns, they were elated.

"Wow! Three of you! Even more perfick! Say, you chicks aren't from Inglarnd, are ya?"

When we said Australia, one asked about kangaroos.

"Do they really box?"

"Yeah, blue," said Kate. "Remarkable animals. They stand up on their hind legs and spin around on their toes. D'ya know, their back legs can rip a dog's guts open."

"You chicks are kinda cute," they said, as we rolled around the marble columns, laughing.

Between them wining and dining us in Athens, we had time to sneak off and enjoy the local boys, who offered bouzouki music, retsina, and smashing plates the Greek way.

247

One evening cops caught three of us on a motorbike heading back to camp with my Greek sweetheart and hauled us into their van for an explanation. No one could speak English. After shrugs, wild smiles, and a caution, the handsome police kissed our fingertips under the twinkling stars and invited us all out for a typical Greek night.

From the overnight crossing to Italy on the *Apia,* where laps of handsome officers were already occupied by blonde tourists (cheap tarts, we named them), we snaked our way up to Rome and Venice, loving the Chianti, art galleries and Romeos. Every girl dreams of being serenaded in a gondola and I scored several, once being stuck on a tiny island unaware that midday siestas last hours.

But Banana was sobbing because hubby Bumfrey had returned to the hotel.

"What's the point of coming to Venice if I can't ride in a gondola?"

He insisted the rides were too expensive.

In the Piazza San Marco, Banana smiled into the face of a tall gondolier. For 4000 lire he offered to take us back to camp, and Banana to her hotel.

"Ooh," I said. "Molto caro. Very dear."

Then added brightly, "For 1000 lire you take us and we sing to you!"

He agreed. And we sang our hearts out.

As we slid through canals beneath a magical red moon, the gondolier crooned and Venetians opened their shutters, waving gently. For the rest of the trip, Banana had a Mona Lisa smile, not unlike the inner smiles we hippie travellers had when parents wanted to know everything.

Some secrets remain locked in our hearts.

Chapter 26
Hitching around Europe

When I wrote home from Edinburgh saying I was working night shifts at a brewery, and keeping warm in a movie theatre during the day since it was cheaper than our flat, Mum replied, "You'll never meet a nice man with that sort of lifestyle. We're too ashamed to tell our friends."

Like many Kiwis and Aussies, I flatted in Earls Court and contributed to a kitty and house rules—£5 a week for a bed or £3 to sleep on the floor. Aussie friends descended with a carton of beer and, after all the singing and guitar playing, party guests you'd never met were writhing on your bed. It was annoying when I had to work the next day, taking a tube into London crammed with dour people of all races. Or I'd find the bathroom sink clogged with black bristles from a Nigerian student.

I longed for home, the golden sands stretching along Pittwater Road, a mum who cared whether I was happy, even ex-boyfriends. My handbag was snatched a day after arriving in London, and a Finnish au pair and I had three guys arrested for indecent exposure and theft.

After hitching around Scotland and touring Ireland by horse and cart, I took an overnight coach to Edinburgh to flat with two Aussies, Ingrad and Margaret. Ingrad, whose parents lived off Pittwater Road, and I remained best friends. We'd been through primary school together and spent teenage hours on the telephone chatting about boys.

While Ingrad was recovering from an emergency appendectomy, Marg and I worked in a noisy brewery. Then Marg did temp nursing, me temp typing and Ingrad relief teaching.

Sometimes our elderly landlord, Playfair Dodds, who lived upstairs, couldn't resist our wicked laughter and came to investigate. Sniffing and lifting up pot lids, he told us how wonderful we were. Addressing me, he thumped on the table apologising, "Miss Strathern-lovely-Scottish-name. I've said it before and I'll say it again. I can't help the weather!"

And he told us not to leave the washing on the line at night for what would the neighbours think?

"It's dark, they can't see," I replied.

"That's not the point Miss Strathern-lovely-Scottish-name. It's just not done here."

I thought that less of a crime than angry students picketing the U.S. Embassy with banners screaming *Nixon NO!* Or drunken Scots roughing up their wives in the streets.

I was curious to visit Russia. Was it truly rampant with spies, mannish women with moustaches, fat toothless peasants wearing printed aprons and scarves around their head, and men in furry headgear drinking vodka?

When Ingrad and I joined a five-week Contiki camping tour to Scandinavia and Russia with ten others, we were searched at the Russian border. Inside panels of the coach were taken apart and the floor jemmied up. Officious guards inspected our belongings before allowing us to proceed with Hermann, our humourless ever-watchful government guide.

Our Kiwi driver snuck off to do some British Museuming, a euphemism for black-marketing. It was dangerous, but the problem was excess money; there was little to buy in the shops and we'd be searched again at the Polish border. Problem solved; we gormandised our way through Russia's fancy restaurants. And if Hermann wasn't visible, students sidled up, saying Psst, got chewing gum? We were bulging with even more useless money after selling tatty jeans, ballpoint pens and sunglasses.

On the way to Poland, the highway was so rough my bra strap broke with us bouncing over potholes. In Germany, vicious dogs snarled at the barbed-wire Berlin Wall as we drove through Checkpoint Charlie. The contrast between East and West Berlin was staggering. When getting our photos processed, we were upset we lost a film of Russia due to border guards tampering with our cameras during the coach search.

In 1970, hitching was a cheap way to see Europe. Sure, we'd heard stories about girls getting raped or murdered but thought they referred to American youngsters. Fed up with our jobs and the Scottish winter, Ingrad and I discussed hitching around the Continent.

First, we would have a dummy run to test our compatibility, capability, clothing and probable distance covered each day. We slept at youth hostels, unaware we'd encounter the coldest Easter of the century.

In high spirits we stuffed packets of soup, cutlery, a map of Europe, passports, a transistor, milk powder and warm clothing into our rucksacks and hitched down to London where kind drivers wanted to mother and feed us.

In France the real test began with hitching from one hostel to another in snow. We'd been given addresses, assured people would love to see us. They weren't. Although hospitable, they'd drive miles to dump us at the closest hostel. In Lille, two youths took us to a cheap pensione where the owner didn't want us because of our packs, but the wife said ooh-la-la and made up a bed. They were justifiably annoyed when the lads kept knocking on our door bringing gifts of shampoo and soap.

Nervous about using the communal toilet down the hall, we piddled into the washbasin in our room. In the morning we found a note: *We are sorry for being of a disturbance. We did not mean any aft pansy. Can we be of assistance to you?*

In one day, we covered 350kms from Arras to Luxemburg in thirteen lifts. We met an exhausted couple who said they had walked all night in Paris because the hostel was full, and the next night they'd slept outside a shoe shop. The girl said she flagged cars to secure a ride for them both while her boyfriend hid in bushes. Two girls hitching together always got the first ride. From Heidelberg we crossed the German-French frontier and walked into a trap.

German Customs ushered us into their office, checked passports, took photographs explaining, "Good relations between Germany and Australia," and pointed to the French border. Our rucksacks were roughly hauled off our backs and our belongings scattered.

"You have hashish?" asked the French officials with a frozen smile.

"Course not," we said.

"Non, non, non," said a uniformed lad running his fingers over the lining of our coats, the soles and heels of our shoes. When my passport revealed a Turkish stamp a woman officer's eye glinted; she hauled me into a concrete cell and ordered me to strip while she probed for heroine punctures or anything

251

else I might have stuck up my arse. I was a kid, just past being a teenager, and appalled. When I cried, she thought I was guilty. Ingrad had milk powder in her rucksack and we spent hours in a cell while it was drug tested. When released, we were wary but thought it might be fun to plan a bigger trip. That sixteen-day trip cost £25.

"Must you hitchhike?" asked our anxious English aunts when we said we were off again. "It seems frightfully dangerous."

Our parents in Australia were equally worried.

Again we packed a sleeping bag sheet, youth hostel card, travellers' cheques, and a change of clothing, togs and soup packets. Hitching out of London, we caught the ferry to Boulogne. Ingrad was the map-planner. I'd been to Europe before and didn't care where I went; I sought adventure and freedom.

The first lift in France began ominously. A swarthy middle-aged man with a baby girl cooing in the back seat took us two kilometres down the road before tweaking our bosoms and shoving us out of his Citroen. But other Frenchmen were charming and we had no trouble getting lifts to Spain, jumping into Jaguars, Volvos, trucks transporting cases of champagne, bread, cakes, and accepting free meals.

The Spanish were more hospitable. Australia, they marvelled, such a long way from home!

Since it was the European summer now, some hostels were full of backpackers, mostly Americans. It was hard at the end of a long ride to find there were no vacancies. Appearing vulnerable, we always found someone who'd feed us, take us home or drive out of his way, looking for a cheap pensione.

Males travelling together had to wait longer for lifts, but we met two ingenious English chaps. They wore top hats, were dapperly dressed and strutted with walking sticks, holding placards indicating their destination. Ingrad and I had a rough idea where we'd like to go but were flexible. That gave us our best and worst experiences.

Our least pleasant experience in Spain was accepting a lift with Jose in his white Renault. Initially gregarious and generous, we became alarmed when he veered off the highway down a beaten track. He couldn't speak English and the day

252

was turning sinister. Fuelled by wine and cognac, he wildly grabbed us. Snatching our rucksacks we tore up a lonely dirt track, panting and laughing hysterically. Fearing he'd kill us, we dived into bushes, our hearts pounding, while he drove up and down looking for us. We lay low for hours.

"What's that awful smell?" asked Ingrad when we finally emerged. I'd lain in a cowpat.

Beneath a full moon, and shivering with cold, we trudged to the highway. We decided to walk all night, but were soon blinded by the headlights of an enormous petrol tanker. It screeched to a halt, its brakes hissing. A cab door flung open.

"Bad man, he takey (sic) us in bushies," I explained as the safe-looking driver hauled us up.

During the night he fed us at workmen's cafes and stopped to point out special landmarks. Arriving pre-dawn in Valladolid, the driver assured us his brother who also drove trucks, was a good boy. Our driver needed a snooze. In our confusion we got separated and I was shoved into a petrol tanker several cabs down. The brother was a creep. I screamed, cried and pleaded for ages before he let me go.

"Ingrad! Where are you?" I called up to identical cabs dotted along the highway.

A strawberry-blonde head cried out of a window.

"Here! The same thing happened to me!"

On the road again, a charming honeymooning couple insisted we breakfast with their friends at their rustic farmhouse. A maid scuttled off to cook bacon and eggs since the hosts had visited England and tasted British fare. Satiated, we then spent all day winding around a mountain pass before being deposited outside a convent. Thinking we'd walked all the way from England, the concerned nuns made up a big fluffy bed and dished out piles of food to the *Sound of Music* LP they procured for our benefit. Deeply touched, we didn't know which way to cross ourselves.

When a Mercedes pulled up the next morning, the nuns filed outside, waving us off.

One ride was with a guy called Angel who showed us around the picturesque port of La Coruna, bought us a slap-up meal with aperitifs and insisted we accompany him to Santiago de Compostela. Called the Jerusalem of the West, this beautiful city was the centre of pilgrimages in the Middle Ages.

Immediately Angel dropped us off, a red Mini-Moke pulled up with three cheerful men. Mondo ran a language school, Joao had been in the cavalry, and Juan, who was a famous sculptor, gave us keys to a luxury flat. In high spirits they sang Galician songs and we sang a dubious version of *Waltzing Matilda*.

"Happy travels. Don't forget your Galician friends. I think you girls are very brave," Juan said the next morning, dropping us off on the highway.

We hitched a ride into Portugal in a bright yellow Renault with a man displaying a dazzling array of crooked gold, silver and black teeth. His caged Alsatian bared its fangs beneath a litter of dismantled doll torsos on the back seat. We spent five weeks weaving in and out of Spain and Portugal. Some days we walked for hours in remote areas or sat on the side of the road during the blistering hot afternoon siesta time when no traffic passed.

At youth hostels we shared experiences and visited places we'd never thought about. With a hitch of a thumb we casually deviated to tiny towns to climb a bell tower or site of historic interest because our lift said we must go there. They often treated us to an oily meal and wine gulped from goatskin bladders. It was hit and miss who picked us up.

Sometimes fat gypsies rescued us on lonely inland stretches. We might travel all day with them or bunny-hop from Fiats, sports cars, or Renaults to hippie vans with a variety of drivers; their nationalities and jobs as diverse as their cars. Some were famous TV personalities or, like Fernando, an Olympic boxer.

In Cascais, in Portugal, Antonio's weeping mum engulfed me in her massive cleavage. Tony was now in the army in Angola but we'd been corresponding since he planted that fervent kiss on my nubile lips years ago in Lisbon. On that voyage Dad had pushed us together. Tony had dreams of going to London and studying drama, his letters becoming increasingly flowery and hippie-laced. Were we going to get married, asked his fat mama, after two days of food and embarrassing kindness? No, I thought, I'm still going to see the world.

During a lift to Lisbon, the radio blared out the funeral service of Senor Salazar, President of Portugal. With our blondish hair, and packs on our backs, we were rarely ignored and had animated conversations with students who couldn't speak English. Keen to eat fish, I pantomimed eating and casting a fishing rod. One youth said, "Discotheque!"

Crossing the Pyrenees after too many churches, bullfights and art galleries, Ingrad declared she'd never look another tortilla in the face!

Hunters, a bookmaker, gendarmes, jazz musicians, businessmen and a tonsured French priest gave us lifts to the Italian border during seven days travelling through the south of France. After the Aussie beaches, we weren't impressed with the French Riviera and, similarly, Monte Carlo wasn't impressed with us, kicking us out of a casino. The highway was littered with hitchhikers, and French girls at youth hostels were inconsiderate and loud, although the youths weren't lecherous. In Avignon we gawked at Picasso's erotic collection of abstruse writhing mass of nudes and three-eyed faces wearing hats of the Elizabethan era.

In Italy we covered 2500kms in a month hitching as far south as Naples and Capri, heading back up to Rome, over to the east coast to Venice, and to the Yugoslav border. In Perugia we ducked into a church for safety after being pursued by soldiers who piously crossed themselves with one hand, pinching us with the other.

A Romeo in a sports car became frisky along the autostrada. He pointed to Ingrad's head.

"What name this in English?"

His hand edged south as she related body parts. When his hand plunged between her legs, and he asked, "What name?" she turned bright pink.

"Don't be so rude," I piped up from the back seat. "That hasn't got a name."

He dumped us on the outskirts of Rome.

It was fun swapping hitching experiences. Two Brisbane girls said they resorted to trains whenever they had a spat, and three Adelaide girls said if they couldn't all fit into one car, they left notes for each other at the first cafe in town. An

American lass drawled, "Ah like to think of the road as mah home."

Another said she decided to surprise her parents after being away from home for three years.

"You must be wanting Linda," said the mother opening her door. "I'm sorry, honey, she doesn't live here anymore."

The disappointed daughter cried, "But, Mom, I'm Linda!"

After an overload of culture, pasta and red wine, I was annoyed with motherly advice from the other side of the world.

"Don't you get tired of roving and carrying heavy swags every day? I'd like it better if you spent more time in youth hostels," she wrote. And, "Don't you dare go to Turkey. It's not worth the risk. Don't trust any Italian or Greek men. Remember, they are very cunning and very poor and if they are nice to you, it's for a good reason."

Also, "You must have missed the tragedy in Venice when all those people drowned in the canal. I suppose you don't know much about current affairs such as the war in Palestine."

Or, "We are bloody worried at the way you wander round late at night drinking with strangers. Anyone can get picked up. It doesn't mean you're popular and charming—just foolhardy."

Dad added, "Watch out in Grease (sic.) A lot of people slip up there!"

Milorad, a teacher from Belgrade, took us to Rijeka in his large silver car. He asked about Australia. The conversation grew lively when Ingrad drew dainty sheep, wheat and opals. After treating us to a typical Yugoslav lunch, he pulled up outside a youth hostel. He was disgusted with the warden swigging from a bottle, passing it around inebriated youngsters. Concerned, he drove to the home of his uncle who had teenage daughters. The excited family took us in. Every evening the girls took us to dances but they were druggy, noisy and psychedelic.

Other hostels down the coast were filthy and undisciplined. But our lifts became classier with rides from doctors, a guy who showed off his chain of hotels and kind Italian salesmen.

From Dubrovnik we got a lift with a German medical student, Martin, with car woes, and we ended up near the

Albanian border having taken a wrong turn. The wind howled and rain raged as we lurched over bumpy roads in the black night before sighting lights in Murino.

Eighty-nine drivers were competing in a Europa Car Rally testing different cars, travelling through Sicily, North Africa and Europe. In return for lodgings, we agreed to act as controllers and check the times cars passed at dawn. These rooms were filthy and the eiderdowns bloodstained, and it was so cold we couldn't sleep.

At 4am cars roared past, overtaking arthritic barefoot women dressed in rags, clutching firewood, cigarettes hanging out of their mouths, school kids with shaven heads, families in wagons and peasants fetching buckets of water.

Our ten-day adventure covered 1580kms to the Greek border. It cost $18.25.

"I think my blood was still frozen from that night in Murino," said Ingrad in Thessaloniki when she sold her blood. "It took a long time to get out."

Minos, a law student, despised the Turks, saying he'd join the army to win Istanbul back for Greece.

"You must be eating *sometink* when you drink," he warned, ordering retsina and giving me a collection of postcards with passionate messages. "I am Greek. I know this."

After climbing part way up Mount Olympus and a 190km lift to Lamia, a schoolgirl told us to follow her.

"We have small house. Not much money, but if the heart is good, you are welcome."

What a humbling experience being cared for by an impoverished family in a shack. At night the mother blew out the candle, muttered a hasty prayer to the Virgin Mary and climbed into bed. The three daughters curled up on the floor having given us their lumpy bed. Their father pretended not to be hungry despite walking to the rice fields, a two-hour journey each way.

Greece was full of adventure and extreme kindness because many Greeks had relatives in Australia.

From Athens, we boarded a boat bound for Crete.

"Croiky, it's bonzer meeting you sheilas," boomed an Aussie voice at the Iraklion youth hostel. "Oi've been havin' a real good bludge here for four flamin' years. Couldn't go home now. All me mates are bloody married, an' all that crap."

In Mallia was a relaxed beach hostel with a vista of fig trees and windmills. The warden, Pandelis, took us out every night, cramming ten of us Aussies and Canadians into his crony's Volkswagen. We ate hot bread and goat cheese and danced in the streets, or in the grounds of the old Minoan palace, to Greek music.

We were thrilled to be invited to a Greek priest's birthday party and chuckled when Pandelis perched on my knee. He irreverently yanked the ponytail of the priest who'd come to fetch us in a borrowed Volkswagen.

"Priests not allowed to laugh in public," he warned as we traipsed across a pitch-black field. "Papas can't speak English."

Papas lit a lantern, took off his robes, and ushered us in to a feast of sizzling chickens stuffed with tomatoes, olives and potatoes. Over bottles of Kokinelli, we clinked glasses crying *kali orexi* and happy birthday, and toasted our countries. Men didn't seem to work in Crete. Pandelis explained, "Bah! Work is for women and donkeys."

When the jovial winking priest played footsy under the table, I was surprised but didn't want to spoil his birthday. Once alone on the balcony gazing at the moon, Papas propositioned me, offering 100 drachmas. Would the parishioners who paid for his lifestyle approve?

The other party guests were in hysterics listening to me resisting Papas' advances.

"In Affstralie, Greek priesties good boys."

I was rescued. And, still laughing, we left this man of God having gulped whisky nightcaps and yelled Happy Birthday.

A day later, two American hitchhikers cried excitedly, "Guess what! We've been invited to a Greek priest's birthday!"

Papas sure loved having birthdays.

Battering in vain on the youth hostel door in Chania, the other end of Crete, we were dismayed to find it closed for winter. Villagers drinking in a square considered our dilemma. An old Egyptian took us home to his one-room hut, with no running water or electricity. Icons and dusty pictures of saints were tacked to the wall. He suggested we share the bed with his mute wife, but we dozed under his bed during the freezing night. Considered prized guests, his relatives fed us so much over the next few days we couldn't do up our jeans, despite dancing to Zorba the Greek and climbing down gorges.

In an Athens' youth hostel toilet, I became hysterical. I couldn't remove a tampon because it had disintegrated.

"Are you crouching the right way?" yelled Ingrad from behind the door.

"I think it's shot up into my stomach," I sobbed. "Go and get some newspapers. This place is a bloodbath. I don't want to die."

Shuffling along the road with a towel between my legs, strangers directed us to a hospital for women's troubles. There I was poked and prodded, legs up in stirrups in full view of passing patients and staff.

"Zere's nothing up zere," said an exasperated junior doctor. "No bebee. Where you from?"

"Australia," I said. "There is something up there. It's a Tampax. Get it out!"

A dozen unmasked medical students, nurses and the chief gynaecologist gathered around my humiliated little body, muttering and whispering. They couldn't figure out what was wrong.

Ingrad showed them a tampon and demonstrated what you were supposed to do with it.

"Ah," said a Cypriot student as the surgeon probed. "Our women don't use those."

"Can you see anything?" I whimpered.

"Bits of wood," translated the cute student stroking my hand. He meant wool. "You need operation and stay overnight. Don't cry."

On awakening at dusk, I was startled to find a young man leaning over me, caressing my hair. His Spanish girlfriend had been wheeled away for an abortion. When she returned he leapt into bed with her, whispering sweet nothings, and they moaned and writhed throughout the night.

Next morning Ingrad and I were reunited; she'd gone to the wrong hospital and panicked, thinking I'd been spirited away.

When I wrote to Mum, she simply said, "I couldn't show that letter to your poor father. Far too sordid and graphic."

We hitched to Bulgaria. The roads were bad and traffic thin as we climbed into shabby sedans and trucks relying on Lebanese, Arabs and locals to help us find food and accommodation.

"Come to Istanbul with us," said Prince Kamul, cousin of King Hussein, as we hopped into his sleek car followed by his entourage of bodyguards and Arab servants.

Instead, we spent a week in Bulgaria covering 750kms for only $10, sleeping in strange places before hitching into Romania by horse and cart. It was an oppressive scary country but two sisters took us home and furtively whispered about life in Bucharest, afraid their conversation would be overheard.

Disillusioned, we took an overnight train to Belgrade and played cards with passengers. One said he was French/Italian. "Top half French, bottom half Italian," he winked passing around tuica (plum brandy.)

In Belgrade we stayed with a biology professor and his family.

"Something is plunging into me and I don't like it," shouted Ingrad as we caught an over-crowded bus full of tall swarthy passengers. Immobilised with packs on our backs we were terrified of suffocating.

"I'm being fiddled with, too," I gasped.

In Budapest we stayed with a doddery Hungarian Jewish doctor but decided to follow our gut instincts and leave. Then we thumbed around Austria, taking in all the major cities and sights. Once a woman driver knew my dream was to visit the Mad King of Bavaria's castle, she drove us there and gave us extra money so we could explore two castles in Fussen. Then she took us home for the night, insisting we have a sauna in her Finnish-style home in the forest.

Our good fortune continued when a guy in a Mustang picked us up in Innsbruck and said he'd take us to the Swiss border. But as we passed ski resorts, he said, "I zink dere is sometink wrong wiv ze engine. I can smell sometink funny."

Ingrad and I exchanged secret smiles. Our jeans were tatty and travel-stained and, since we were running out of money, we had tied plastic bags over our disintegrating boots.

After being dumped in the middle of nowhere, a German student from Stuttgart took us to Zurich where we gazed, homesick, at Christmas decorations. Local folk tutted sympathetically and pulled us into cafes for hot chocolate. It was snowing and very cold.

Not expecting our adventures to last so long, we only had summer clothes and wore a ragged assortment over our jeans. Our remaining precious coins were spent buying safety pins as the zips had broken and the seams torn. Into our sixth month, we reached Brussels. Drenched yet elated, we boarded the *Princesse Astrid* to Dover eating Swiss bread rolls, Austrian meat paste, Hungarian jam and German soup.

"Up you come, ducks," said the jolly driver of a big yellow truck with Brain Haulage emblazoned on it. "Cor lummy!" he gasped when we told him where we'd been. "Reckon your brains might need a good over-haul."

Scraping together loose change, we caught a bus to Aldgate and a tube to Ingrad's Auntie Mary's at Finchley, where Ingrad's rucksack fell apart at the front gate.

"Stay there," shouted Auntie Mary. "Don't move." She dashed inside to place newspaper in the hallway and up the staircase. Then she ran a deep bath. Ordering us to strip in the laundry, she used a long pole to deposit our clothes outside to be fumigated.

Our 151-day adventure covering 12,000 miles cost $350.

It was time to go home and find a husband.

Epilogue

Finding it difficult settling back into normal life in Sydney, Ingrad and I jumped on a ship to New Zealand. We picked and packed apples on my uncle's orchard in Mapua, near Nelson, then hitchhiked around the South Island.

We found husbands in New Zealand who'd also done the hippie trail. Little did I realise I'd adopt several children from orphanages in the communist countries we had visited. I never knew they existed then. *How Many Planes to Get Me?* is the story of a journey to create a family.

When my parents retired to New Zealand, my sister became homesick in Scotland; she settled back here. Jasper stayed on in Australia. The sun, the surf, and his mates were important to him. Although my parents remained disappointed he didn't follow in his uncle's footsteps and become an admiral, Dad tried to extend the proverbial olive branch to Jasper, reflecting on Australian life.

"Would you like a cup of tea—or a beer?" asked Jasper hopefully.

He now rented a house on Pittwater Road, where the waves crashed beyond and his blonde-headed youngsters squealed happily in a plastic rubber pool.

Mum said tea, and Dad agreed. Then he changed his mind.

"Er, give us a beer, old chap. Reckon you might have been right all along. I can see why you like this country."

Jasper grinned.

Yes, Dad said, Aussies were basically good blokes. They might be a bit rough around the edges but they were cheerful, solid and generally decent. In fact, said Dad, he'd thought long and hard about the secret to an Aussie bloke's happiness. Simple.

Jasper was keen to hear Dad's profound thoughts.

"A Holden full of beer."

Jonquil Graham

Author Jonquil Graham grew up in Sydney on Pittwater Road. After hitchhiking around the world, she married a Kiwi and together they adopted nine children. She helped establish I-CANZ (Inter-country Adoption New Zealand) and wrote *How Many Planes to Get Me?* about her experience of fostering and adoption. Jonquil now has lots of grandchildren and a collection of Liberace memorabilia.

Also by Jonquil Graham

How Many Planes To Get Me?

How do you end up adopting nine children - five of them, including two sets of twins from Eastern Europe?

This began for Jonquil and Bryan Graham with the simple idea of fostering a few New Zealand kids. After all, they had the ideal family home - a rambling old house on a kiwifruit orchard in glorious Golden Bay.

And fostering is what they engaged with, not only the nine who became their own but many others over the years, giving the Grahams what they consider to be the richest of experiences.

Jonquil Graham's account is candid, heart-warming and often extremely funny. It also shows us the tragedy of children without families, and the difference that true parenting makes to both the parents and the children they take to their hearts.

Love fairly jumps off the pages, along with all the ups and downs of a riotous family life.

How Many Planes to Get Me? was originally published by Cape Catley. To enquire about ordering a print copy or eBook contact the author at jonquil.graham@gmail.com.

www.ingramcontent.com/pod-product-compliance
Lightning Source LLC
LaVergne TN
LVHW051542080426
835510LV00020B/2814